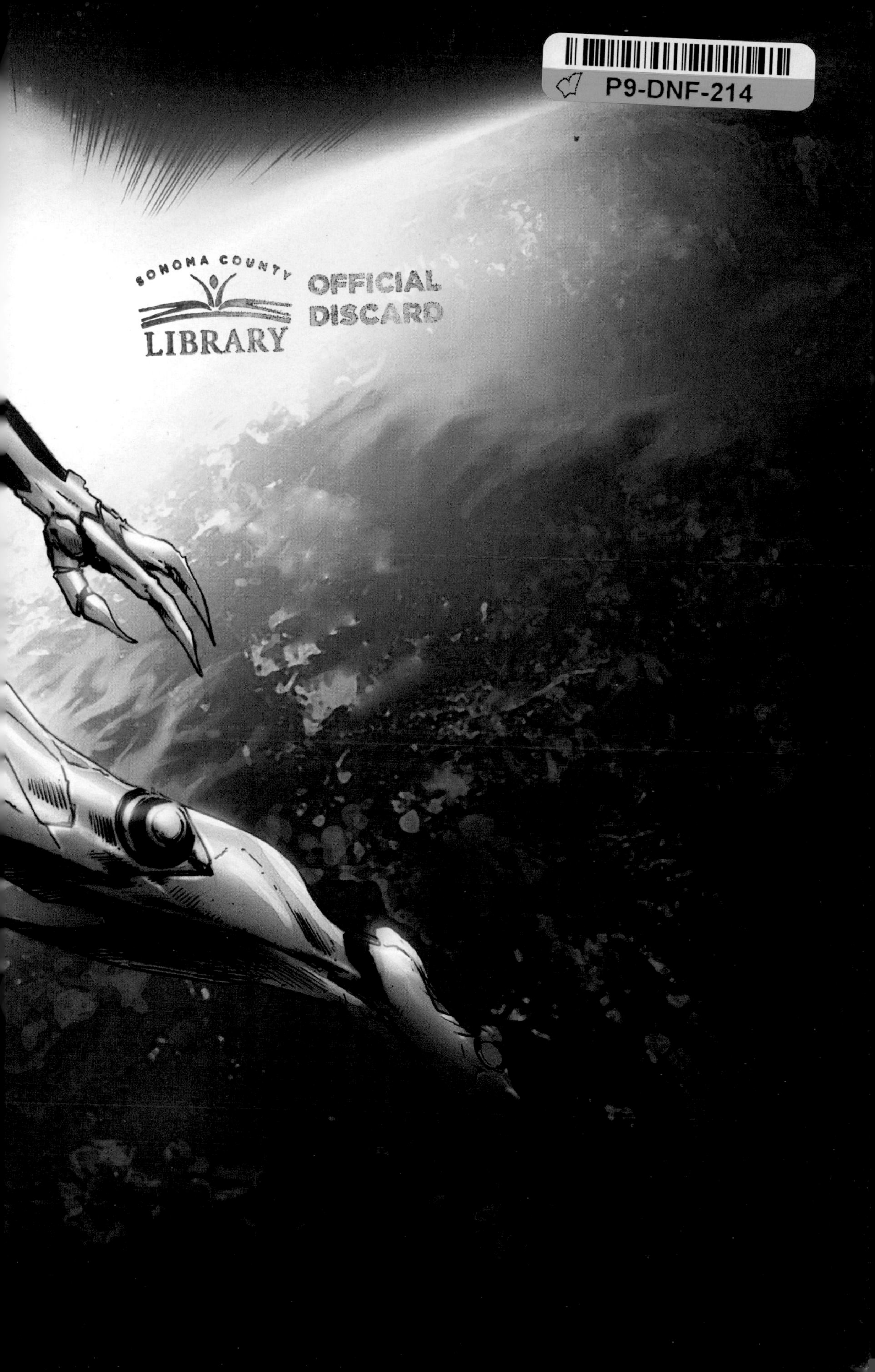

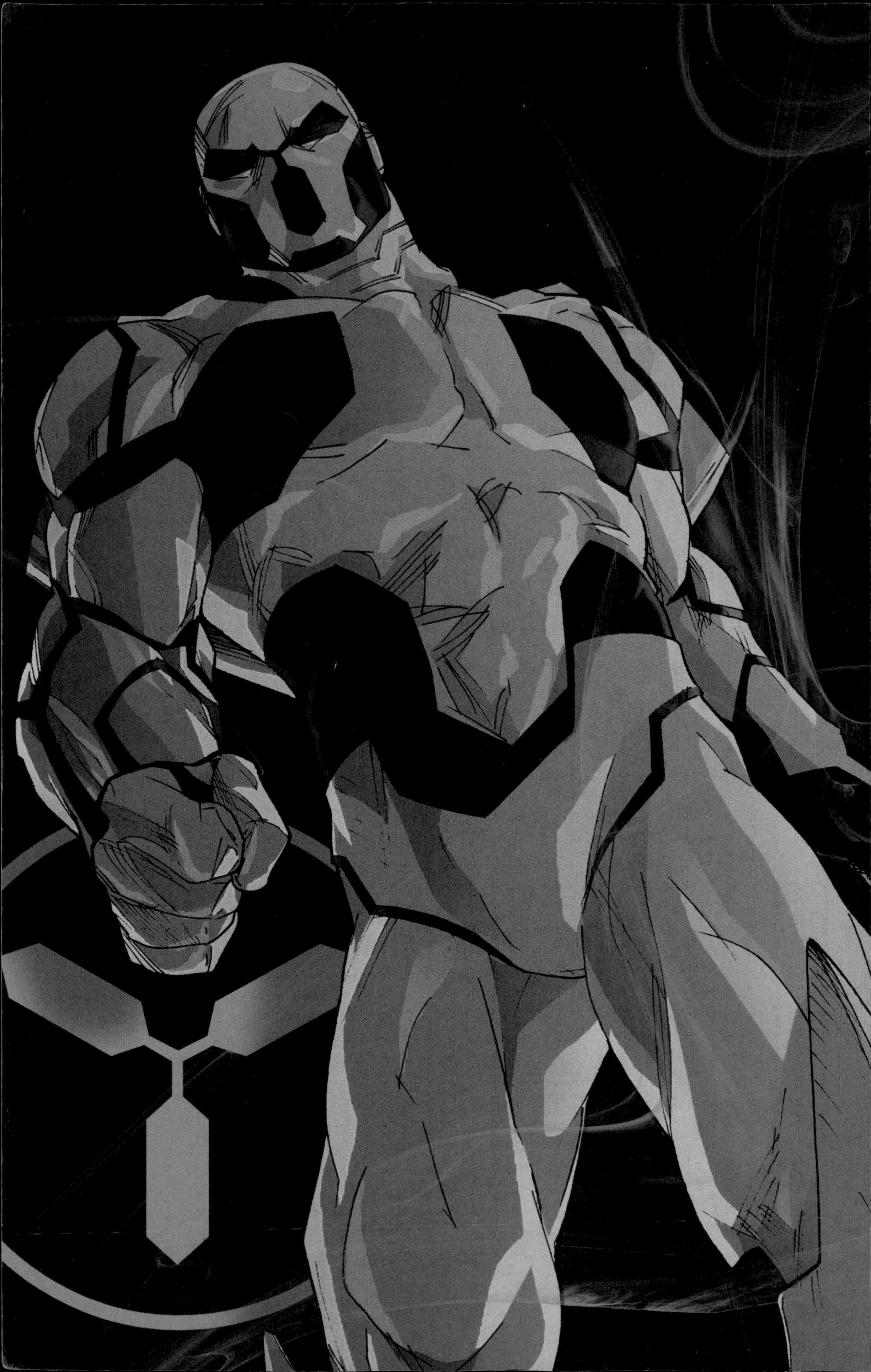

Ross Richie - Chief Executive Officer

Matt Gagnon - Editor-in-Chief

Adam Fortier - VP-New Business

Wes Harris - VP-Publishing

Lance Kreiter - VP-Licensing & Merchandising

Chip Mosher - Marketing Director

Bryce Carlson - Managing Editor

Ian Brill - Editor

Dafna Pleban - Editor

Christopher Burns - Editor

Christopher Meyer - Editor

Shannon Watters - Assistant Editor

Eric Harburn - Assistant Editor

Adam Staffaroni - Assistant Editor

Brian Latimer - Lead Graphic Designer

Stephanie Gonzaga - Graphic Designer

Travis Beaty - Traffic Coordinator

Devin Funches - Marketing Assistant

Ivan Salazar - Marketing Assistant

Brett Grinnell - Executive Assistant

ONE SMALL STEP FOR MAN

STAN LEE
PAUL CORNELL

SOLDIER ZERO

JAVIER PINA
SERGIO ARIÑO

VOLUME ONE

GRAND POOBAH
STAN LEE

WRITTEN BY
PAUL CORNELL

ART BY
JAVIER PINA & SERGIO ARIÑO

COLORS BY
ALFRED ROCKEFELLER & ARCHIE VAN BUREN

LETTERS BY
ED DUKESHIRE

SOLDIER ZERO
CHARACTER DESIGN
DAVE JOHNSON

COVER
TREVOR HAIRSINE
WITH ALFRED ROCKEFELLER

GRAPHIC DESIGNER
BRIAN LATIMER

EDITOR
BRYCE CARLSON

EDITOR-IN-CHIEF
MATT GAGNON

PUBLISHER
ROSS RICHIE

SPECIAL THANKS
GILL CHAMPION, TONY PARKER

BOOM! STUDIOS
Stan Lee's POW! ENTERTAINMENT

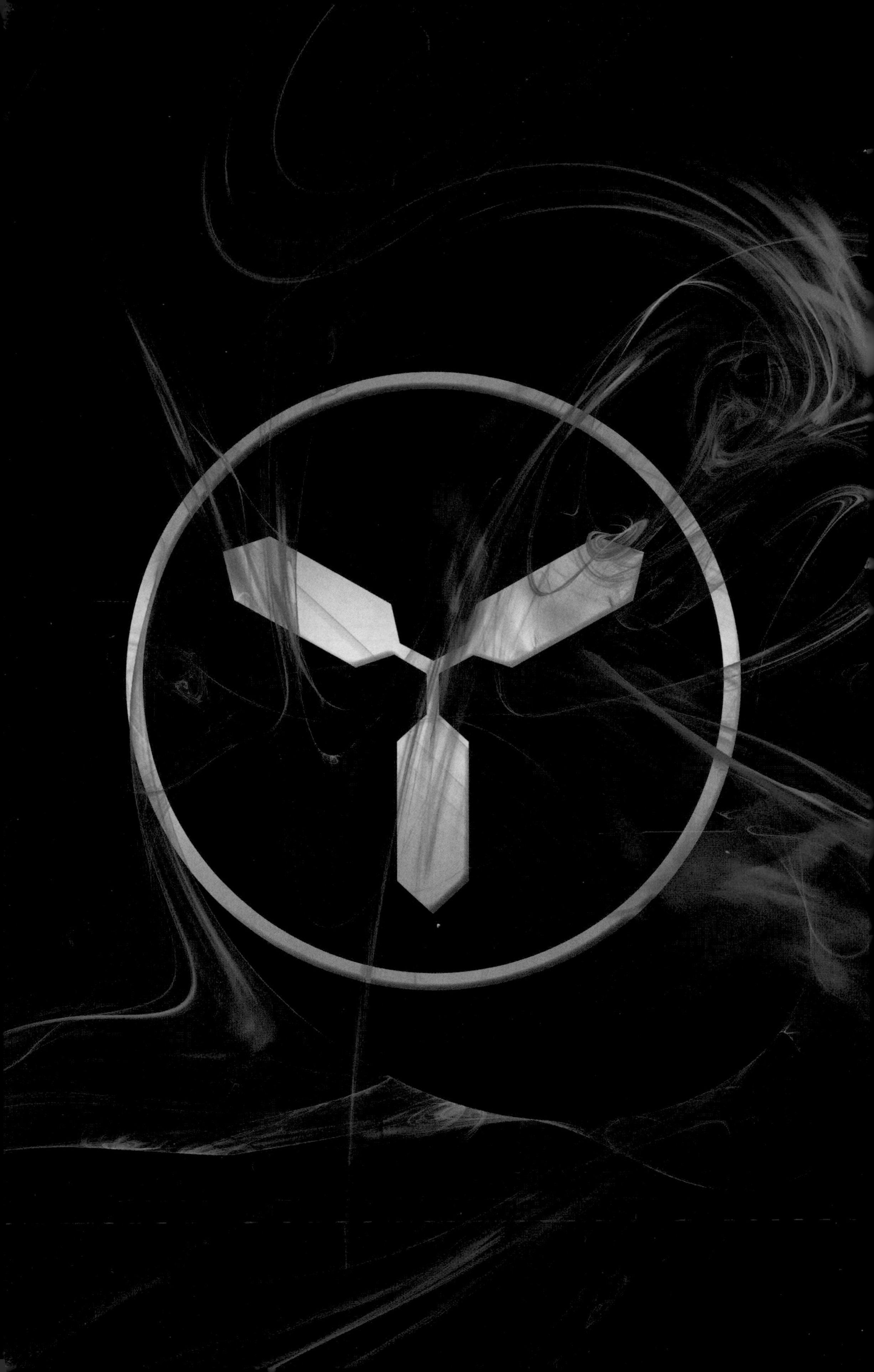

"MAN, COME ON!
"I TRY OUT SOMEPLACE NEW--
"--AND THIS IS WHAT I GET?"
SIR, HE WILL CONTINUE TO EVADE OUR MANIFOLD RAMS. EASILY, SIR.
THE HYBRID IS PREDICTIVE, TRACKING THE MOVEMENTS OF THE SHIP'S EMPLACEMENTS.
SOLDIER ZERO in ONE SMALL STEP FOR MAN

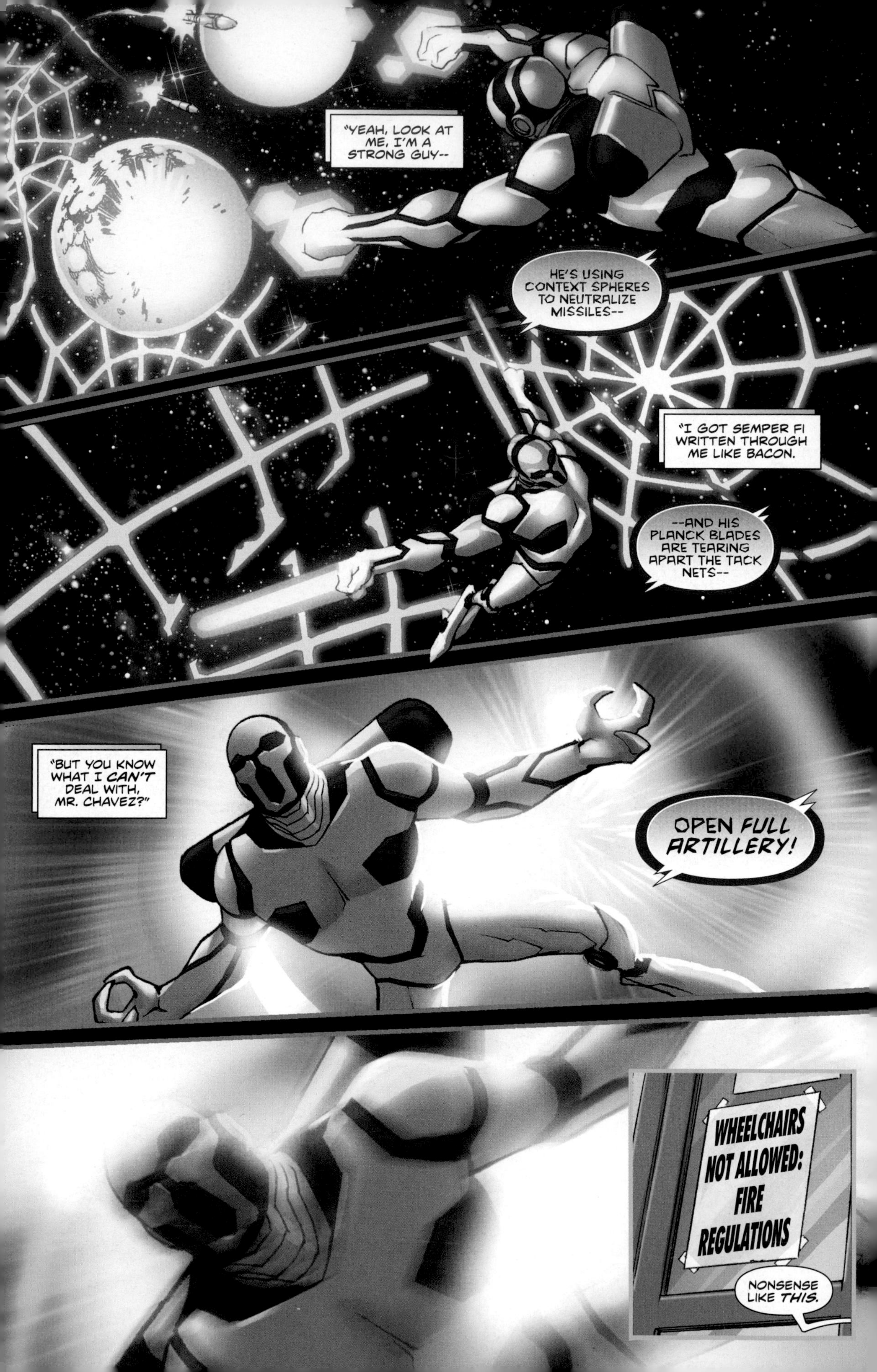
"YEAH, LOOK AT ME, I'M A STRONG GUY--
HE'S USING CONTEXT SPHERES TO NEUTRALIZE MISSILES--
"I GOT SEMPER FI WRITTEN THROUGH ME LIKE BACON.
--AND HIS PLANCK BLADES ARE TEARING APART THE TACK NETS--
"BUT YOU KNOW WHAT I *CAN'T* DEAL WITH, MR. CHAVEZ?"
OPEN *FULL ARTILLERY!*
WHEELCHAIRS NOT ALLOWED: FIRE REGULATIONS
NONSENSE LIKE *THIS.*

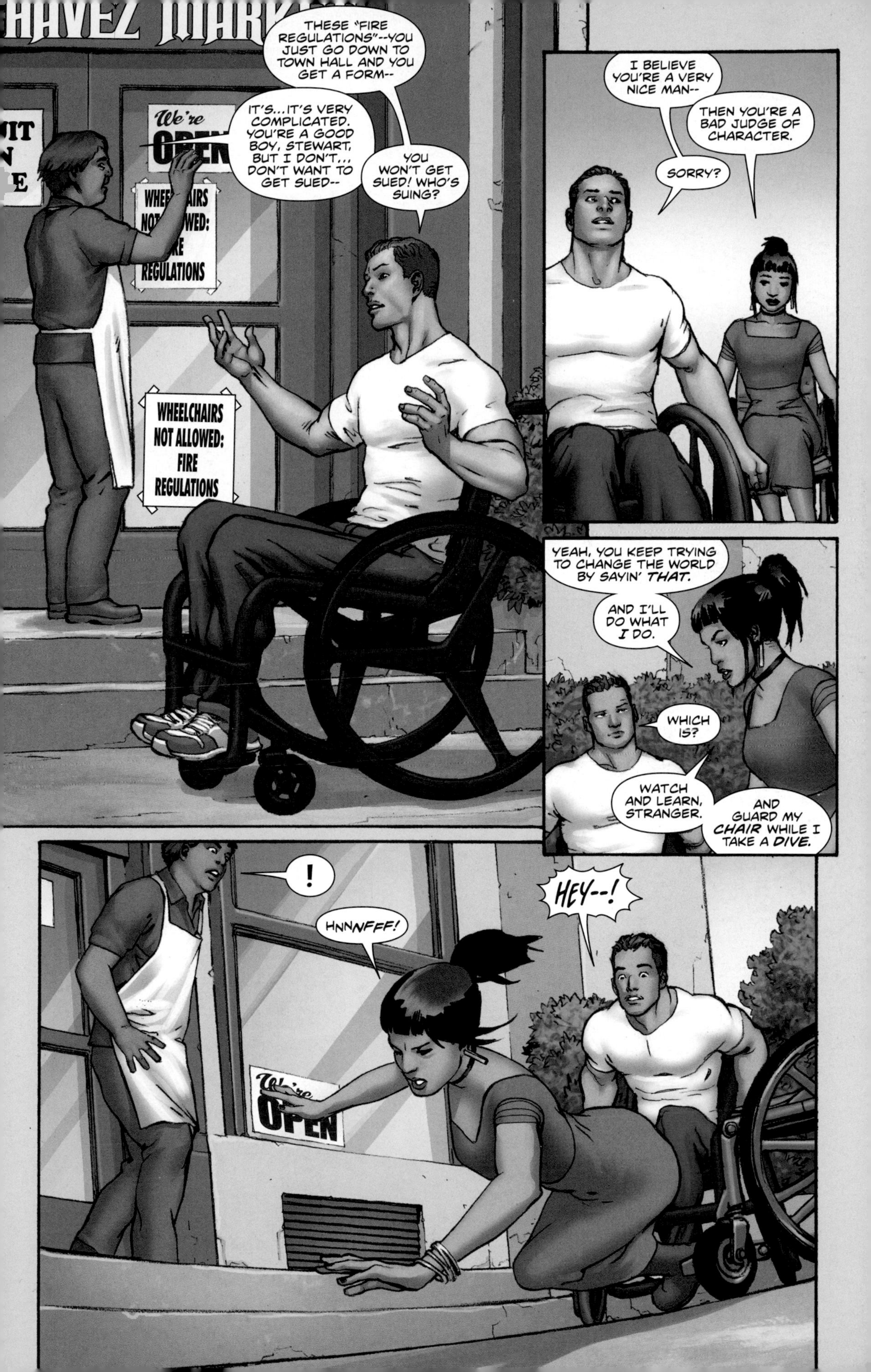

We're OPEN
WHEELCHAIRS NOT ALLOWED: FIRE REGULATIONS
THESE "FIRE REGULATIONS"--YOU JUST GO DOWN TO TOWN HALL AND YOU GET A FORM--
IT'S...IT'S VERY COMPLICATED. YOU'RE A GOOD BOY, STEWART, BUT I DON'T... DON'T WANT TO GET SUED--
YOU WON'T GET SUED! WHO'S SUING?
I BELIEVE YOU'RE A VERY NICE MAN--
THEN YOU'RE A BAD JUDGE OF CHARACTER.
SORRY?
YEAH, YOU KEEP TRYING TO CHANGE THE WORLD BY SAYIN' *THAT.*
AND I'LL DO WHAT *I* DO.
WHICH IS?
WATCH AND LEARN, STRANGER.
AND GUARD MY *CHAIR* WHILE I TAKE A *DIVE.*
!
HEY--!
HNN*NFFF!*

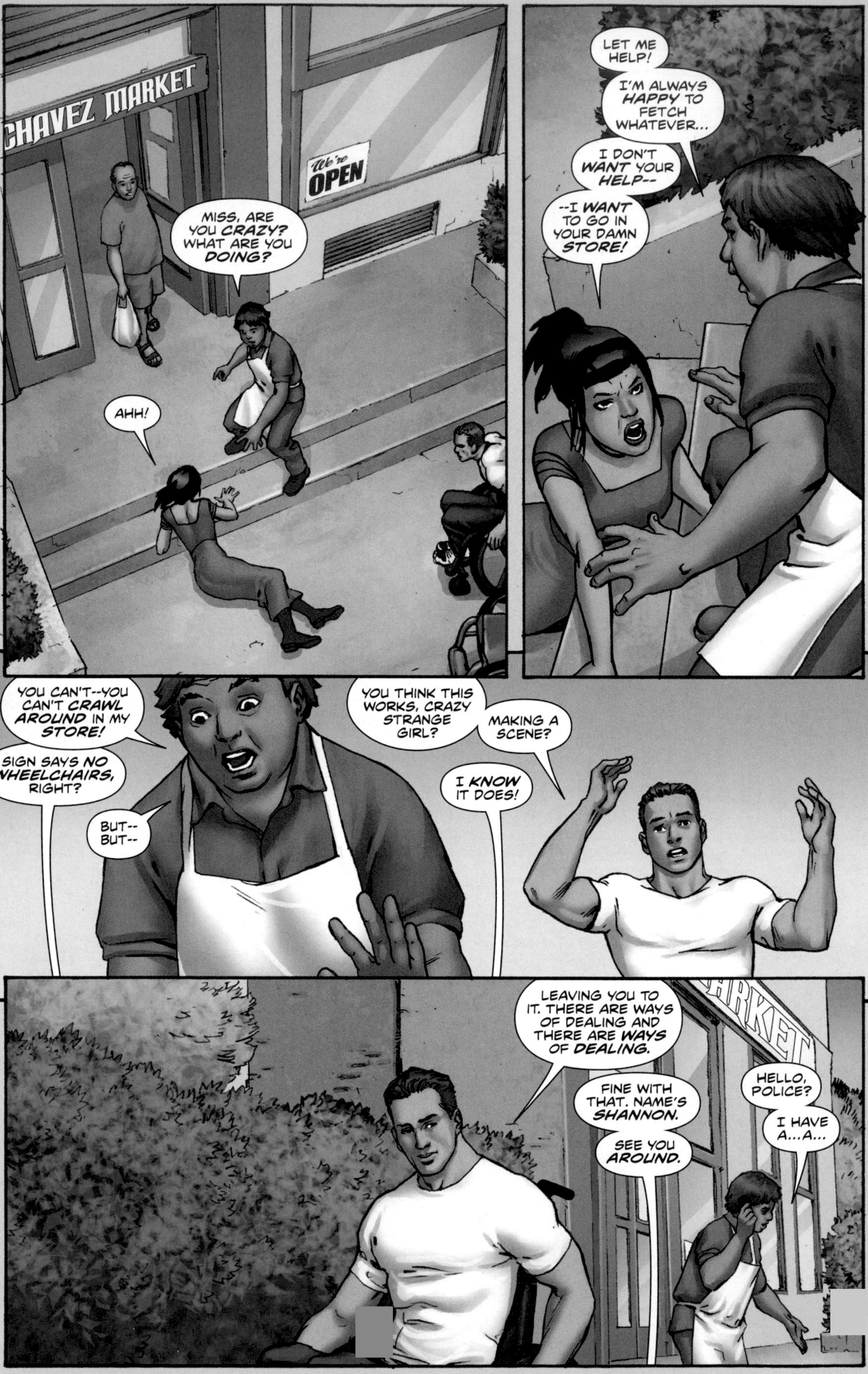
CHAVEZ MARKET
We're OPEN
MISS, ARE YOU CRAZY? WHAT ARE YOU DOING?
AHH!
LET ME HELP!
I'M ALWAYS HAPPY TO FETCH WHATEVER...
I DON'T WANT YOUR HELP--
--I WANT TO GO IN YOUR DAMN STORE!
YOU CAN'T--YOU CAN'T CRAWL AROUND IN MY STORE!
SIGN SAYS NO WHEELCHAIRS, RIGHT?
BUT-- BUT--
YOU THINK THIS WORKS, CRAZY STRANGE GIRL?
MAKING A SCENE?
I KNOW IT DOES!
LEAVING YOU TO IT. THERE ARE WAYS OF DEALING AND THERE ARE WAYS OF DEALING.
FINE WITH THAT. NAME'S SHANNON.
SEE YOU AROUND.
HELLO, POLICE?
I HAVE A...A...

*"...I DON'T KNOW **WHAT** I HAVE."*

HEY, BRO.

BRO.

HOW'S **CAPT. STEWART TRAUTMANN,** THE GREAT HERO OF THE AFGHANISTAN WAR TODAY?

YOU SEEING L--

HEY--! **HEY!**

JAMES--!

YOU MAKING FUN OF MY BROTHER?

JAMES, THEY'RE **NOT**--

--JAMES, IT'S **FINE.**

《SIGH》

I'VE BEEN THROUGH SO MUCH **WORSE...**

GOT THAT SORTED OUT.

SORRY IF I OVERREACTED.

IT'S JUST... Y'KNOW, YOU'RE MY BROTHER. I WANNA WATCH OUT FOR YOU.

YOU DON'T HAVE TO.

CAN'T HELP IT. SO AS I WAS SAYING...YOU SEEING **LILY** TONIGHT?

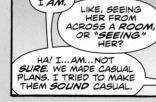

YEAH, I **AM.**

LIKE, SEEING HER FROM ACROSS A **ROOM,** OR "**SEEING**" HER?

HA! I...AM...NOT **SURE.** WE MADE CASUAL PLANS. I TRIED TO MAKE THEM **SOUND** CASUAL.

YOU DON'T HAVE A CASUAL BONE IN YOUR BODY.

WHATEVER. I AM **BOUND AND DETERMINED** TO **TALK** TO HER TONIGHT--

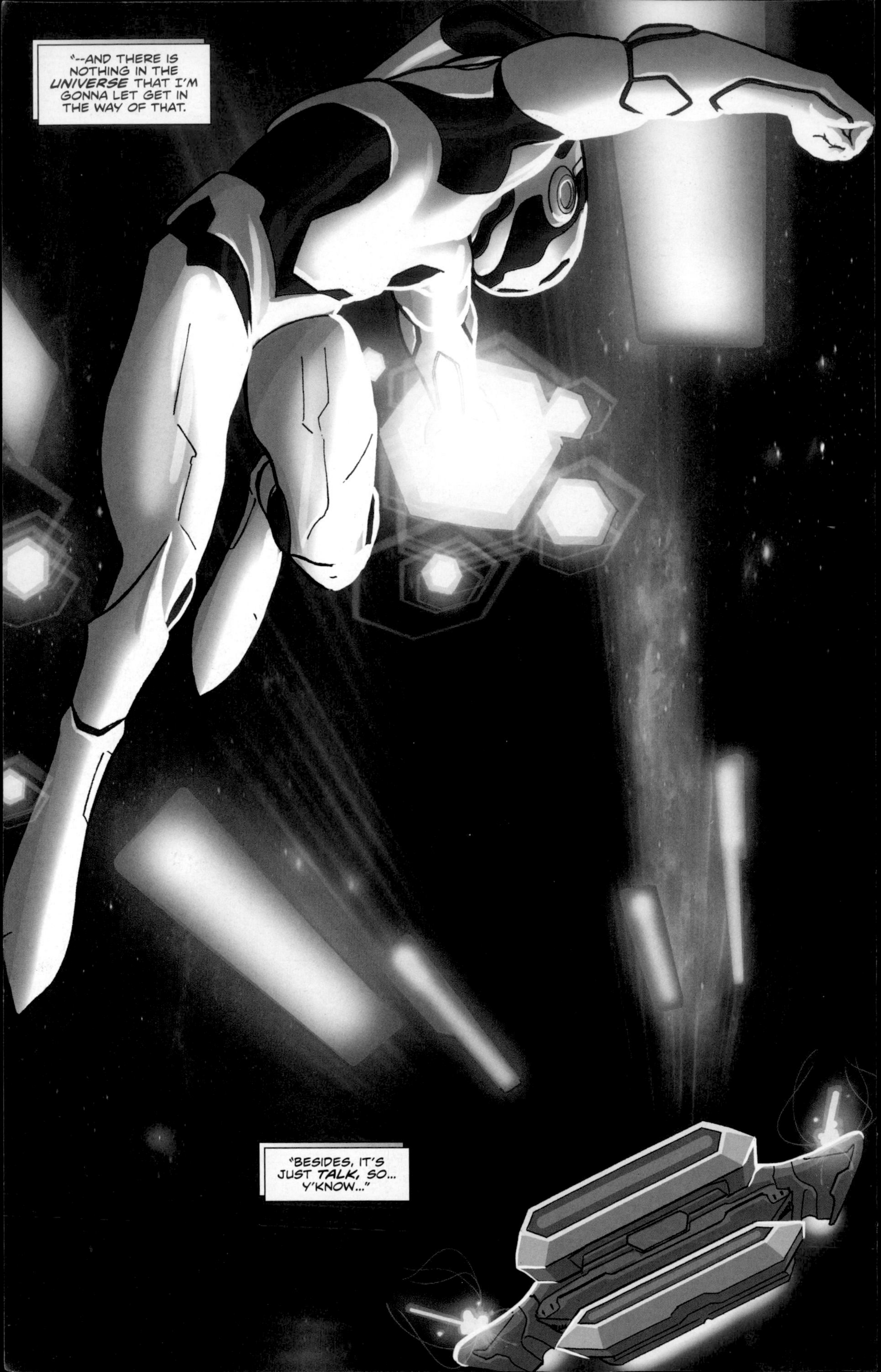
"--AND THERE IS NOTHING IN THE *UNIVERSE* THAT I'M GONNA LET GET IN THE WAY OF THAT.
"BESIDES, IT'S JUST *TALK*, SO... Y'KNOW..."

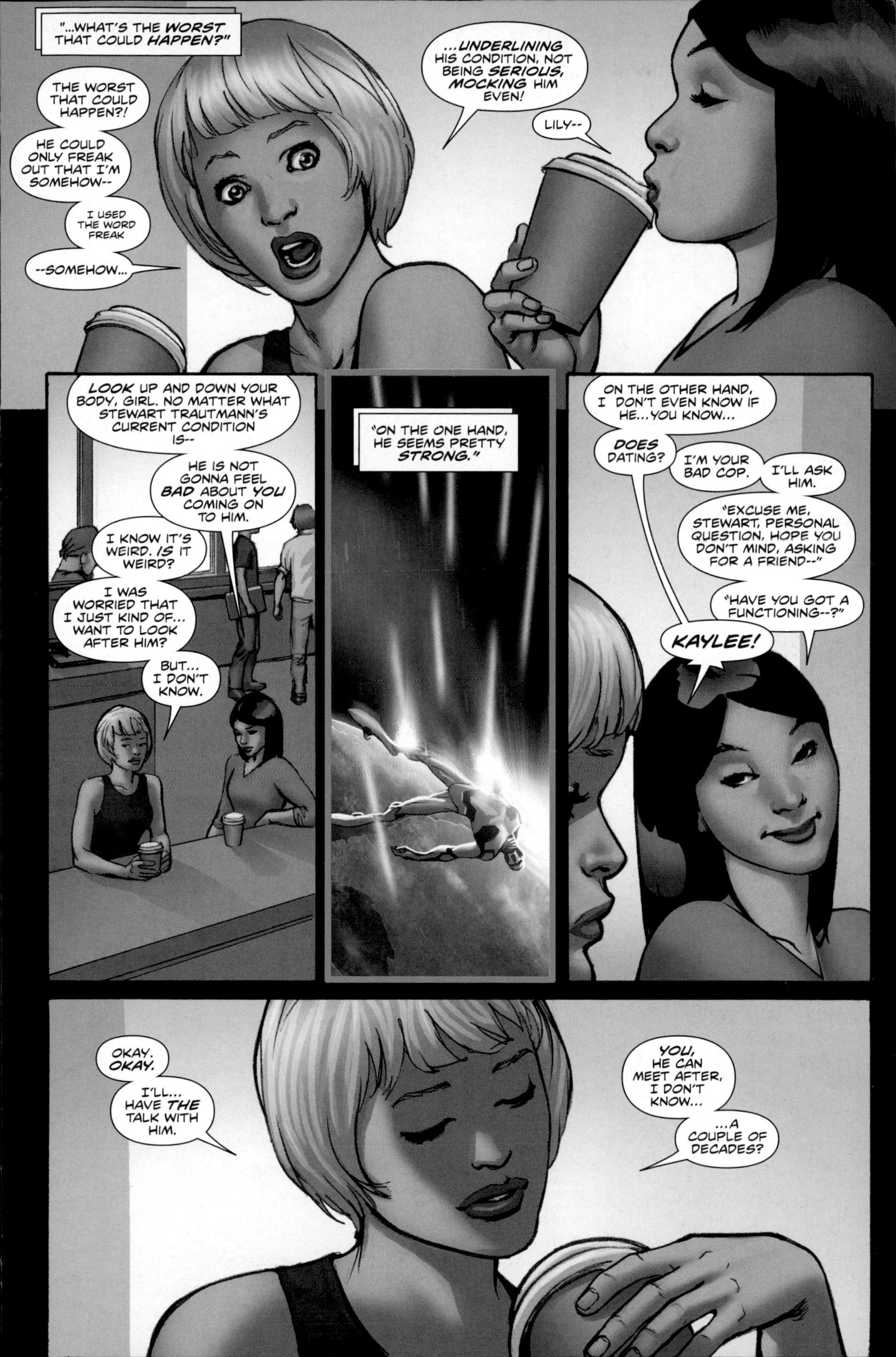

"...WHAT'S THE WORST THAT COULD HAPPEN?"
THE WORST THAT COULD HAPPEN?!
HE COULD ONLY FREAK OUT THAT I'M SOMEHOW--
I USED THE WORD FREAK
--SOMEHOW...
...UNDERLINING HIS CONDITION, NOT BEING SERIOUS, MOCKING HIM EVEN!
LILY--
LOOK UP AND DOWN YOUR BODY, GIRL. NO MATTER WHAT STEWART TRAUTMANN'S CURRENT CONDITION IS--
HE IS NOT GONNA FEEL BAD ABOUT YOU COMING ON TO HIM.
I KNOW IT'S WEIRD. IS IT WEIRD?
I WAS WORRIED THAT I JUST KIND OF... WANT TO LOOK AFTER HIM?
BUT... I DON'T KNOW.
"ON THE ONE HAND, HE SEEMS PRETTY STRONG."
ON THE OTHER HAND, I DON'T EVEN KNOW IF HE...YOU KNOW...
DOES DATING?
I'M YOUR BAD COP.
I'LL ASK HIM.
"EXCUSE ME, STEWART, PERSONAL QUESTION, HOPE YOU DON'T MIND, ASKING FOR A FRIEND--"
"HAVE YOU GOT A FUNCTIONING--?"
KAYLEE!
OKAY. OKAY.
I'LL... HAVE THE TALK WITH HIM.
YOU, HE CAN MEET AFTER, I DON'T KNOW...
...A COUPLE OF DECADES?

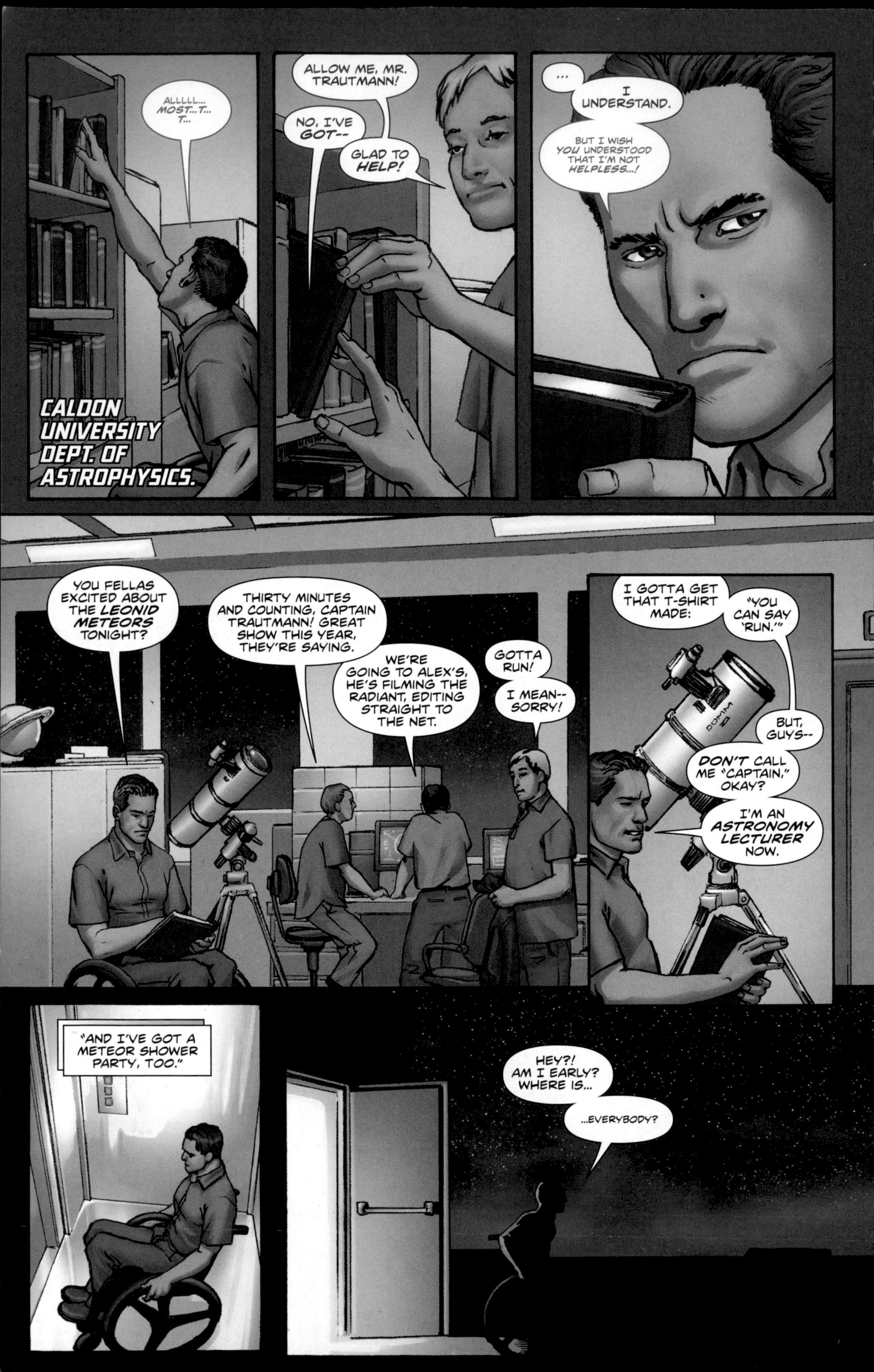
CALDON UNIVERSITY DEPT. OF ASTROPHYSICS.
ALLLLLL... MOST...T... T...
ALLOW ME, MR. TRAUTMANN!
NO, I'VE GOT--
GLAD TO HELP!
...
I UNDERSTAND.
BUT I WISH YOU UNDERSTOOD THAT I'M NOT HELPLESS...!
YOU FELLAS EXCITED ABOUT THE LEONID METEORS TONIGHT?
THIRTY MINUTES AND COUNTING, CAPTAIN TRAUTMANN! GREAT SHOW THIS YEAR, THEY'RE SAYING.
WE'RE GOING TO ALEX'S, HE'S FILMING THE RADIANT, EDITING STRAIGHT TO THE NET.
GOTTA RUN!
I MEAN-- SORRY!
I GOTTA GET THAT T-SHIRT MADE:
"YOU CAN SAY 'RUN.'"
BUT, GUYS--
DON'T CALL ME "CAPTAIN," OKAY?
I'M AN ASTRONOMY LECTURER NOW.
"AND I'VE GOT A METEOR SHOWER PARTY, TOO."
HEY?! AM I EARLY? WHERE IS...
...EVERYBODY?

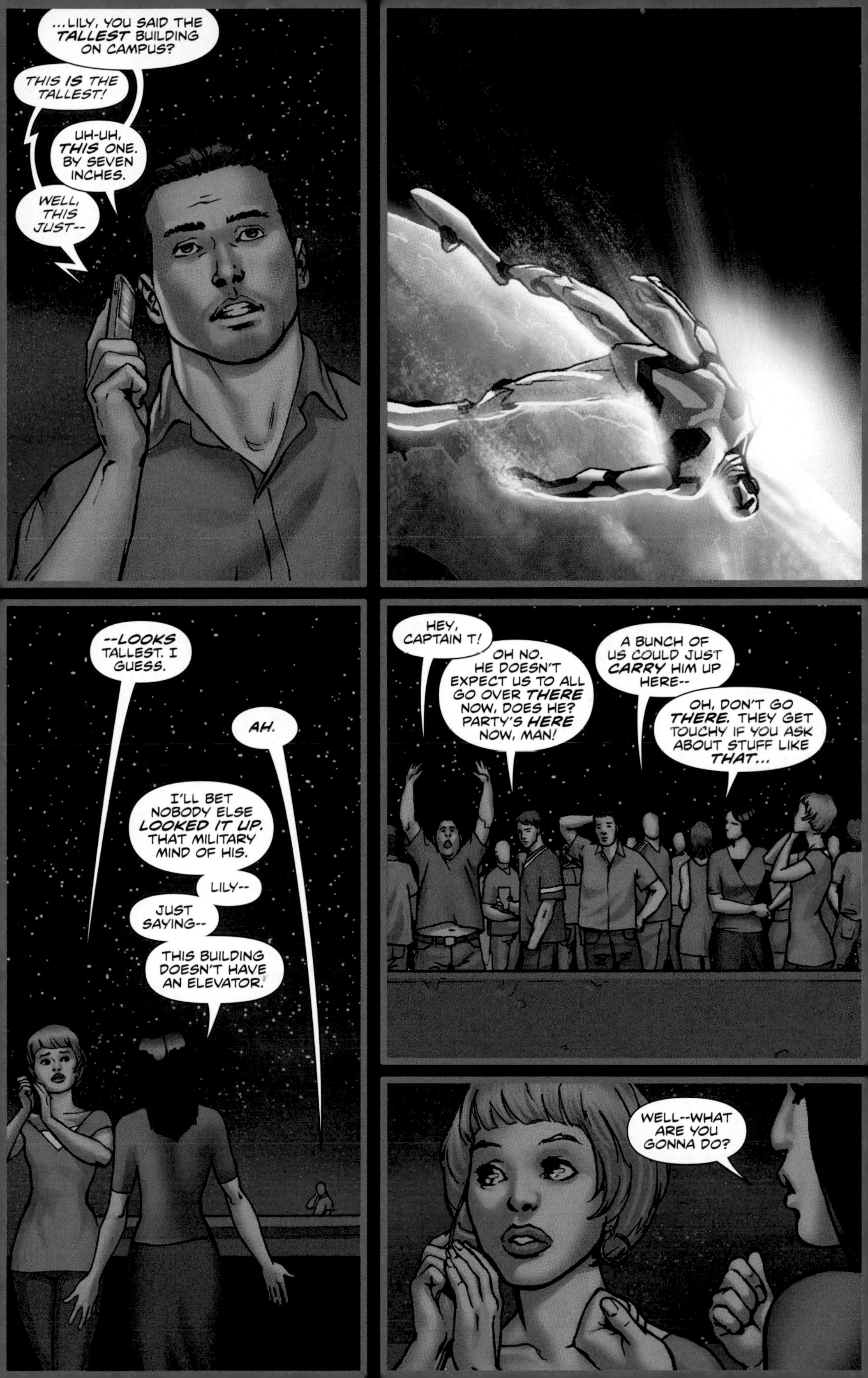
...LILY, YOU SAID THE TALLEST BUILDING ON CAMPUS?
THIS IS THE TALLEST!
UH-UH, THIS ONE. BY SEVEN INCHES.
WELL, THIS JUST--
--LOOKS TALLEST. I GUESS.
AH.
I'LL BET NOBODY ELSE LOOKED IT UP. THAT MILITARY MIND OF HIS.
LILY--
JUST SAYING--
THIS BUILDING DOESN'T HAVE AN ELEVATOR.
HEY, CAPTAIN T!
OH NO. HE DOESN'T EXPECT US TO ALL GO OVER THERE NOW, DOES HE? PARTY'S HERE NOW, MAN!
A BUNCH OF US COULD JUST CARRY HIM UP HERE--
OH, DON'T GO THERE. THEY GET TOUCHY IF YOU ASK ABOUT STUFF LIKE THAT...
WELL--WHAT ARE YOU GONNA DO?

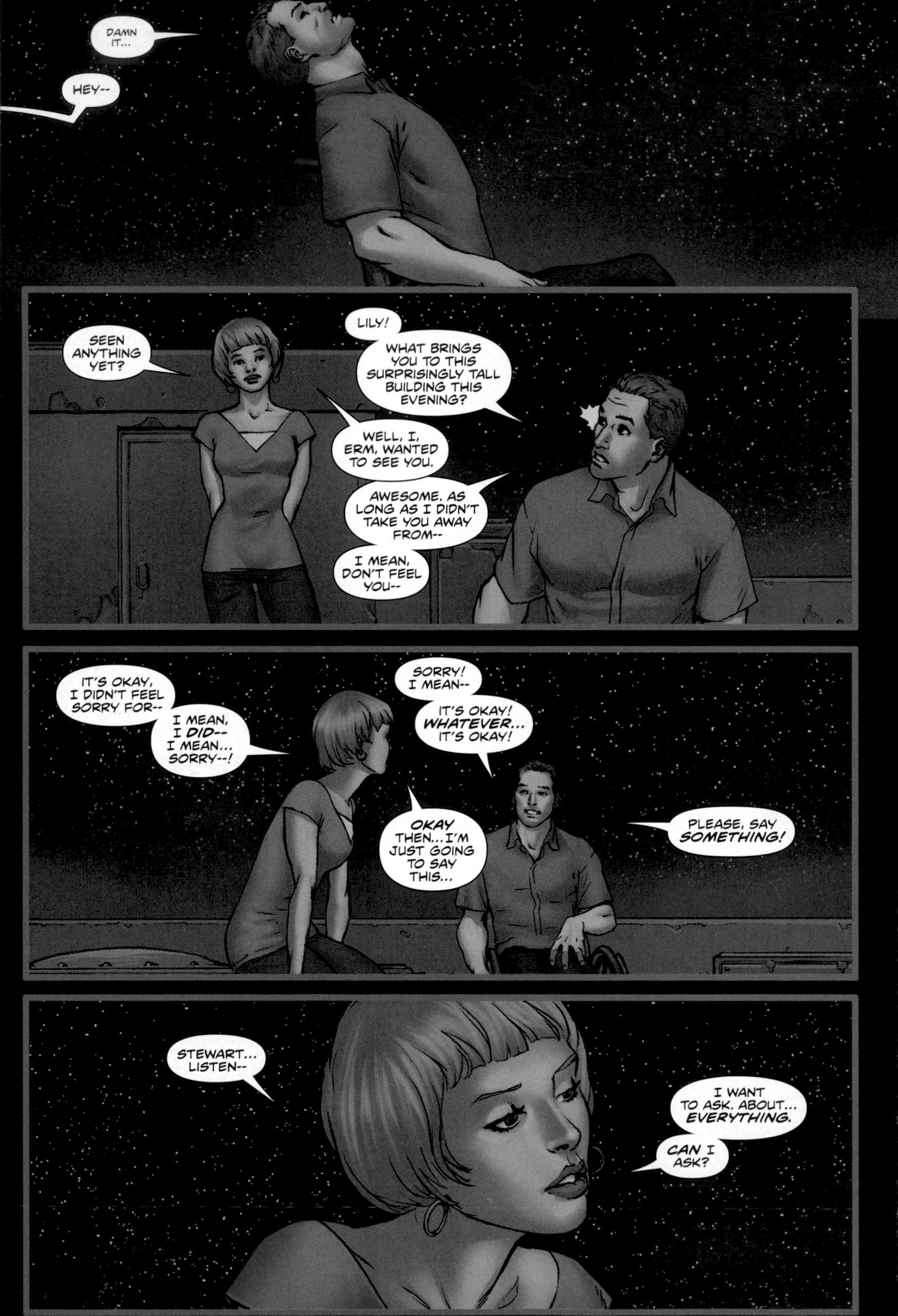
DAMN IT...
HEY--
SEEN ANYTHING YET?
LILY!
WHAT BRINGS YOU TO THIS SURPRISINGLY TALL BUILDING THIS EVENING?
WELL, I, ERM, WANTED TO SEE YOU.
AWESOME. AS LONG AS I DIDN'T TAKE YOU AWAY FROM--
I MEAN, DON'T FEEL YOU--
IT'S OKAY, I DIDN'T FEEL SORRY FOR--
I MEAN, I DID-- I MEAN... SORRY--!
SORRY! I MEAN--
IT'S OKAY! WHATEVER... IT'S OKAY!
OKAY THEN... I'M JUST GOING TO SAY THIS...
PLEASE, SAY SOMETHING!
STEWART... LISTEN--
I WANT TO ASK. ABOUT... EVERYTHING.
CAN I ASK?

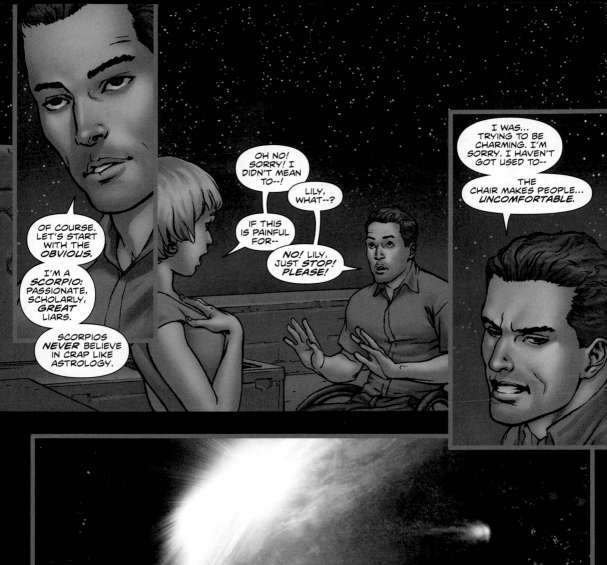

OF COURSE. LET'S START WITH THE *OBVIOUS*.

I'M A *SCORPIO*: PASSIONATE, SCHOLARLY, *GREAT* LIARS.

SCORPIOS *NEVER* BELIEVE IN CRAP LIKE ASTROLOGY.

OH NO! SORRY! I DIDN'T MEAN TO--!

LILY, WHAT--?

IF THIS IS PAINFUL FOR--

NO! LILY, JUST *STOP*! PLEASE!

I WAS... TRYING TO BE CHARMING. I'M SORRY. I HAVEN'T GOT USED TO--

THE CHAIR MAKES PEOPLE... *UNCOMFORTABLE*.

I'M NOT! I'M--

COMFORTABLE! COMPLETELY...

THIS IS SO NOT GOING HOW--

NEVER MIND THAT.

YOU WANT TO KNOW HOW I GOT IN THE CHAIR.

HOW I JUST TELL YOU?

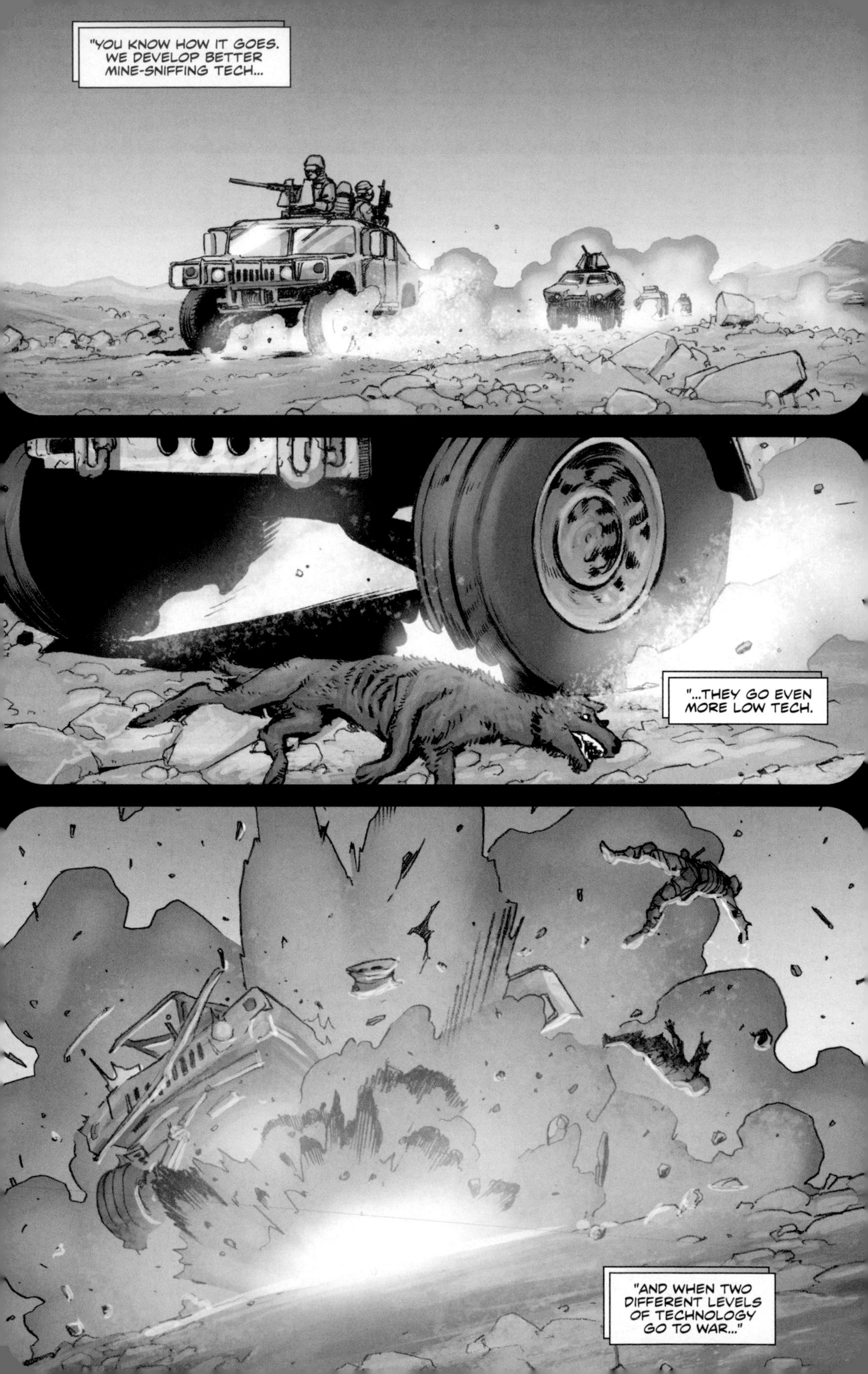
"YOU KNOW HOW IT GOES. WE DEVELOP BETTER MINE-SNIFFING TECH...
"...THEY GO EVEN MORE LOW TECH.
"AND WHEN TWO DIFFERENT LEVELS OF TECHNOLOGY GO TO WAR..."

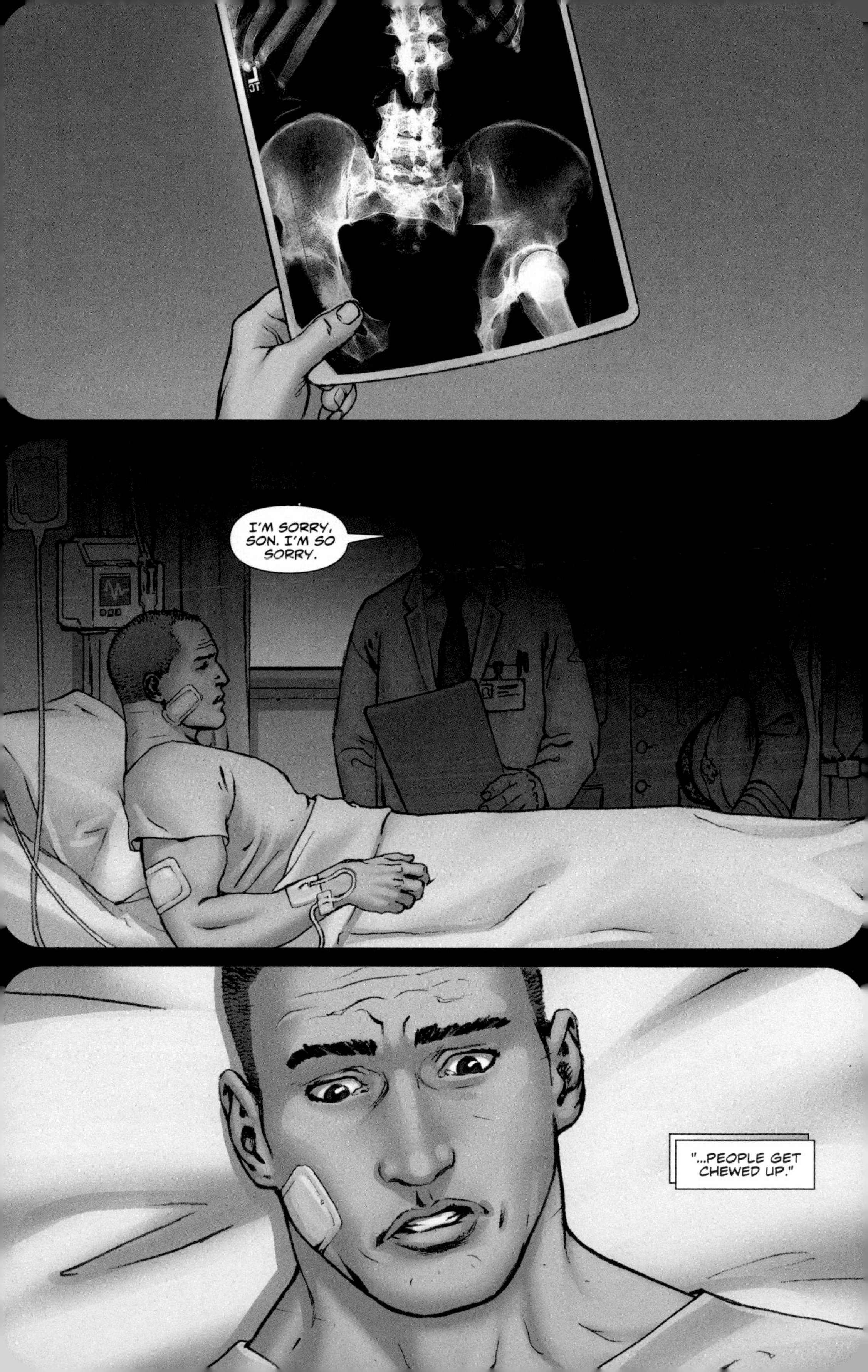
I'M SORRY, SON. I'M SO SORRY.
"...PEOPLE GET CHEWED UP."

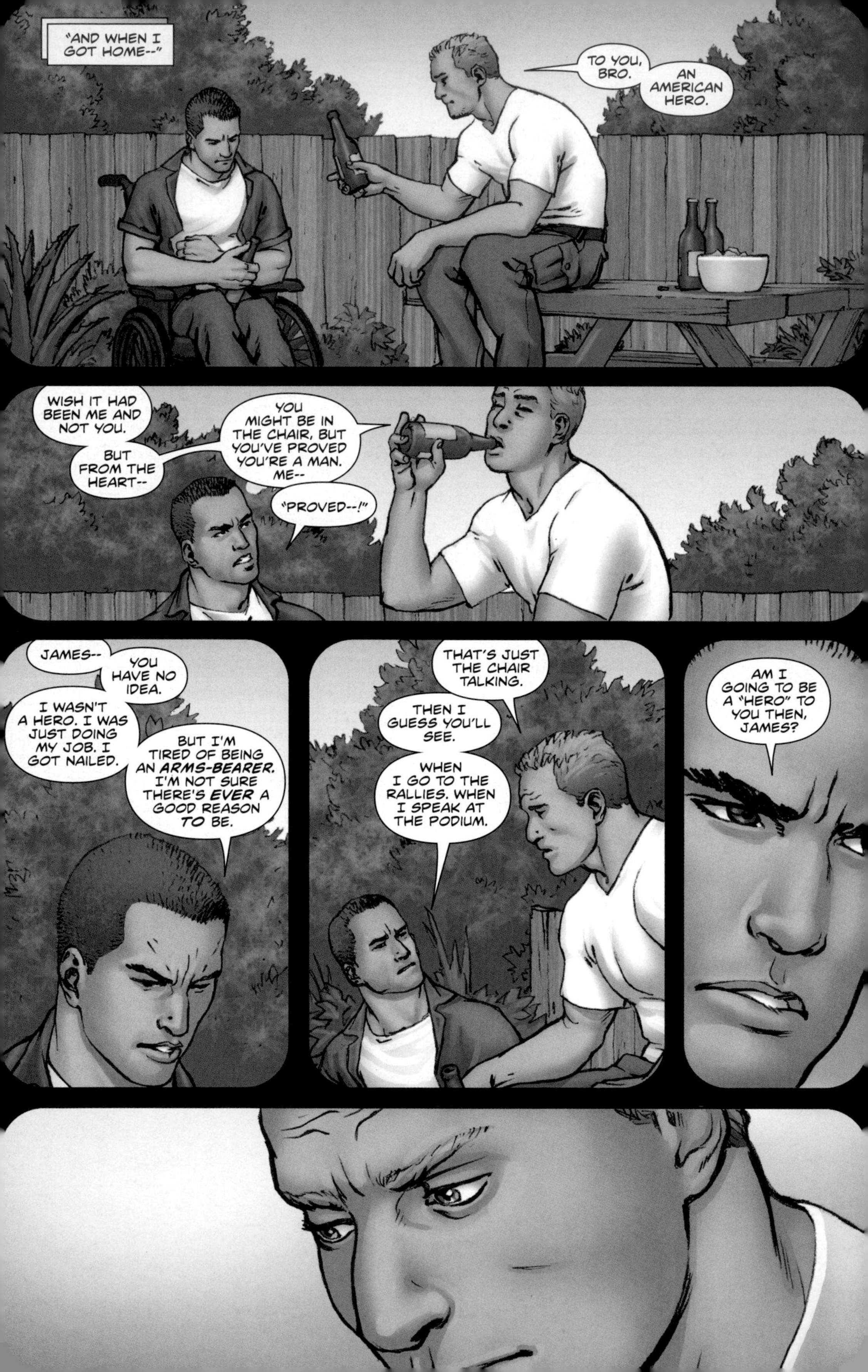
"AND WHEN I GOT HOME--"
TO YOU, BRO.
AN AMERICAN HERO.
WISH IT HAD BEEN ME AND NOT YOU.
BUT FROM THE HEART--
YOU MIGHT BE IN THE CHAIR, BUT YOU'VE PROVED YOU'RE A MAN. ME--
"PROVED--!"
JAMES--
YOU HAVE NO IDEA.
I WASN'T A HERO. I WAS JUST DOING MY JOB. I GOT NAILED.
BUT I'M TIRED OF BEING AN ARMS-BEARER. I'M NOT SURE THERE'S EVER A GOOD REASON TO BE.
THAT'S JUST THE CHAIR TALKING.
THEN I GUESS YOU'LL SEE.
WHEN I GO TO THE RALLIES. WHEN I SPEAK AT THE PODIUM.
AM I GOING TO BE A "HERO" TO YOU THEN, JAMES?

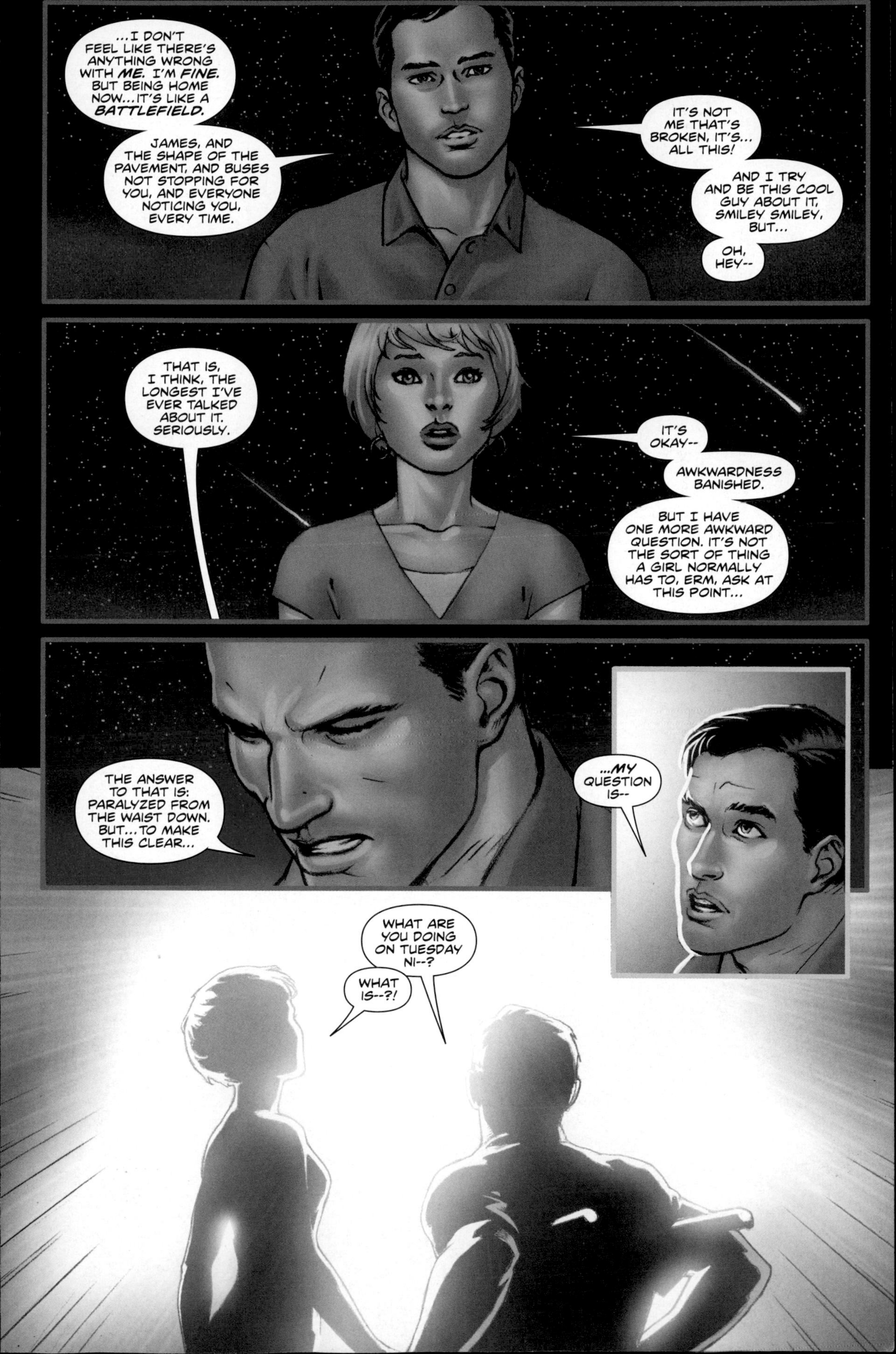
...I DON'T FEEL LIKE THERE'S ANYTHING WRONG WITH *ME.* I'M *FINE.* BUT BEING HOME NOW...IT'S LIKE A *BATTLEFIELD.*
JAMES, AND THE SHAPE OF THE PAVEMENT, AND BUSES NOT STOPPING FOR YOU, AND EVERYONE NOTICING YOU, EVERY TIME.
IT'S NOT ME THAT'S BROKEN, IT'S... ALL THIS!
AND I TRY AND BE THIS COOL GUY ABOUT IT, SMILEY SMILEY, BUT...
OH, HEY--
THAT IS, I THINK, THE LONGEST I'VE EVER TALKED ABOUT IT. SERIOUSLY.
IT'S OKAY--
AWKWARDNESS BANISHED.
BUT I HAVE ONE MORE AWKWARD QUESTION. IT'S NOT THE SORT OF THING A GIRL NORMALLY HAS TO, ERM, ASK AT THIS POINT...
THE ANSWER TO THAT IS: PARALYZED FROM THE WAIST DOWN. BUT...TO MAKE THIS CLEAR...
...*MY* QUESTION IS--
WHAT ARE YOU DOING ON TUESDAY NI--?
WHAT IS--?!

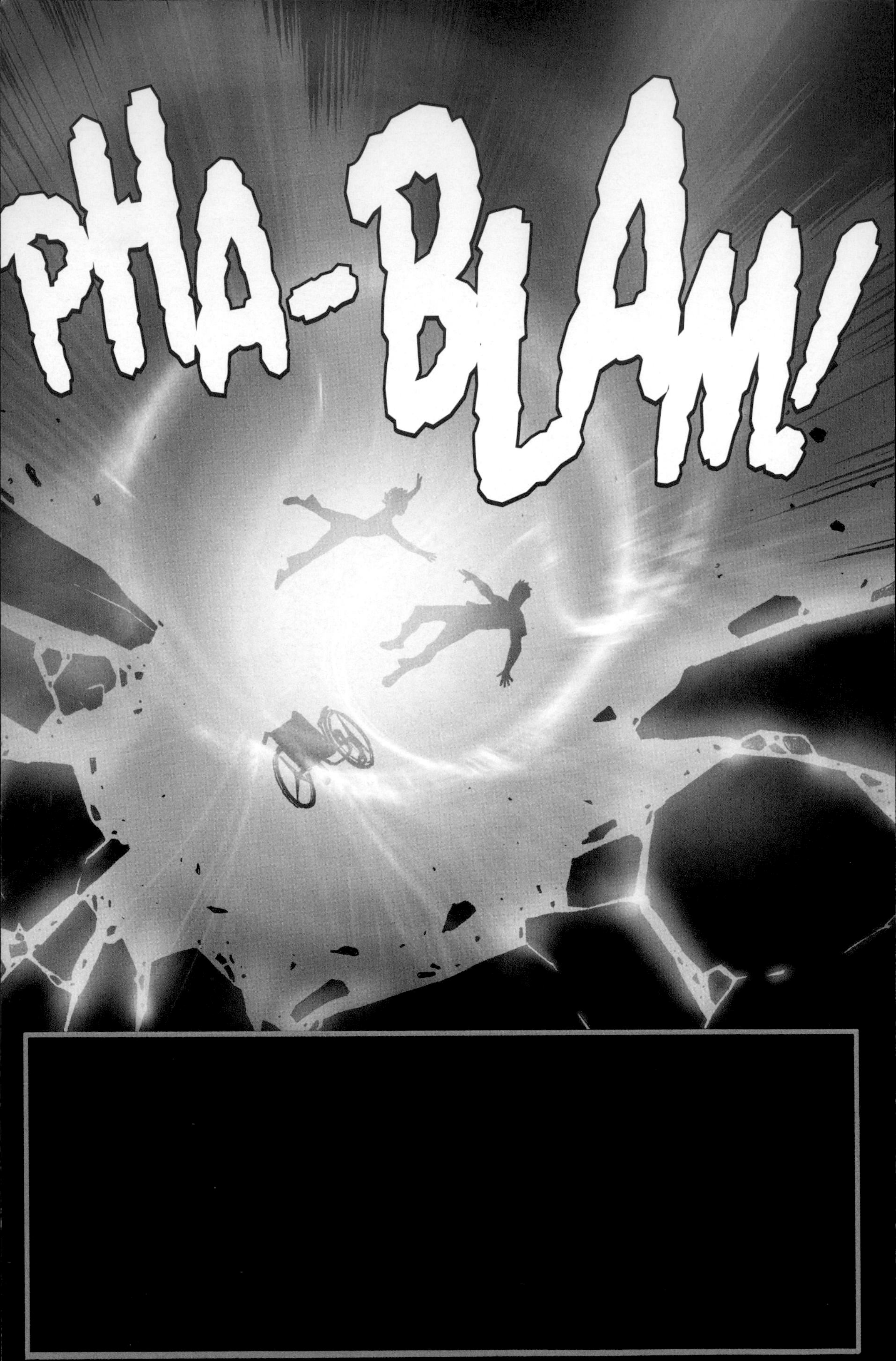
PHA-BLAM!

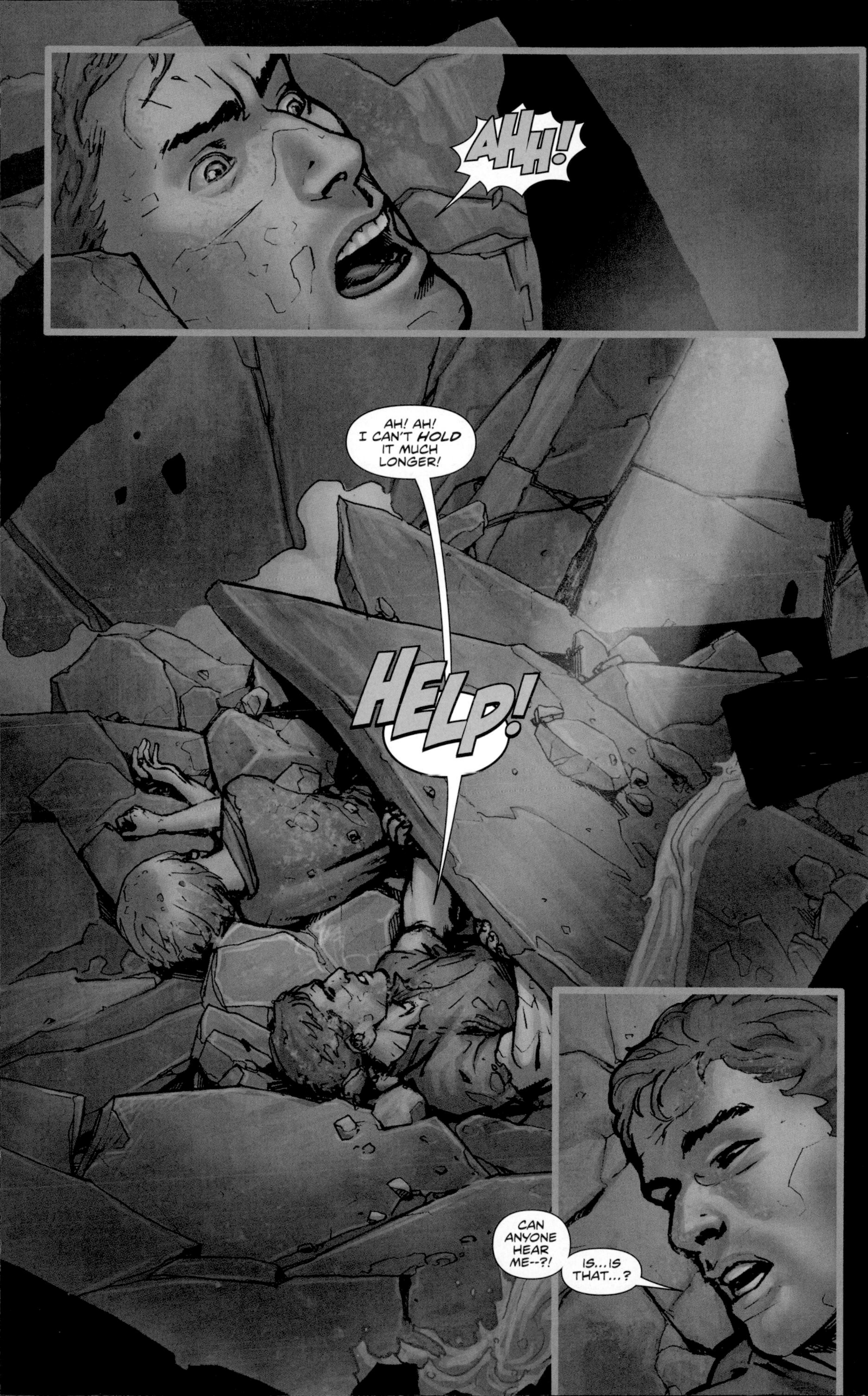
AHH!
AH! AH! I CAN'T HOLD IT MUCH LONGER!
HELP!
CAN ANYONE HEAR ME--?!
IS...IS THAT...?

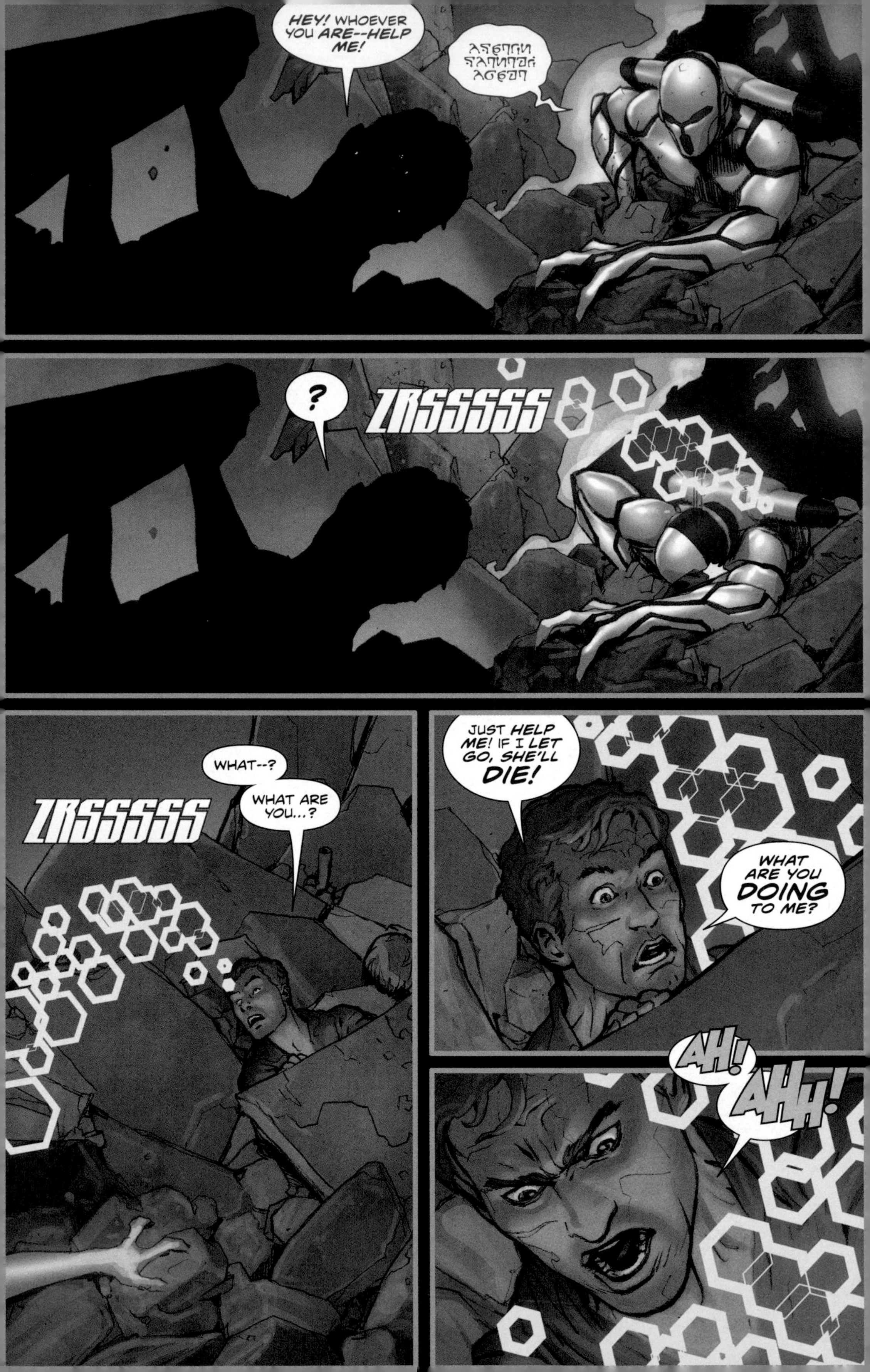
HEY! WHOEVER YOU ARE--HELP ME!
?
ZRSSSSS
ZRSSSSS
WHAT--?
WHAT ARE YOU...?
JUST HELP ME! IF I LET GO, SHE'LL DIE!
WHAT ARE YOU DOING TO ME?
AH! AHH!

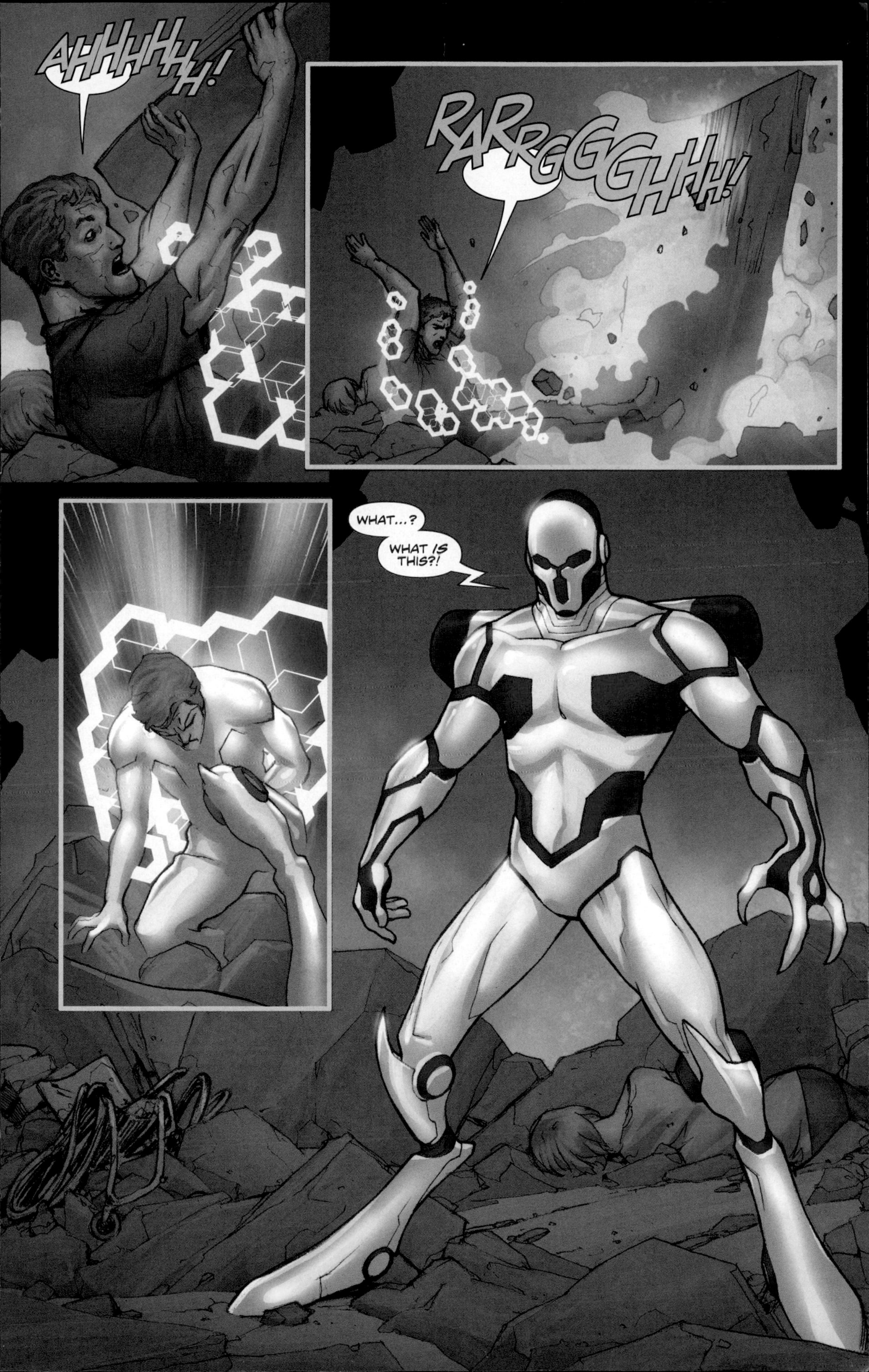
AHHHHHH!
RARRGGGHHH!
WHAT...?
WHAT IS THIS?!

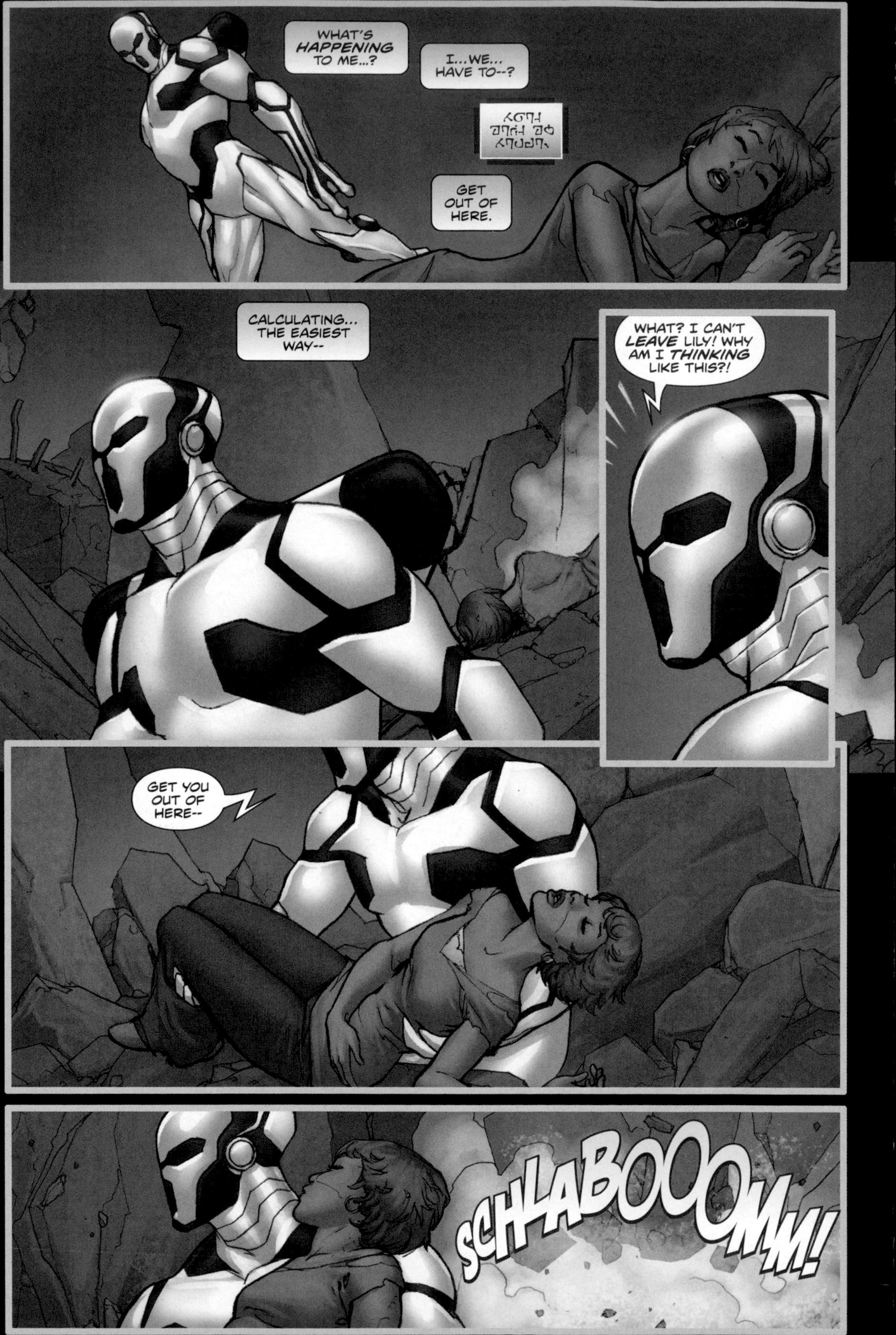
WHAT'S HAPPENING TO ME...?
I...WE... HAVE TO--?
GET OUT OF HERE.
CALCULATING... THE EASIEST WAY--
WHAT? I CAN'T LEAVE LILY! WHY AM I THINKING LIKE THIS?!
GET YOU OUT OF HERE--
SCHLABOOOMM!

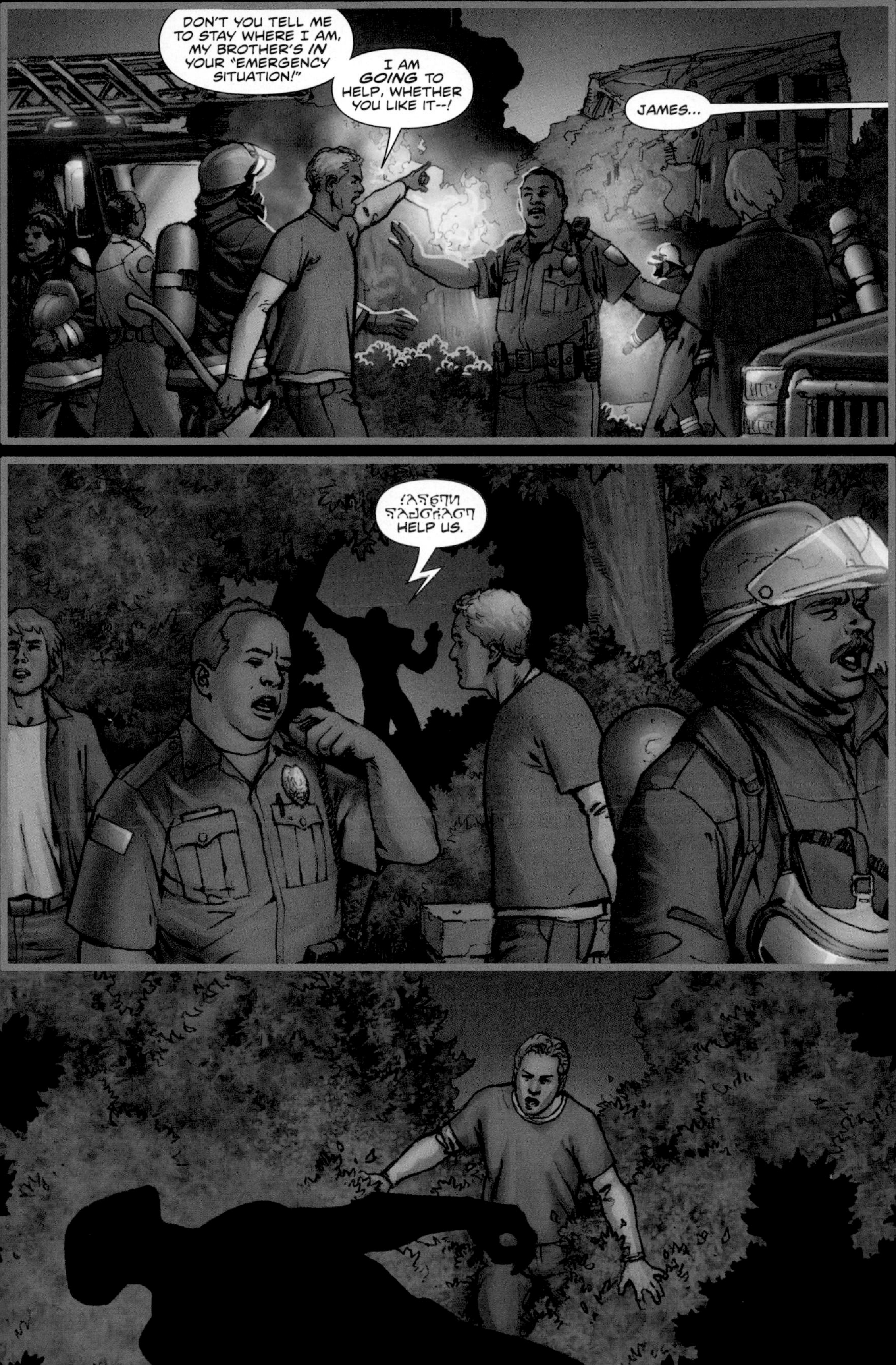
DON'T YOU TELL ME TO STAY WHERE I AM, MY BROTHER'S *IN* YOUR "EMERGENCY SITUATION!"
I AM *GOING* TO HELP, WHETHER YOU LIKE IT--!
JAMES...
HELP US.

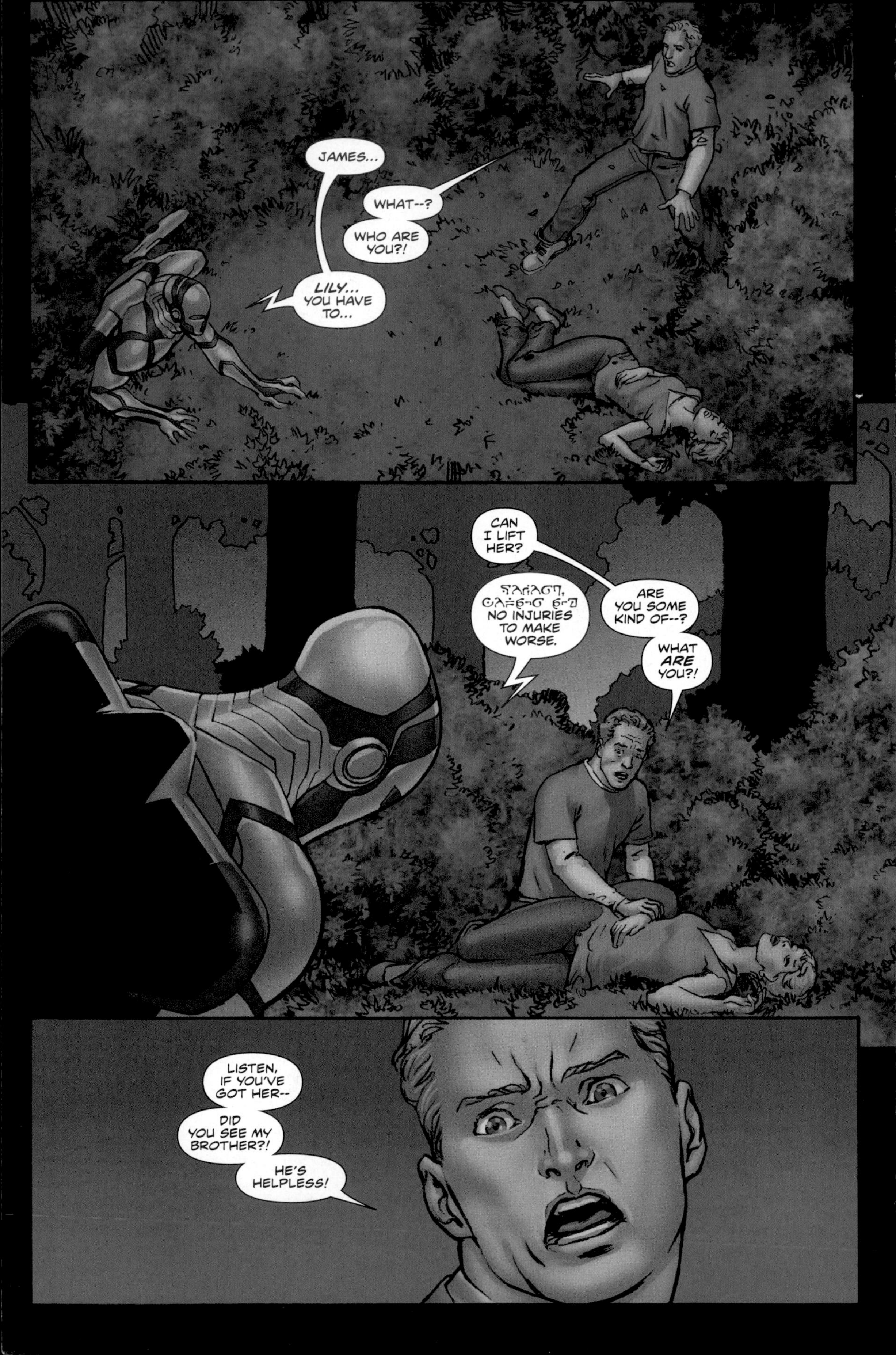
JAMES...
WHAT--?
WHO ARE YOU?!
LILY... YOU HAVE TO...
CAN I LIFT HER?
NO INJURIES TO MAKE WORSE.
ARE YOU SOME KIND OF--?
WHAT ARE YOU?!
LISTEN, IF YOU'VE GOT HER--
DID YOU SEE MY BROTHER?!
HE'S HELPLESS!

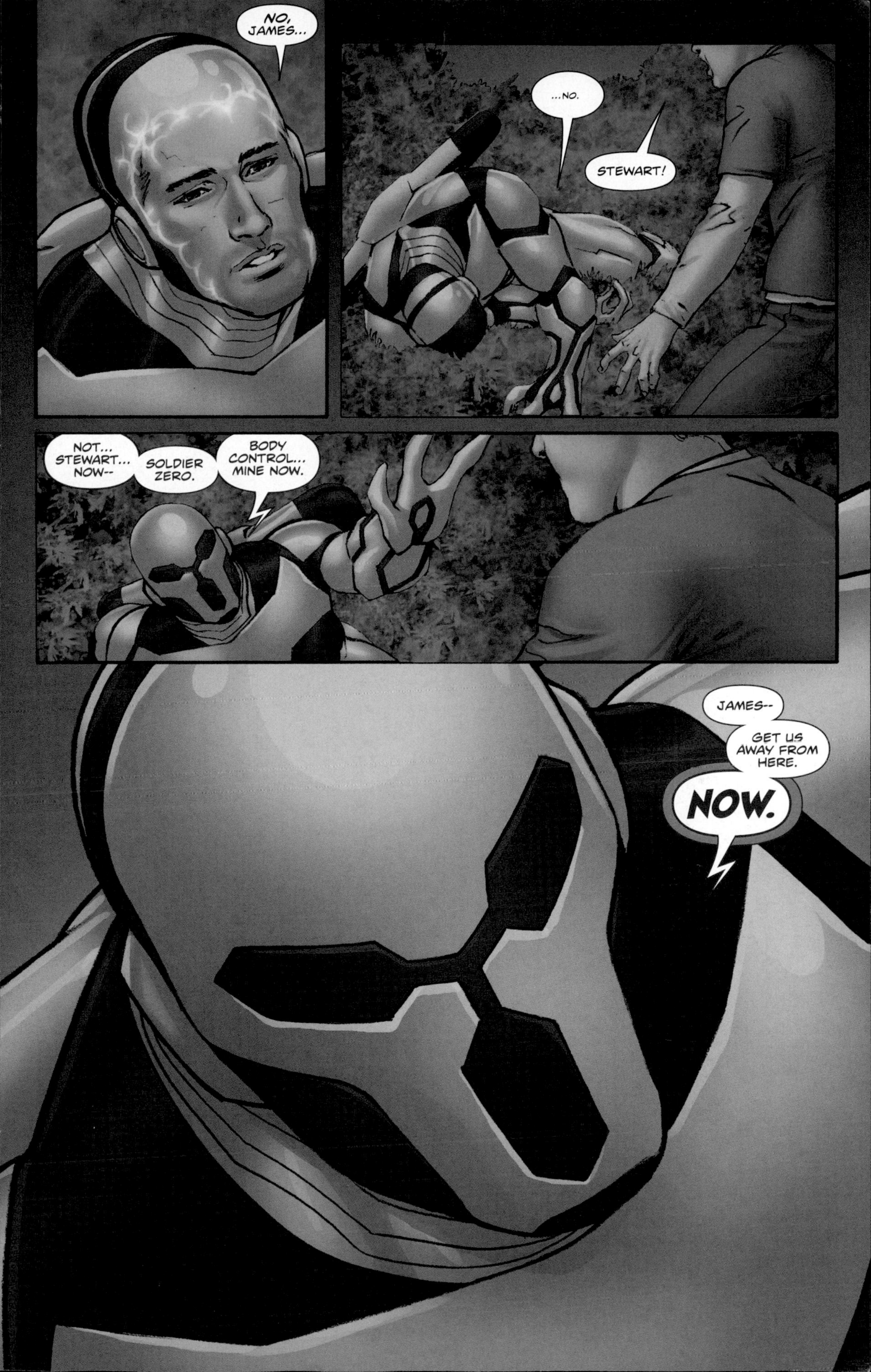
NO, JAMES...
...NO.
STEWART!
NOT... STEWART... NOW--
SOLDIER ZERO.
BODY CONTROL... MINE NOW.
JAMES--
GET US AWAY FROM HERE.
NOW.

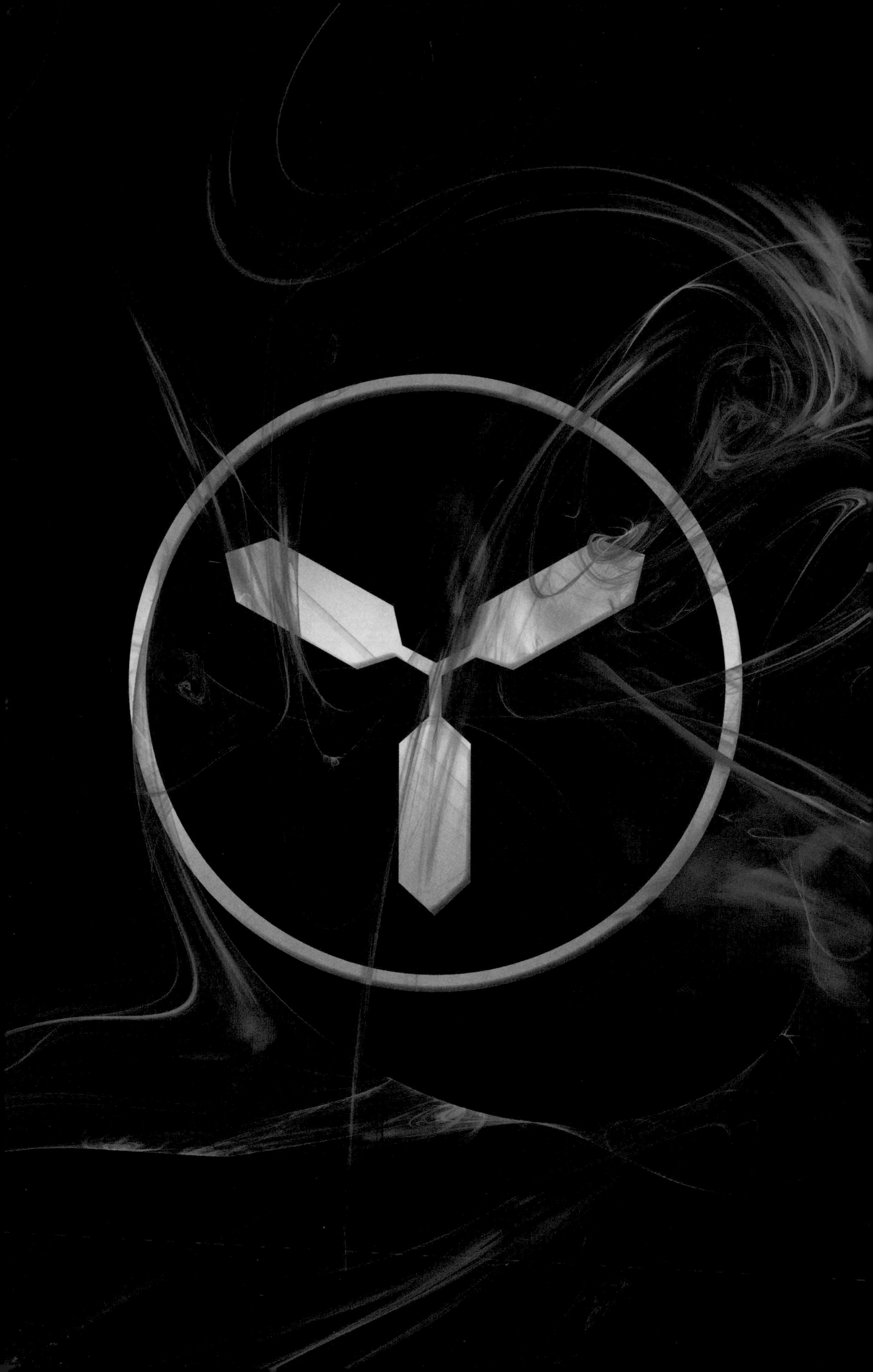

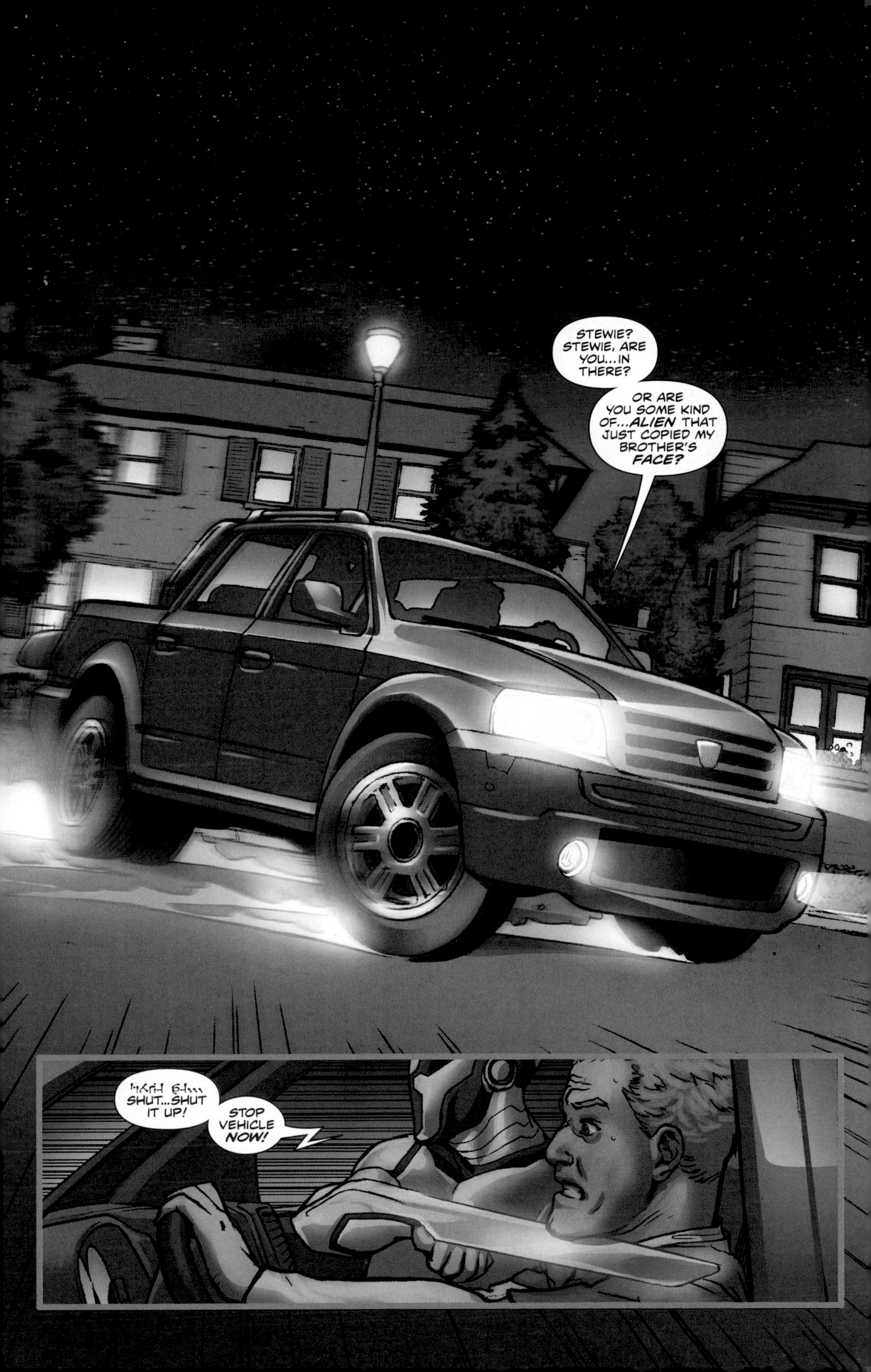
STEWIE? STEWIE, ARE YOU...IN THERE?
OR ARE YOU SOME KIND OF...ALIEN THAT JUST COPIED MY BROTHER'S FACE?
SHUT...SHUT IT UP!
STOP VEHICLE NOW!

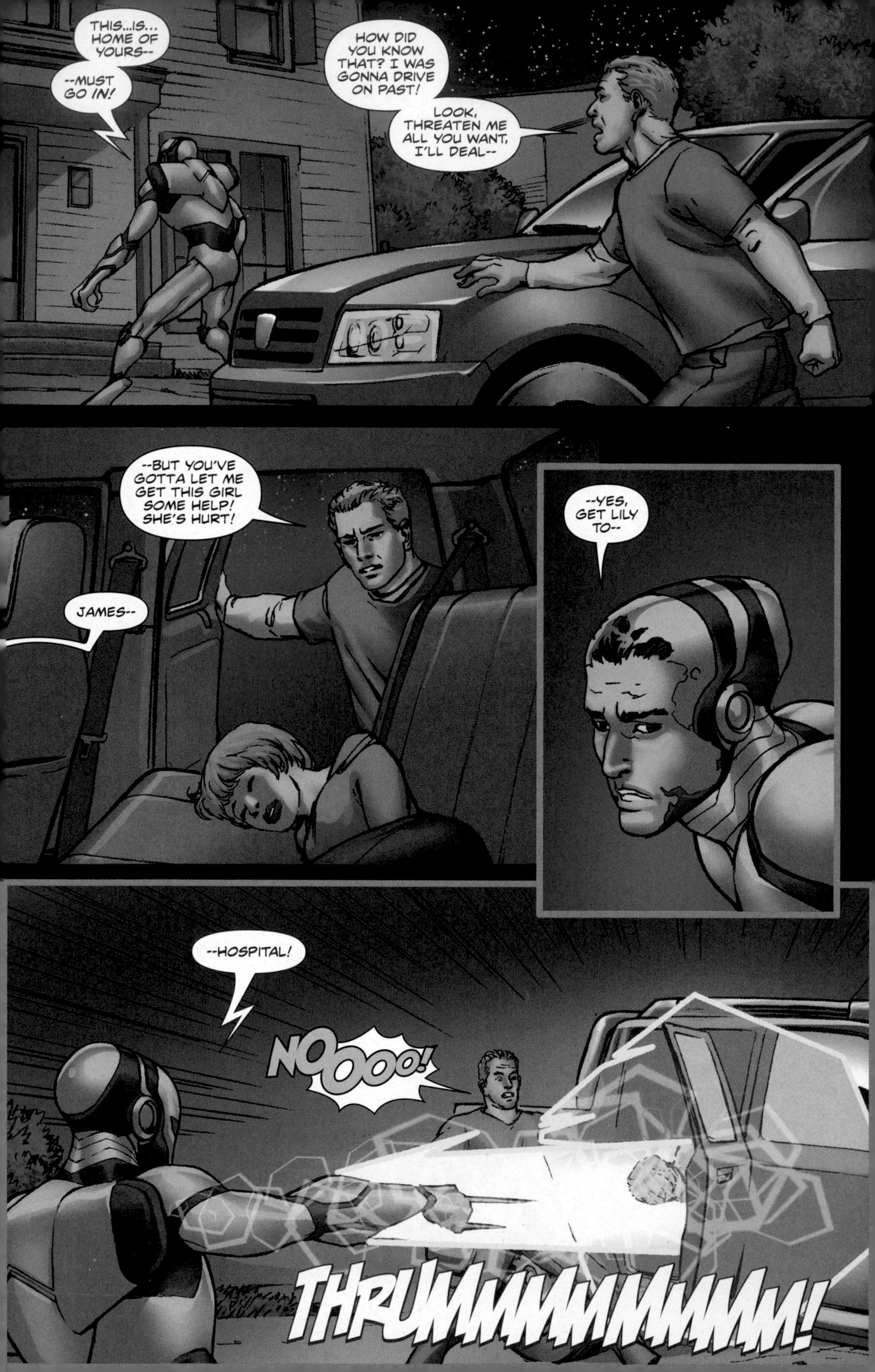
THIS...IS... HOME OF YOURS--
--MUST GO IN!
HOW DID YOU KNOW THAT? I WAS GONNA DRIVE ON PAST!
LOOK, THREATEN ME ALL YOU WANT, I'LL DEAL--
--BUT YOU'VE GOTTA LET ME GET THIS GIRL SOME HELP! SHE'S HURT!
JAMES--
--YES, GET LILY TO--
--HOSPITAL!
NOOOOO!
THRUMMMMMMMMMM!

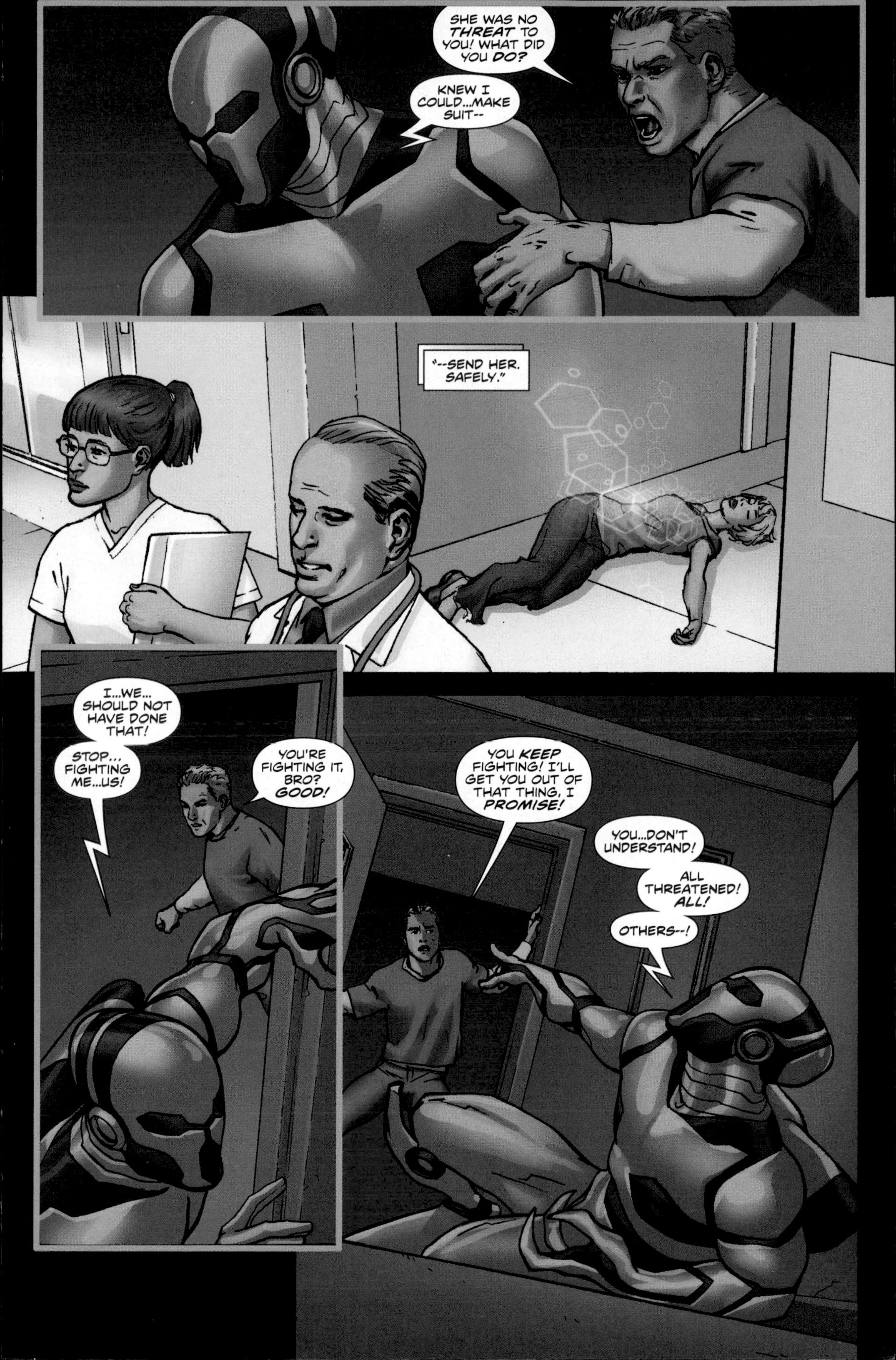
SHE WAS NO THREAT TO YOU! WHAT DID YOU DO?
KNEW I COULD...MAKE SUIT--
"--SEND HER. SAFELY."
I...WE... SHOULD NOT HAVE DONE THAT!
STOP... FIGHTING ME...US!
YOU'RE FIGHTING IT, BRO? GOOD!
YOU KEEP FIGHTING! I'LL GET YOU OUT OF THAT THING, I PROMISE!
YOU...DON'T UNDERSTAND!
ALL THREATENED! ALL!
OTHERS--!

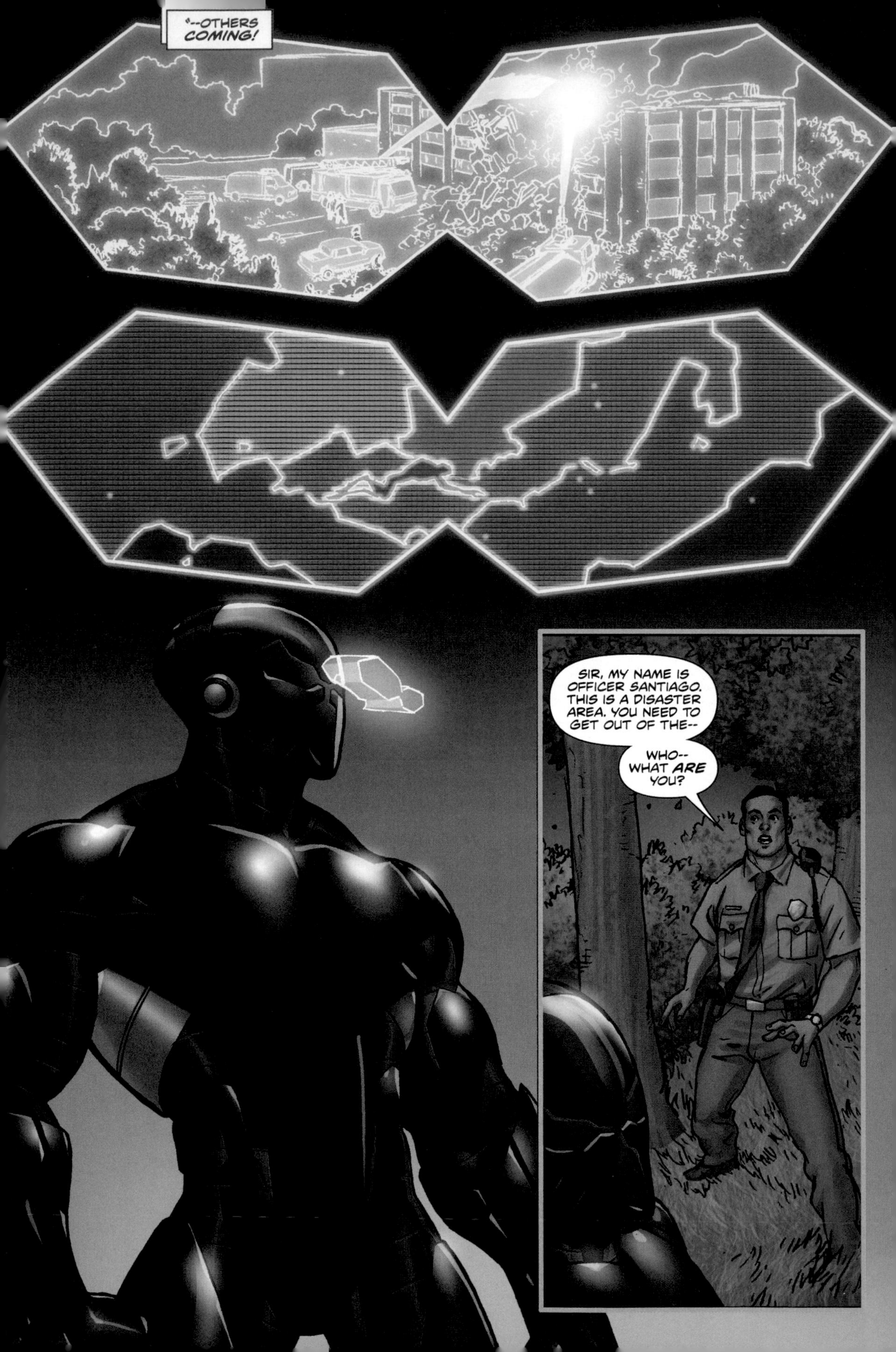
"--OTHERS COMING!
SIR, MY NAME IS OFFICER SANTIAGO. THIS IS A DISASTER AREA. YOU NEED TO GET OUT OF THE--
WHO-- WHAT ARE YOU?

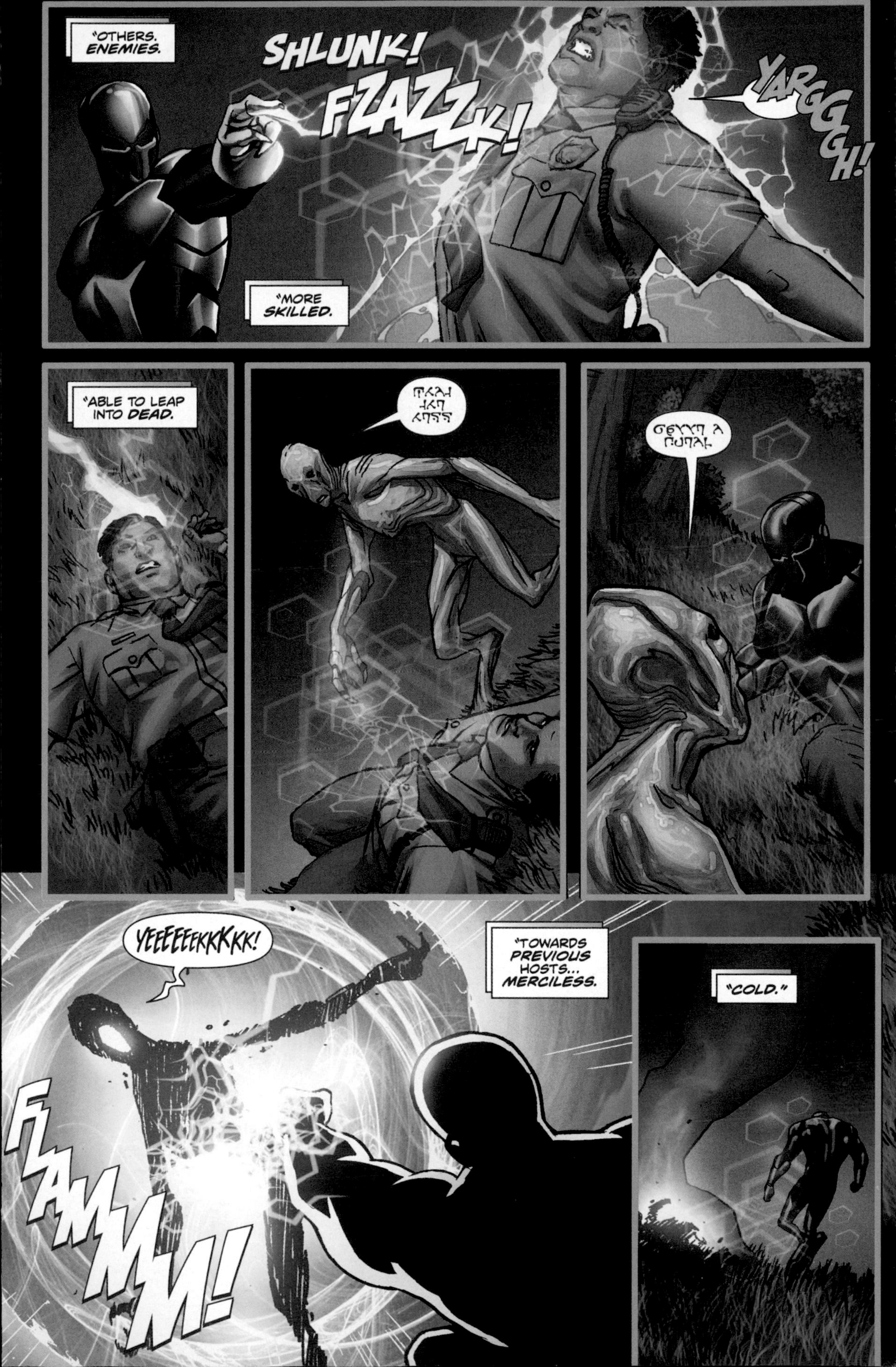
"OTHERS. ENEMIES.
SHLUNK!
FZAZZK!
YARGGGH!
"MORE SKILLED.
"ABLE TO LEAP INTO DEAD.
YEEEEEEKKKKK!
"TOWARDS PREVIOUS HOSTS... MERCILESS.
FLAMMM!
"COLD."

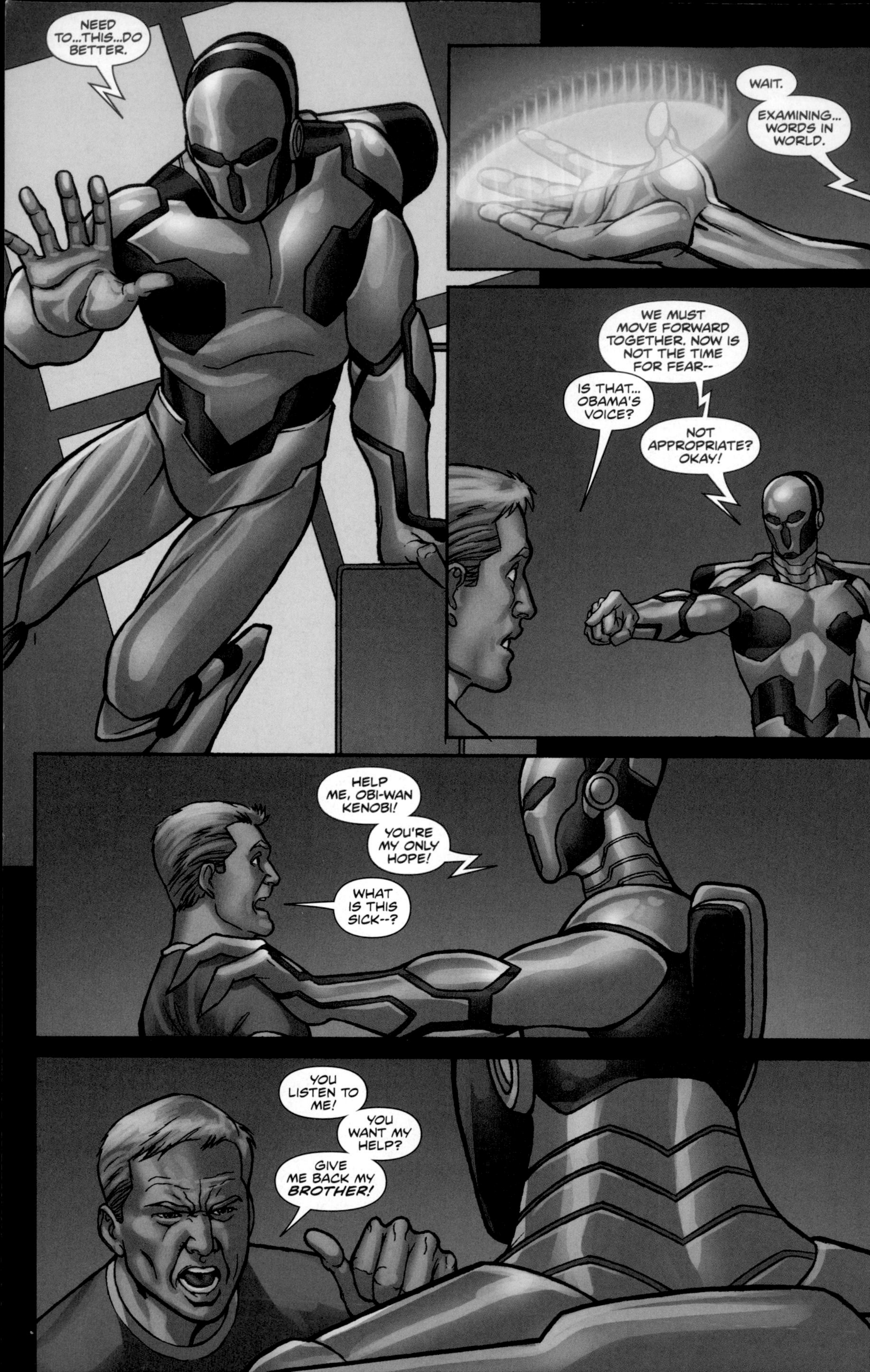
NEED TO...THIS...DO BETTER.
WAIT.
EXAMINING... WORDS IN WORLD.
WE MUST MOVE FORWARD TOGETHER. NOW IS NOT THE TIME FOR FEAR--
IS THAT... OBAMA'S VOICE?
NOT APPROPRIATE? OKAY!
HELP ME, OBI-WAN KENOBI!
YOU'RE MY ONLY HOPE!
WHAT IS THIS SICK--?
YOU LISTEN TO ME!
YOU WANT MY HELP?
GIVE ME BACK MY BROTHER!

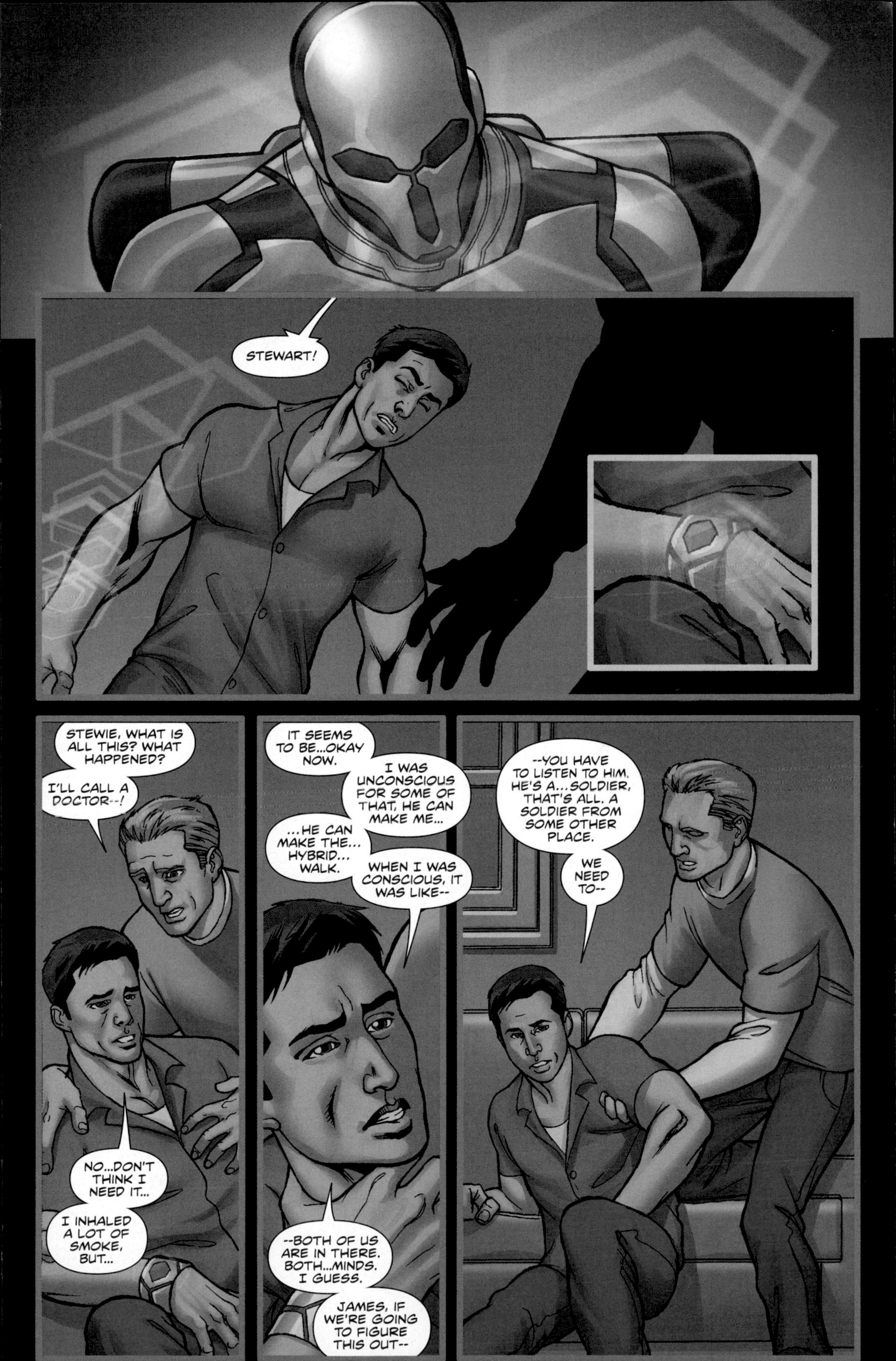
STEWART!
STEWIE, WHAT IS ALL THIS? WHAT HAPPENED?
I'LL CALL A DOCTOR--!
NO...DON'T THINK I NEED IT...
I INHALED A LOT OF SMOKE, BUT...
IT SEEMS TO BE...OKAY NOW.
I WAS UNCONSCIOUS FOR SOME OF THAT, HE CAN MAKE ME...
...HE CAN MAKE THE... HYBRID... WALK.
WHEN I WAS CONSCIOUS, IT WAS LIKE--
--BOTH OF US ARE IN THERE. BOTH...MINDS. I GUESS.
JAMES, IF WE'RE GOING TO FIGURE THIS OUT--
--YOU HAVE TO LISTEN TO HIM. HE'S A...SOLDIER, THAT'S ALL. A SOLDIER FROM SOME OTHER PLACE.
WE NEED TO--

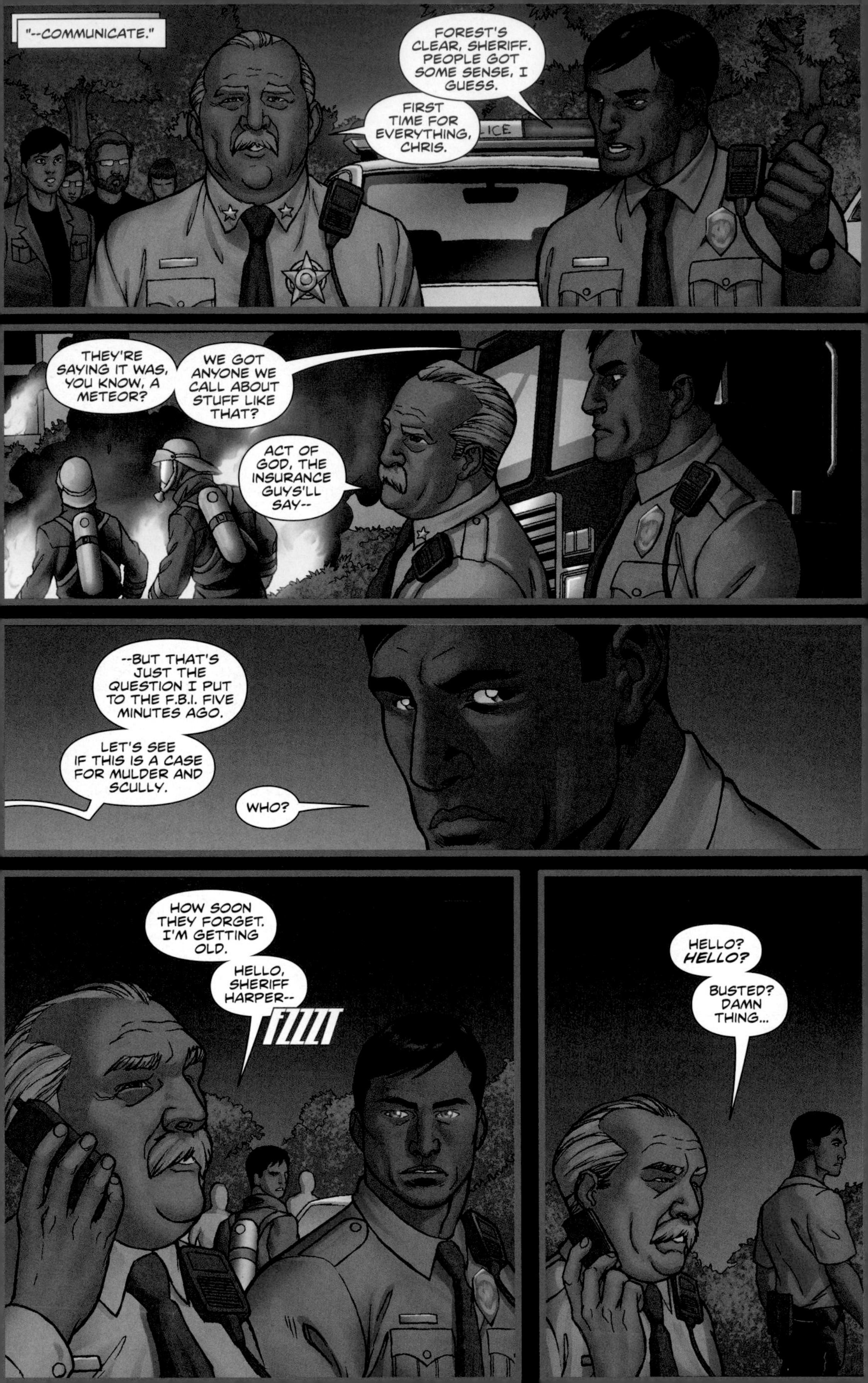
"--COMMUNICATE."
FOREST'S CLEAR, SHERIFF. PEOPLE GOT SOME SENSE, I GUESS.
FIRST TIME FOR EVERYTHING, CHRIS.
THEY'RE SAYING IT WAS, YOU KNOW, A METEOR?
WE GOT ANYONE WE CALL ABOUT STUFF LIKE THAT?
ACT OF GOD, THE INSURANCE GUYS'LL SAY--
--BUT THAT'S JUST THE QUESTION I PUT TO THE F.B.I. FIVE MINUTES AGO.
LET'S SEE IF THIS IS A CASE FOR MULDER AND SCULLY.
WHO?
HOW SOON THEY FORGET. I'M GETTING OLD.
HELLO, SHERIFF HARPER--
FZZZT
HELLO? *HELLO?*
BUSTED? DAMN THING...

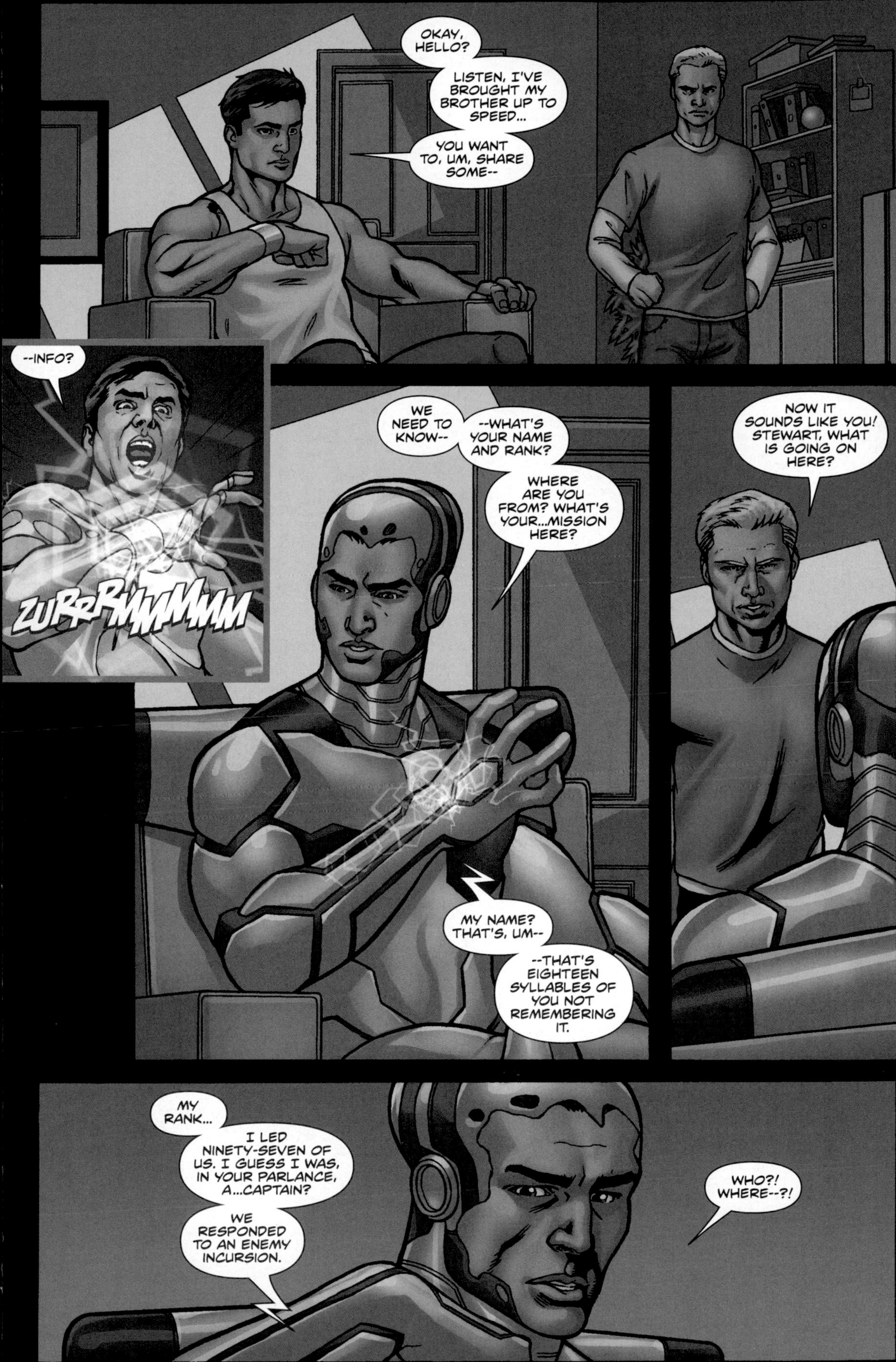
OKAY, HELLO?
LISTEN, I'VE BROUGHT MY BROTHER UP TO SPEED...
YOU WANT TO, UM, SHARE SOME--
--INFO?
ZURRRMMMMMM
WE NEED TO KNOW--
--WHAT'S YOUR NAME AND RANK?
WHERE ARE YOU FROM? WHAT'S YOUR...MISSION HERE?
NOW IT SOUNDS LIKE YOU! STEWART, WHAT IS GOING ON HERE?
MY NAME? THAT'S, UM--
--THAT'S EIGHTEEN SYLLABLES OF YOU NOT REMEMBERING IT.
MY RANK...
I LED NINETY-SEVEN OF US. I GUESS I WAS, IN YOUR PARLANCE, A...CAPTAIN?
WE RESPONDED TO AN ENEMY INCURSION.
WHO?! WHERE--?!

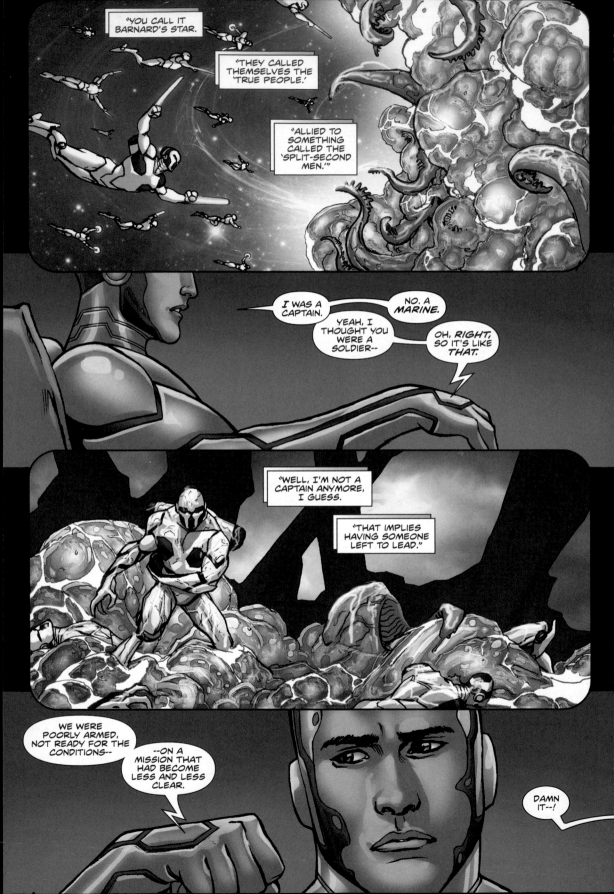

"YOU CALL IT BARNARD'S STAR.

"THEY CALLED THEMSELVES THE 'TRUE PEOPLE.'

"ALLIED TO SOMETHING CALLED THE 'SPLIT-SECOND MEN.'"

I WAS A CAPTAIN.

NO. A MARINE.

YEAH, I THOUGHT YOU WERE A SOLDIER--

OH, RIGHT, SO IT'S LIKE THAT.

"WELL, I'M NOT A CAPTAIN ANYMORE, I GUESS.

"THAT IMPLIES HAVING SOMEONE LEFT TO LEAD."

WE WERE POORLY ARMED, NOT READY FOR THE CONDITIONS--

--ON A MISSION THAT HAD BECOME LESS AND LESS CLEAR.

DAMN IT--!

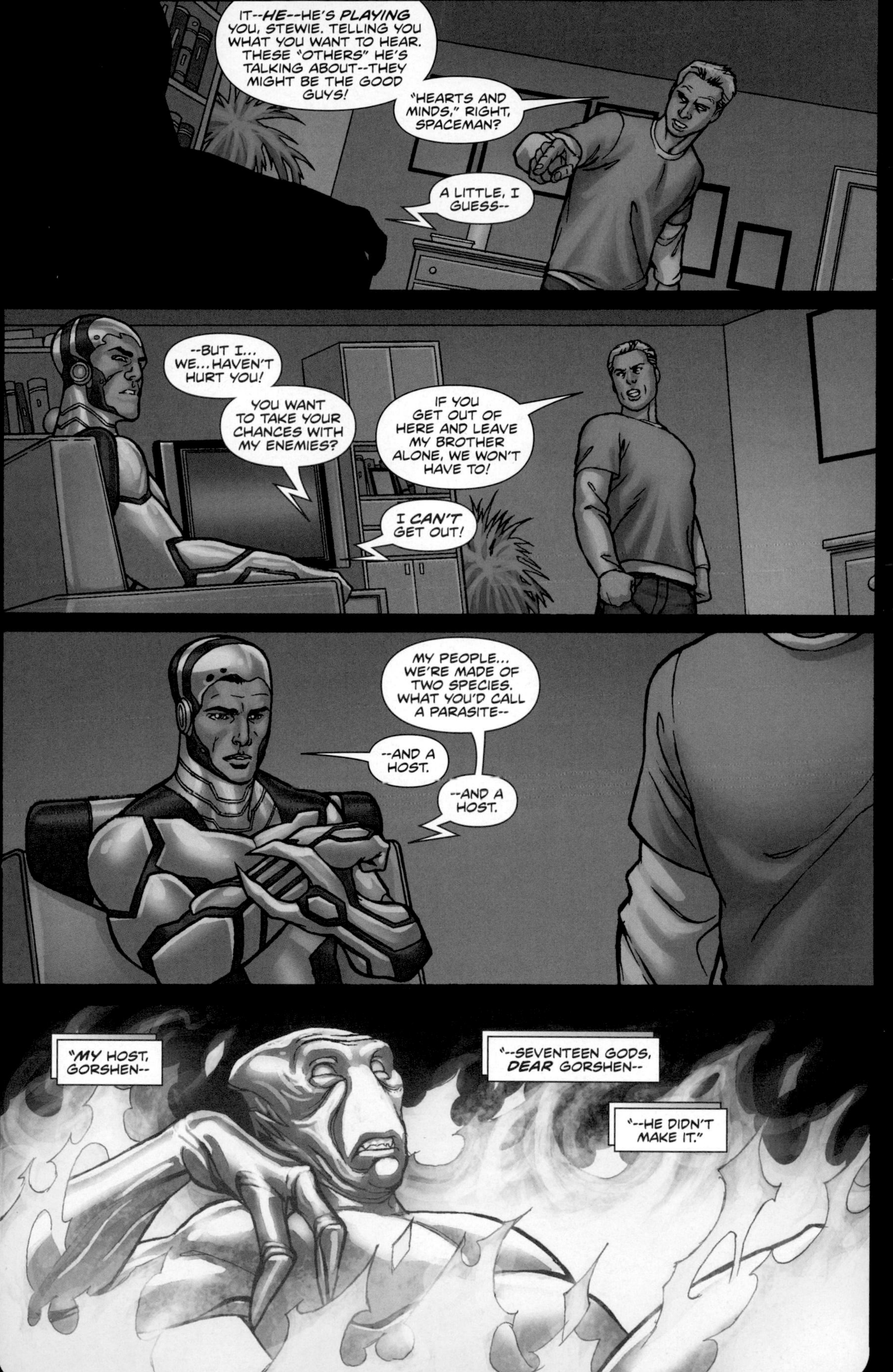

IT--*HE*--HE'S *PLAYING* YOU, STEWIE. TELLING YOU WHAT YOU WANT TO HEAR. THESE "OTHERS" HE'S TALKING ABOUT--THEY MIGHT BE THE GOOD GUYS!
"HEARTS AND MINDS," RIGHT, SPACEMAN?
A LITTLE, I GUESS--
--BUT I... WE... HAVEN'T HURT YOU!
YOU WANT TO TAKE YOUR CHANCES WITH MY ENEMIES?
IF YOU GET OUT OF HERE AND LEAVE MY BROTHER ALONE, WE WON'T HAVE TO!
I *CAN'T* GET OUT!
MY PEOPLE... WE'RE MADE OF TWO SPECIES. WHAT YOU'D CALL A PARASITE--
--AND A HOST.
--AND A HOST.
"*MY* HOST, GORSHEN--
"--SEVENTEEN GODS, *DEAR* GORSHEN--
"--HE DIDN'T MAKE IT."

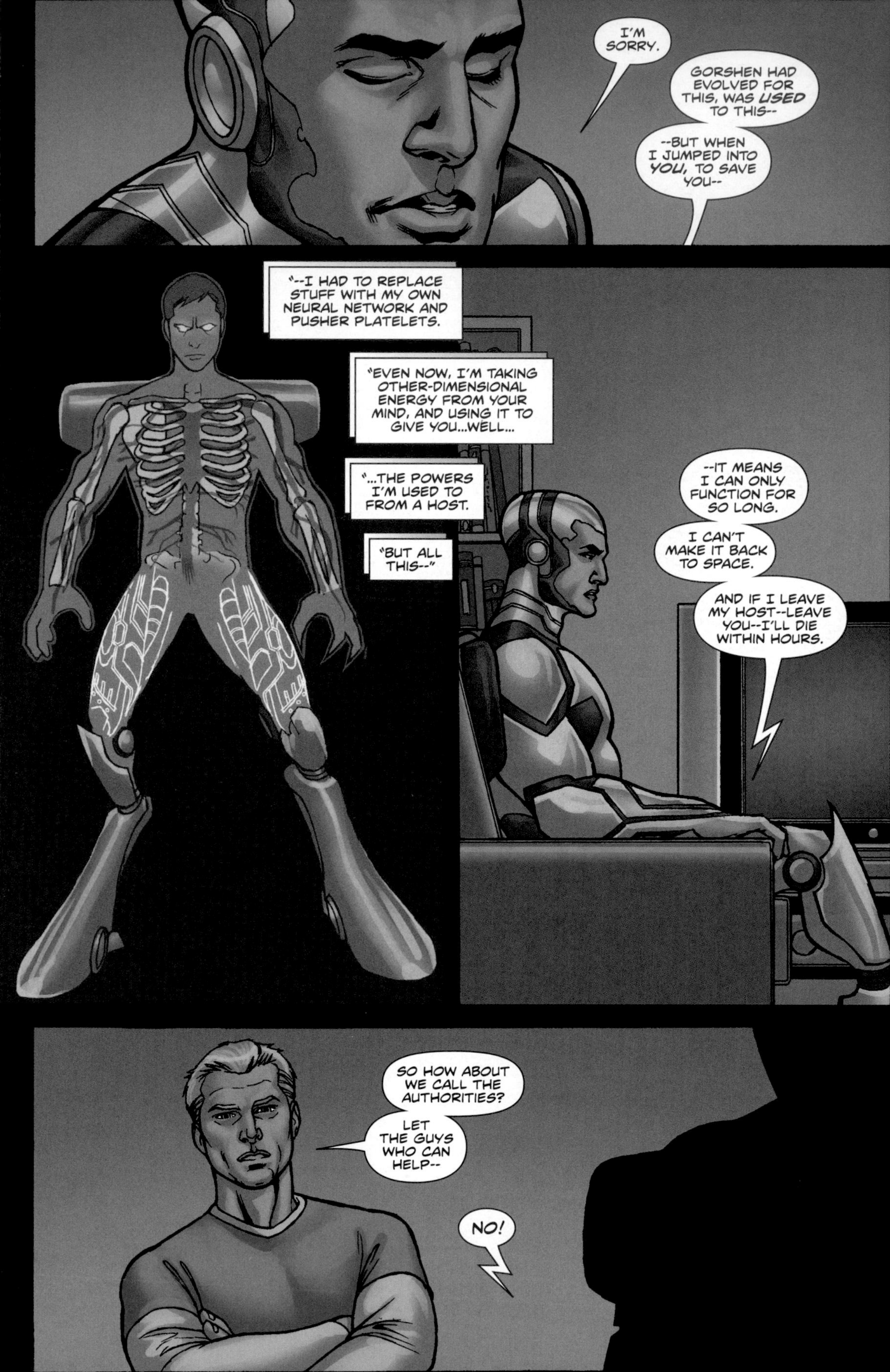
I'M SORRY.
GORSHEN HAD EVOLVED FOR THIS, WAS USED TO THIS--
--BUT WHEN I JUMPED INTO YOU, TO SAVE YOU--
"--I HAD TO REPLACE STUFF WITH MY OWN NEURAL NETWORK AND PUSHER PLATELETS.
"EVEN NOW, I'M TAKING OTHER-DIMENSIONAL ENERGY FROM YOUR MIND, AND USING IT TO GIVE YOU...WELL...
"...THE POWERS I'M USED TO FROM A HOST.
"BUT ALL THIS--"
--IT MEANS I CAN ONLY FUNCTION FOR SO LONG.
I CAN'T MAKE IT BACK TO SPACE.
AND IF I LEAVE MY HOST--LEAVE YOU--I'LL DIE WITHIN HOURS.
SO HOW ABOUT WE CALL THE AUTHORITIES?
LET THE GUYS WHO CAN HELP--
NO!

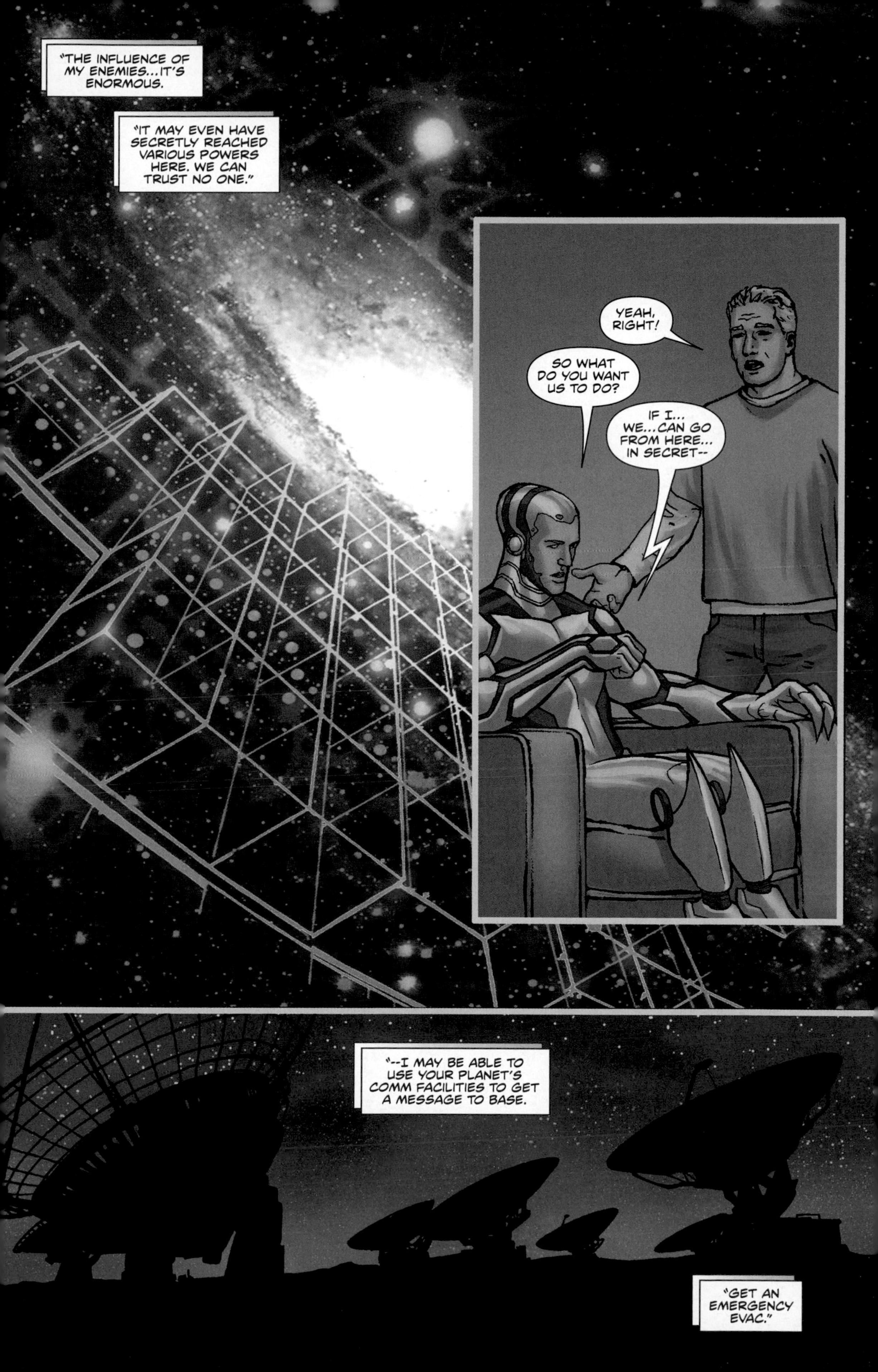
"THE INFLUENCE OF MY ENEMIES...IT'S ENORMOUS.
"IT MAY EVEN HAVE SECRETLY REACHED VARIOUS POWERS HERE. WE CAN TRUST NO ONE."
YEAH, RIGHT!
SO WHAT DO YOU WANT US TO DO?
IF I... WE...CAN GO FROM HERE... IN SECRET--
"--I MAY BE ABLE TO USE YOUR PLANET'S COMM FACILITIES TO GET A MESSAGE TO BASE.
"GET AN EMERGENCY EVAC."

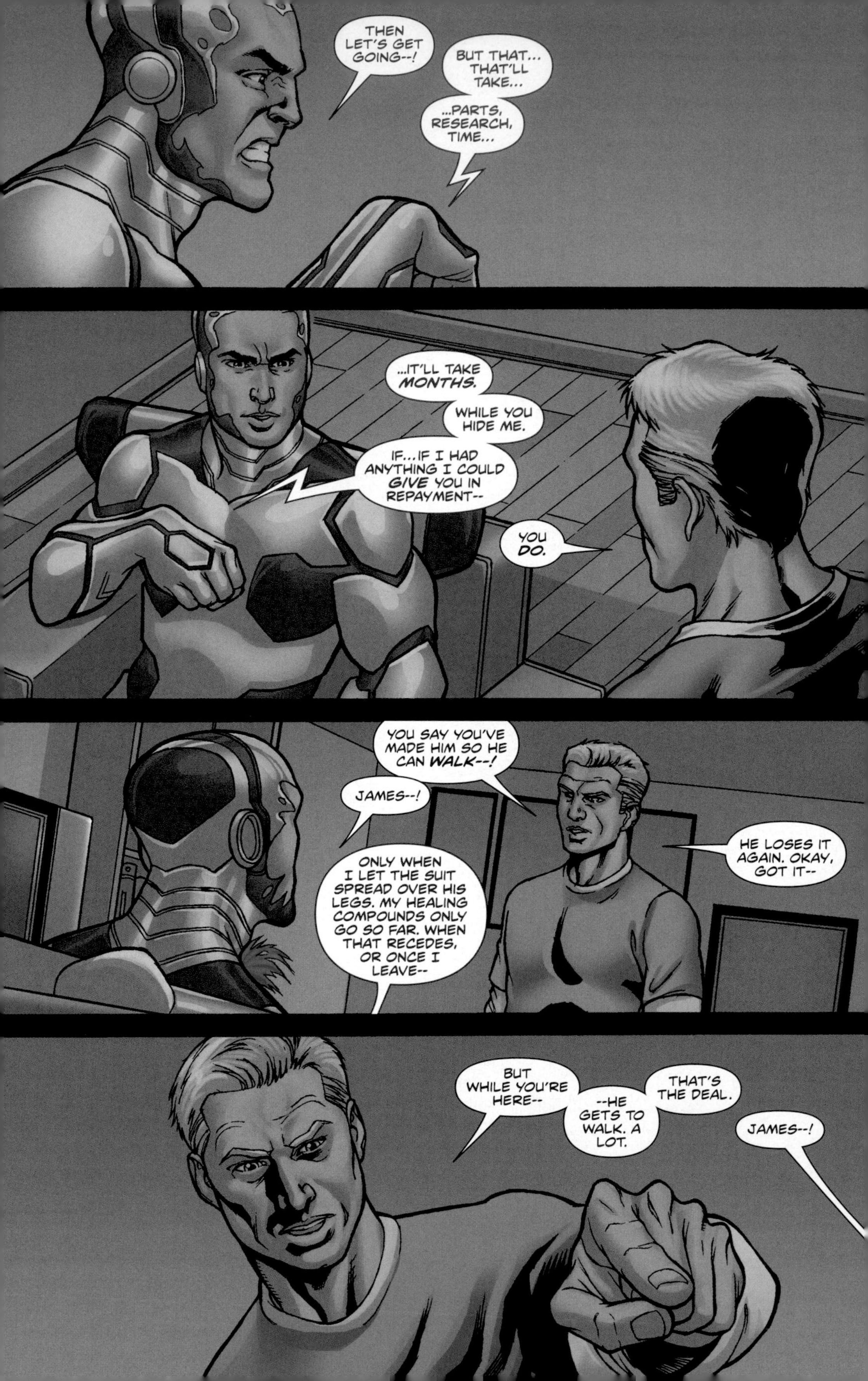
THEN LET'S GET GOING--!
BUT THAT... THAT'LL TAKE...
...PARTS, RESEARCH, TIME...
...IT'LL TAKE MONTHS.
WHILE YOU HIDE ME.
IF... IF I HAD ANYTHING I COULD GIVE YOU IN REPAYMENT--
YOU DO.
YOU SAY YOU'VE MADE HIM SO HE CAN WALK--!
JAMES--!
ONLY WHEN I LET THE SUIT SPREAD OVER HIS LEGS. MY HEALING COMPOUNDS ONLY GO SO FAR. WHEN THAT RECEDES, OR ONCE I LEAVE--
HE LOSES IT AGAIN. OKAY, GOT IT--
BUT WHILE YOU'RE HERE--
--HE GETS TO WALK. A LOT.
THAT'S THE DEAL.
JAMES--!

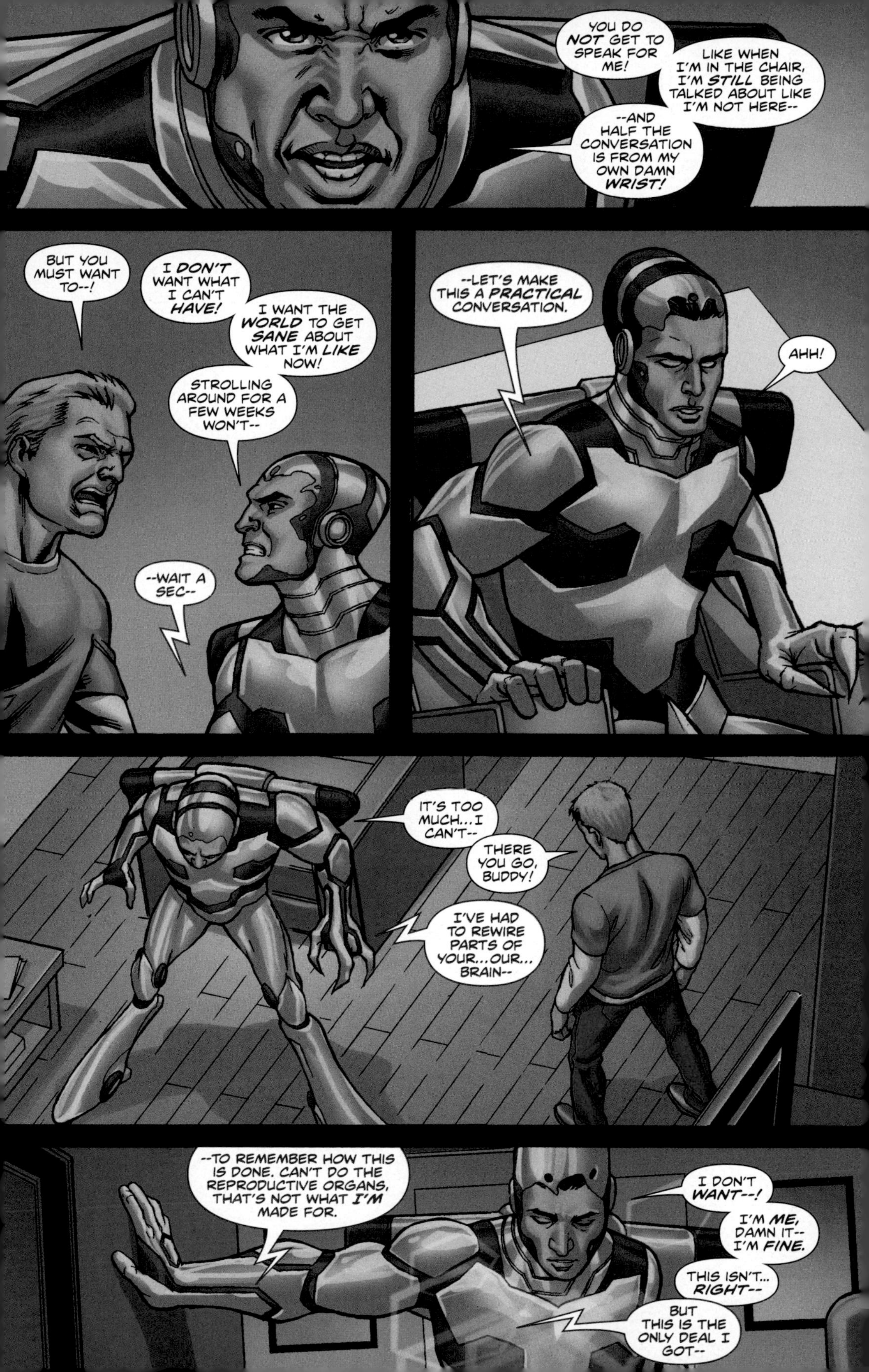
YOU DO NOT GET TO SPEAK FOR ME!
LIKE WHEN I'M IN THE CHAIR, I'M STILL BEING TALKED ABOUT LIKE I'M NOT HERE--
--AND HALF THE CONVERSATION IS FROM MY OWN DAMN WRIST!
BUT YOU MUST WANT TO--!
I DON'T WANT WHAT I CAN'T HAVE!
I WANT THE WORLD TO GET SANE ABOUT WHAT I'M LIKE NOW!
STROLLING AROUND FOR A FEW WEEKS WON'T--
--WAIT A SEC--
--LET'S MAKE THIS A PRACTICAL CONVERSATION.
AHH!
IT'S TOO MUCH... I CAN'T--
THERE YOU GO, BUDDY!
I'VE HAD TO REWIRE PARTS OF YOUR... OUR... BRAIN--
--TO REMEMBER HOW THIS IS DONE. CAN'T DO THE REPRODUCTIVE ORGANS, THAT'S NOT WHAT I'M MADE FOR.
I DON'T WANT--!
I'M ME, DAMN IT-- I'M FINE.
THIS ISN'T... RIGHT--
BUT THIS IS THE ONLY DEAL I GOT--

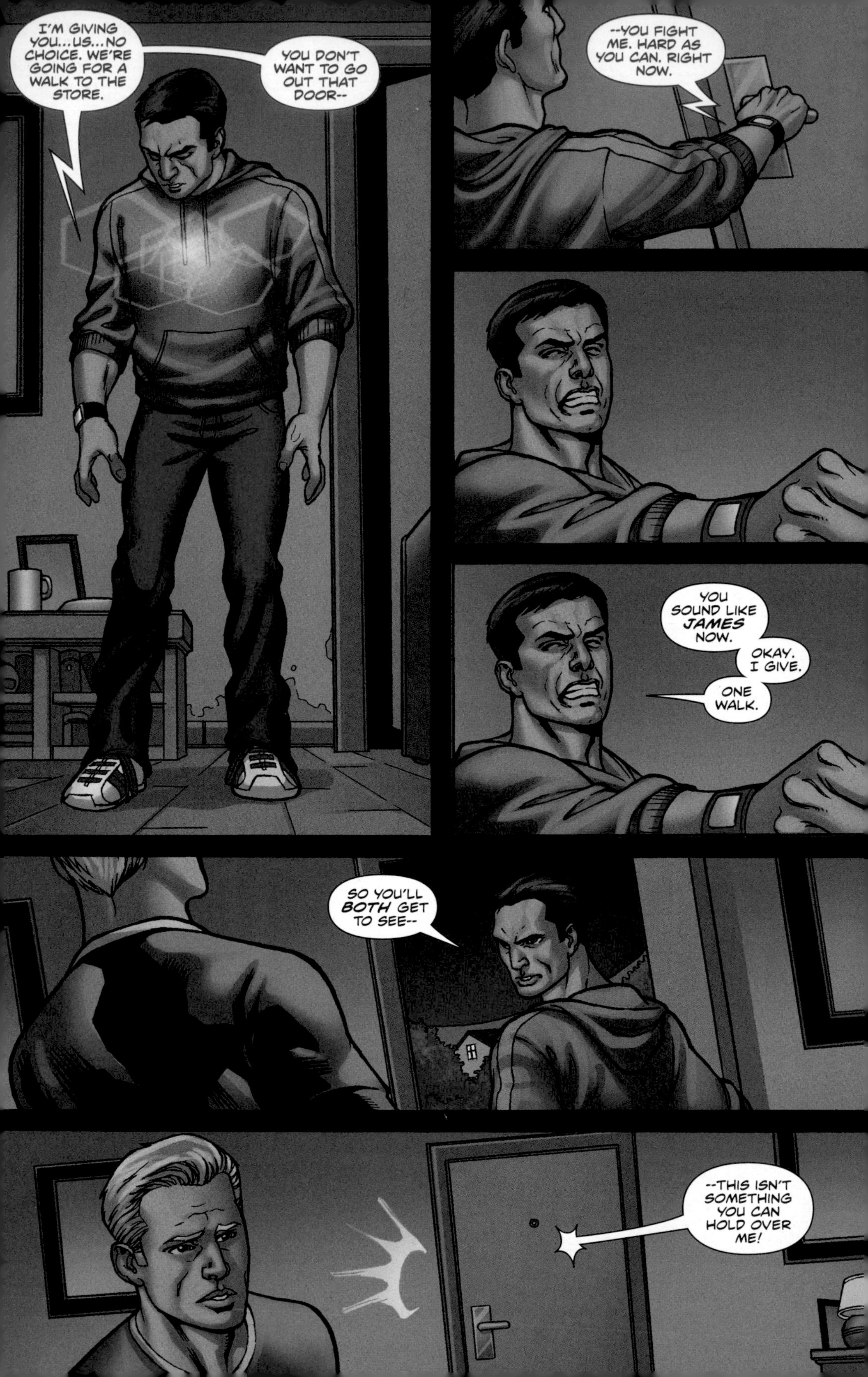
I'M GIVING YOU...US...NO CHOICE. WE'RE GOING FOR A WALK TO THE STORE.
YOU DON'T WANT TO GO OUT THAT DOOR--
--YOU FIGHT ME. HARD AS YOU CAN. RIGHT NOW.
YOU SOUND LIKE JAMES NOW.
OKAY. I GIVE.
ONE WALK.
SO YOU'LL BOTH GET TO SEE--
--THIS ISN'T SOMETHING YOU CAN HOLD OVER ME!

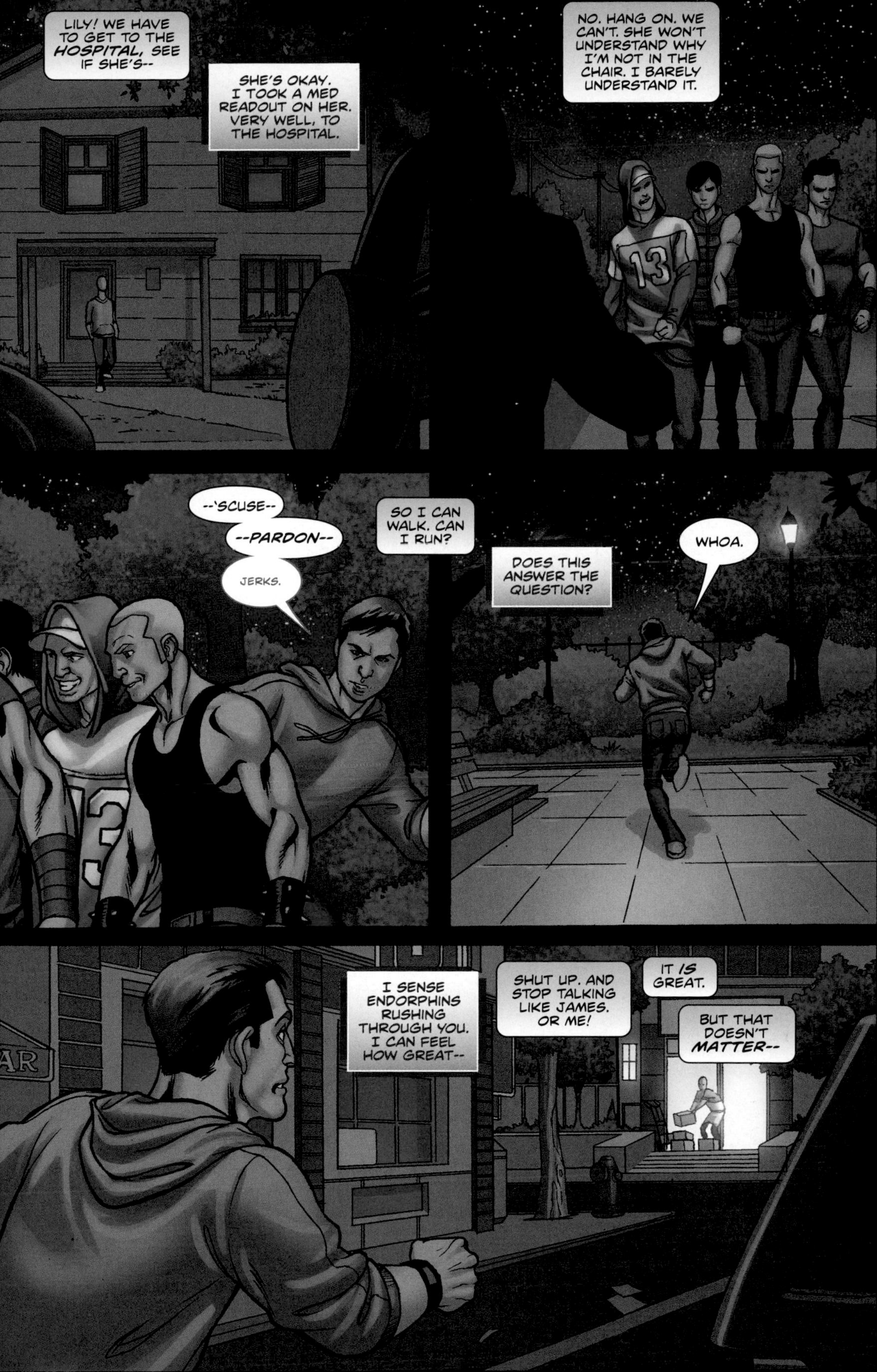

LILY! WE HAVE TO GET TO THE *HOSPITAL*, SEE IF SHE'S--
SHE'S OKAY. I TOOK A MED READOUT ON HER. VERY WELL, TO THE HOSPITAL.
NO. HANG ON. WE CAN'T. SHE WON'T UNDERSTAND WHY I'M NOT IN THE CHAIR. I BARELY UNDERSTAND IT.
--'SCUSE--
--*PARDON*--
JERKS.
SO I CAN WALK. CAN I RUN?
DOES THIS ANSWER THE QUESTION?
WHOA.
I SENSE ENDORPHINS RUSHING THROUGH YOU. I CAN FEEL HOW GREAT--
SHUT UP. AND STOP TALKING LIKE JAMES. OR ME!
IT *IS* GREAT.
BUT THAT DOESN'T *MATTER*--

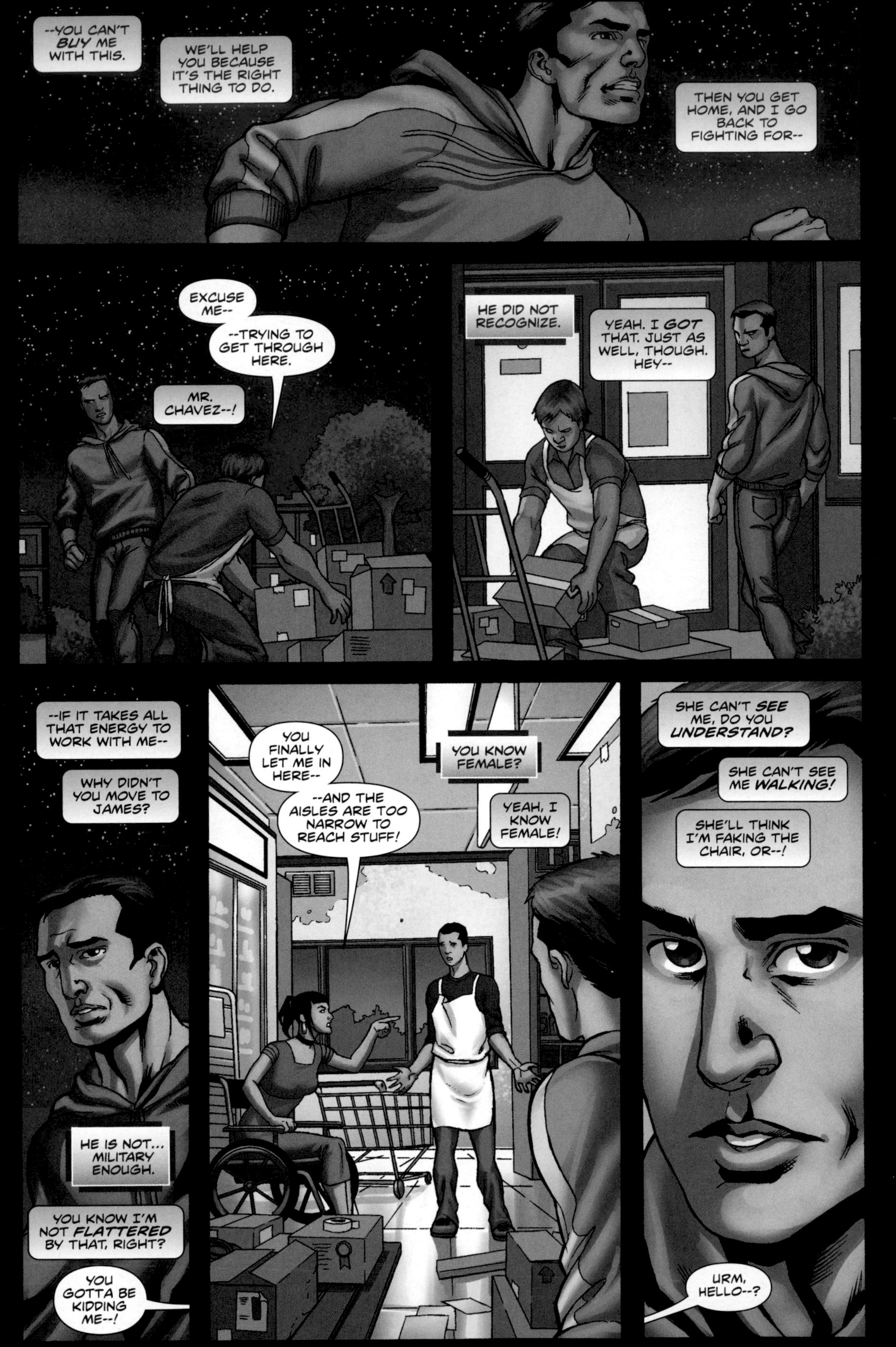
--YOU CAN'T *BUY* ME WITH THIS.
WE'LL HELP YOU BECAUSE IT'S THE RIGHT THING TO DO.
THEN YOU GET HOME, AND I GO BACK TO FIGHTING FOR--
EXCUSE ME--
--TRYING TO GET THROUGH HERE.
MR. CHAVEZ--!
HE DID NOT RECOGNIZE.
YEAH. I *GOT* THAT. JUST AS WELL, THOUGH. HEY--
--IF IT TAKES ALL THAT ENERGY TO WORK WITH ME--
WHY DIDN'T YOU MOVE TO JAMES?
HE IS NOT... MILITARY ENOUGH.
YOU KNOW I'M NOT *FLATTERED* BY THAT, RIGHT?
YOU GOTTA BE KIDDING ME--!
YOU FINALLY LET ME IN HERE--
--AND THE AISLES ARE TOO NARROW TO REACH STUFF!
YOU KNOW FEMALE?
YEAH, I KNOW FEMALE!
SHE CAN'T *SEE* ME, DO YOU *UNDERSTAND?*
SHE CAN'T SEE ME *WALKING!*
SHE'LL THINK I'M FAKING THE CHAIR, OR--!
URM, HELLO--?

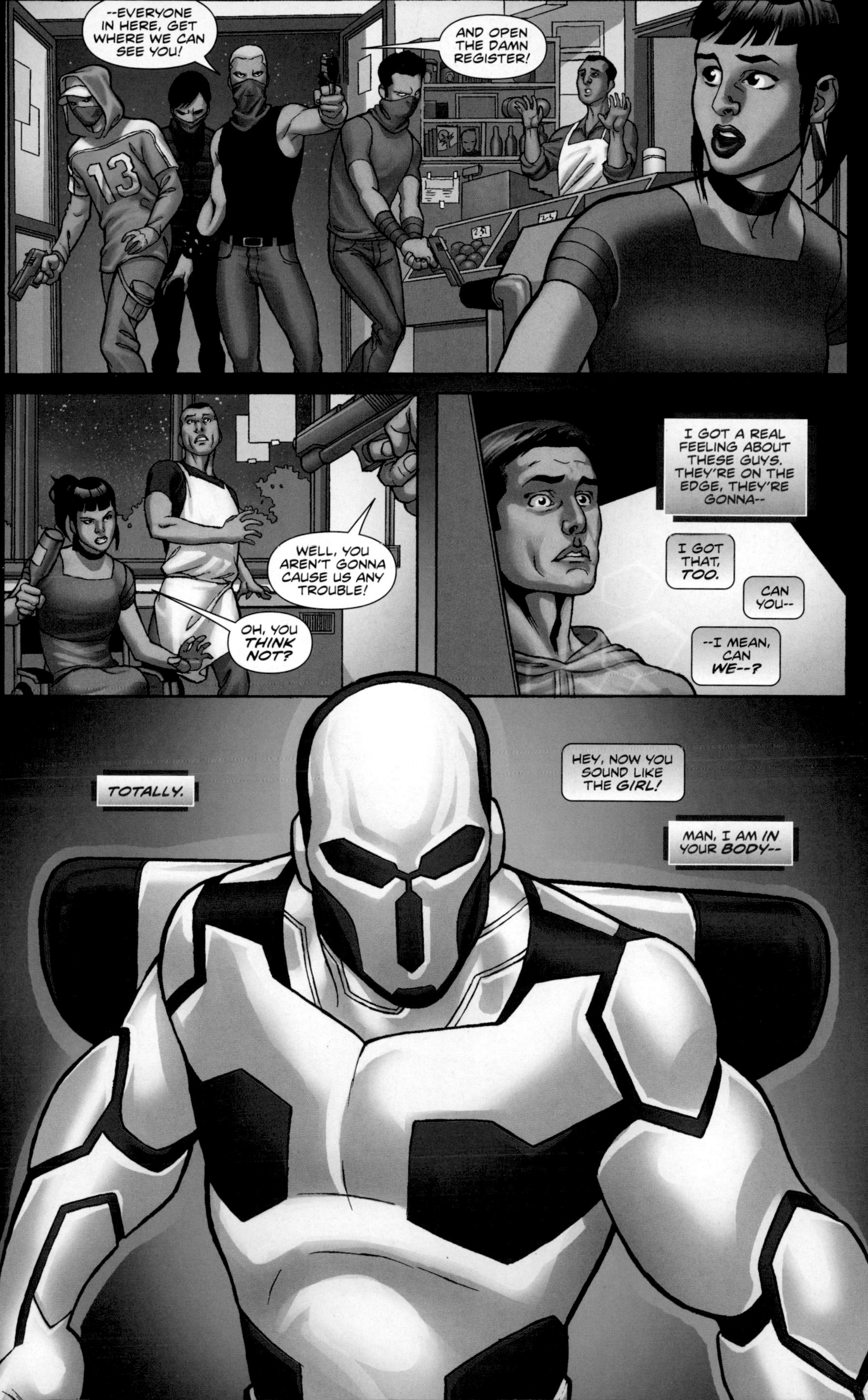
--EVERYONE IN HERE, GET WHERE WE CAN SEE YOU!
AND OPEN THE DAMN REGISTER!
WELL, YOU AREN'T GONNA CAUSE US ANY TROUBLE!
OH, YOU THINK NOT?
I GOT A REAL FEELING ABOUT THESE GUYS. THEY'RE ON THE EDGE, THEY'RE GONNA--
I GOT THAT, TOO.
CAN YOU--
--I MEAN, CAN WE--?
TOTALLY.
HEY, NOW YOU SOUND LIKE THE GIRL!
MAN, I AM IN YOUR BODY--

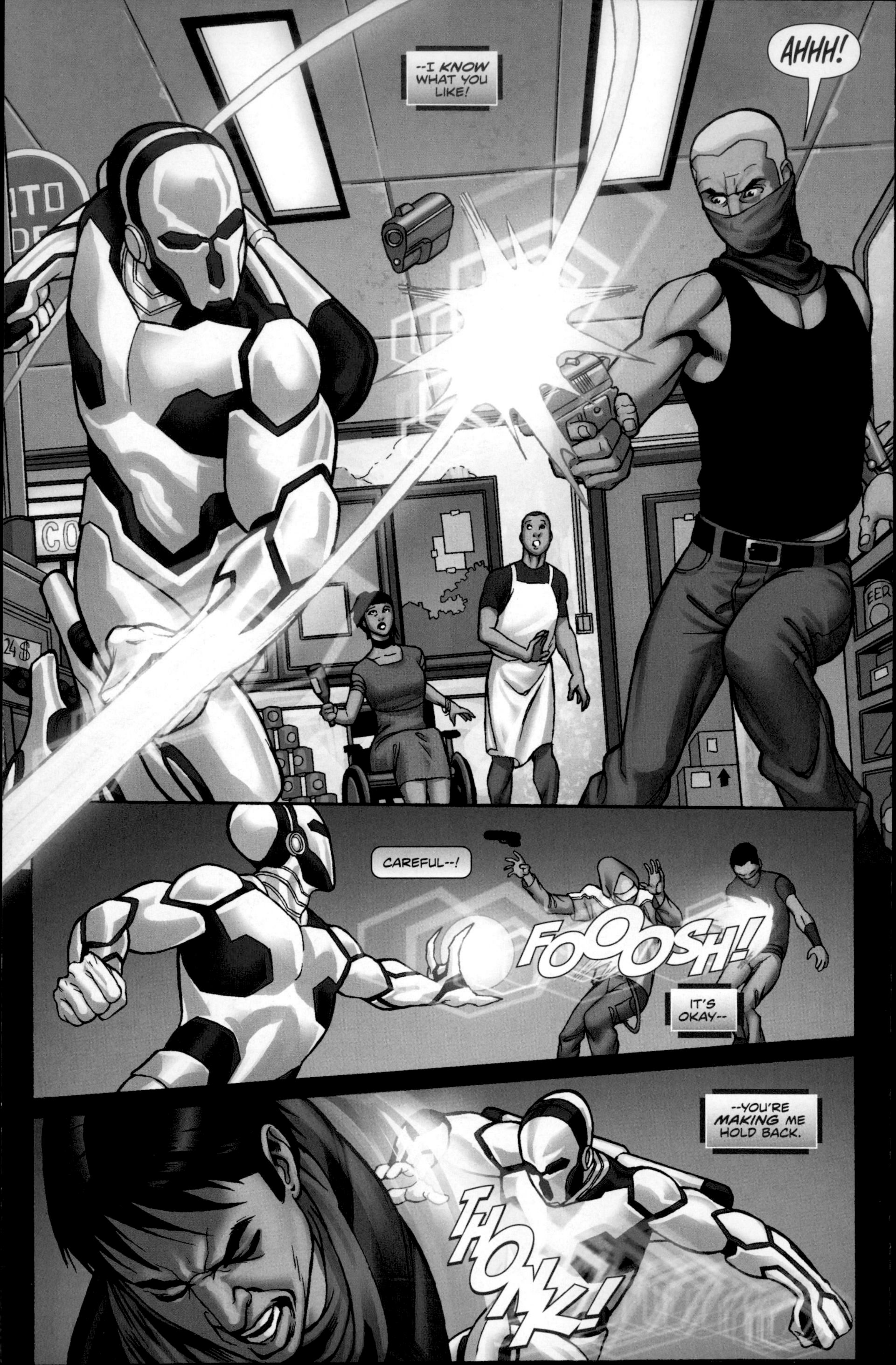
--I KNOW WHAT YOU LIKE!
AHHH!
CAREFUL--!
FOOOOSH!
IT'S OKAY--
--YOU'RE MAKING ME HOLD BACK.
THONK!

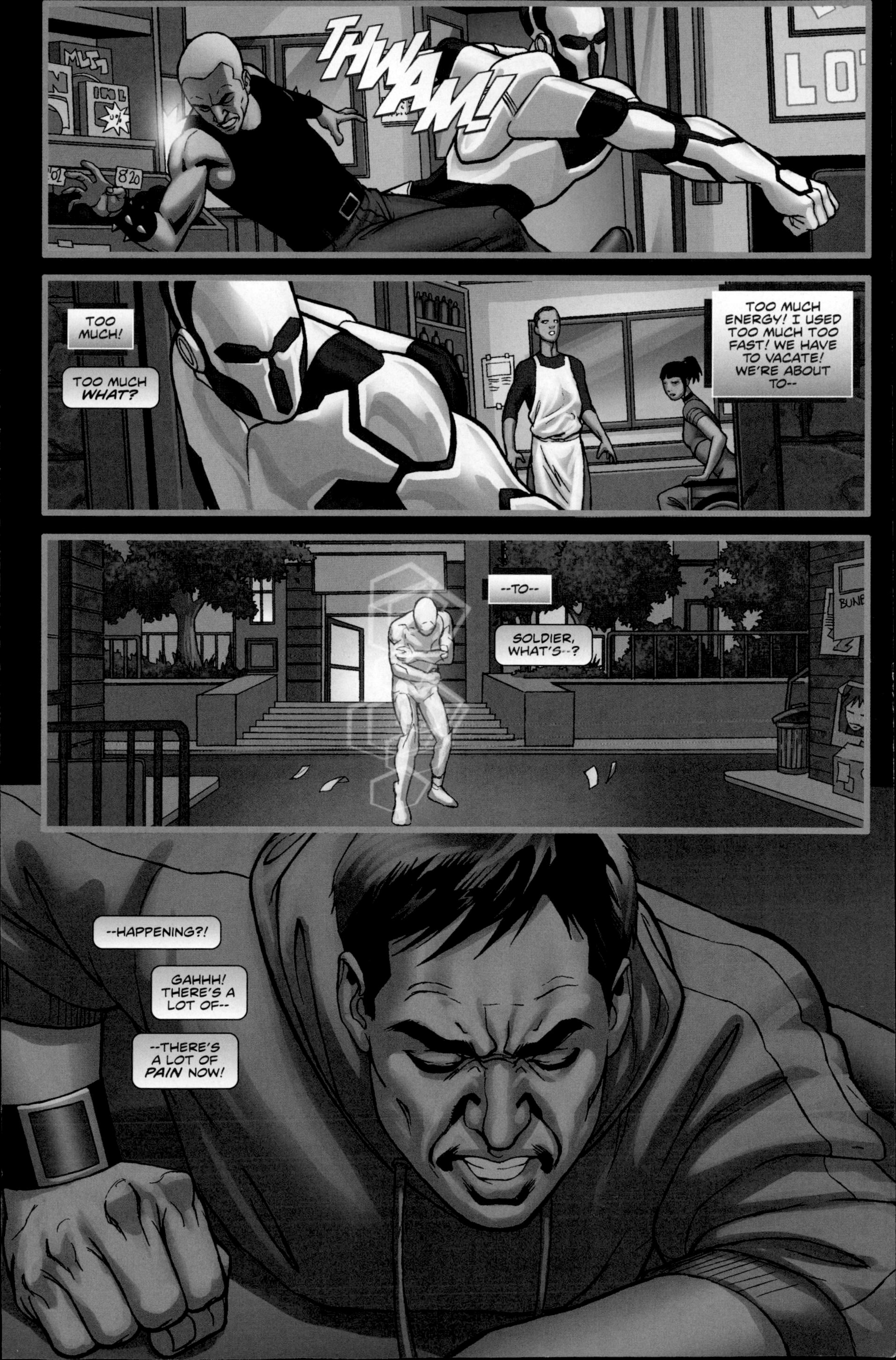
THWAM!
TOO MUCH!
TOO MUCH WHAT?
TOO MUCH ENERGY! I USED TOO MUCH TOO FAST! WE HAVE TO VACATE! WE'RE ABOUT TO--
--TO--
SOLDIER, WHAT'S--?
--HAPPENING?!
GAHHH! THERE'S A LOT OF--
--THERE'S A LOT OF PAIN NOW!

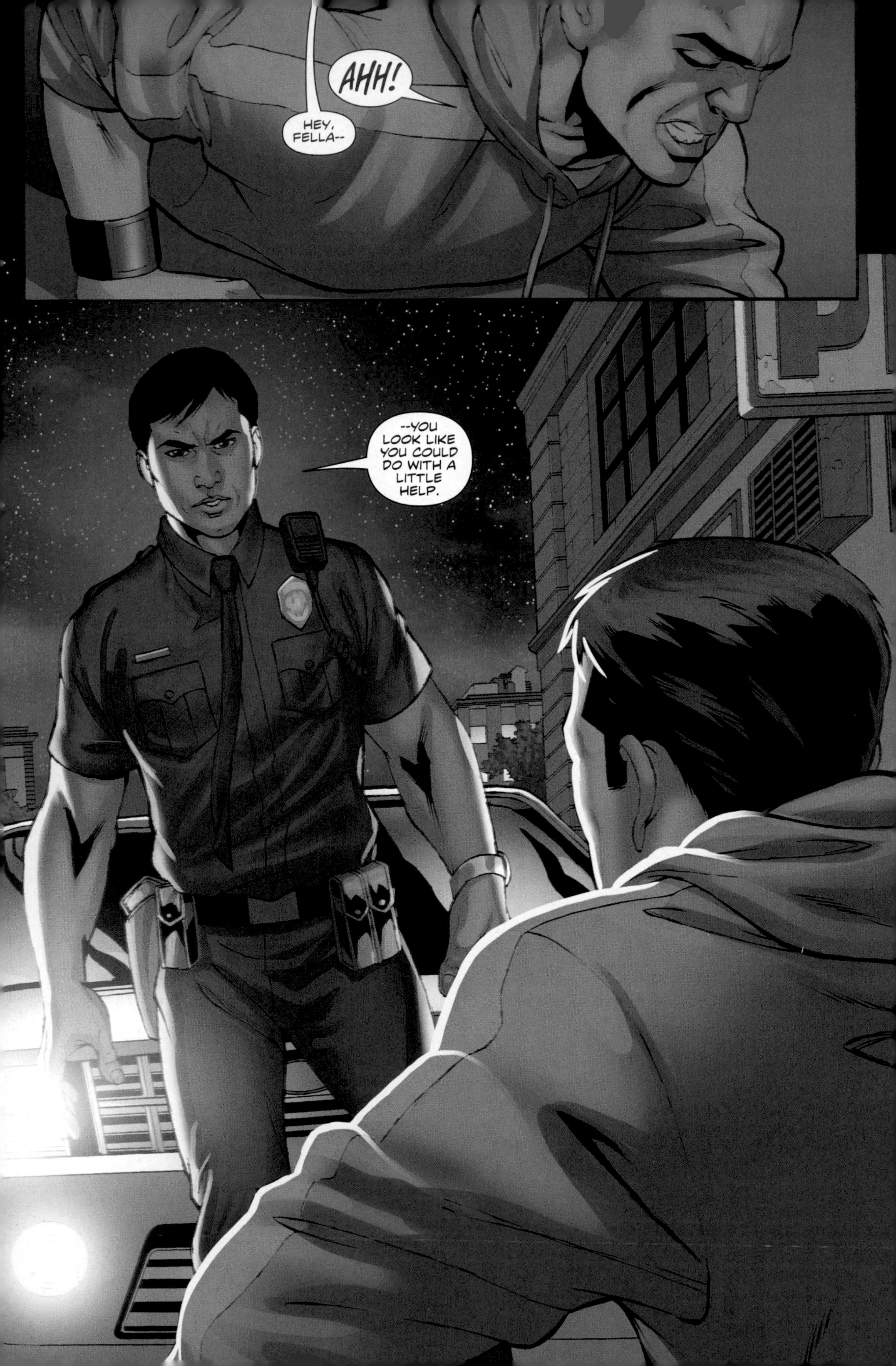
AHH!
HEY, FELLA--
--YOU LOOK LIKE YOU COULD DO WITH A LITTLE HELP.

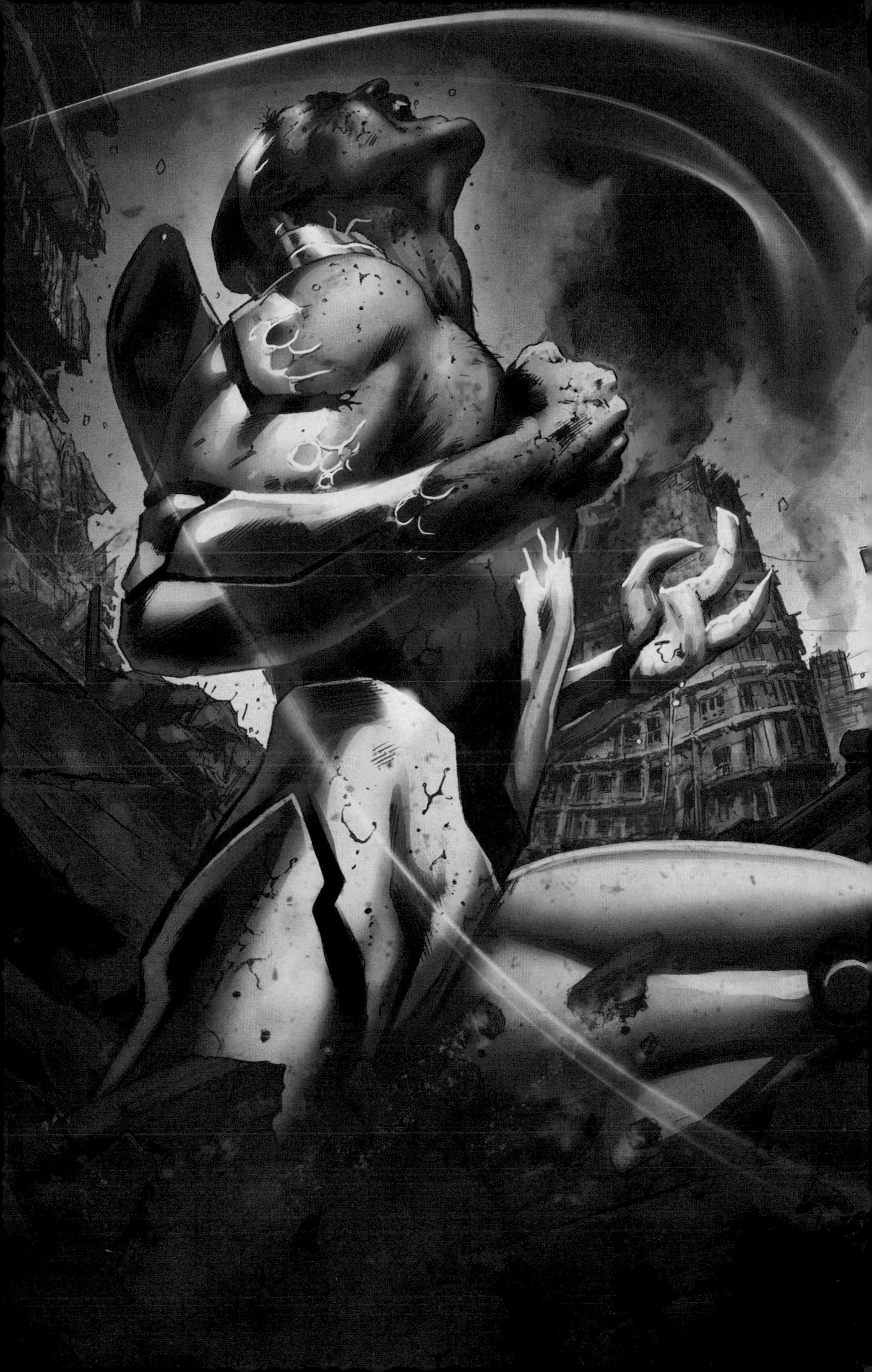

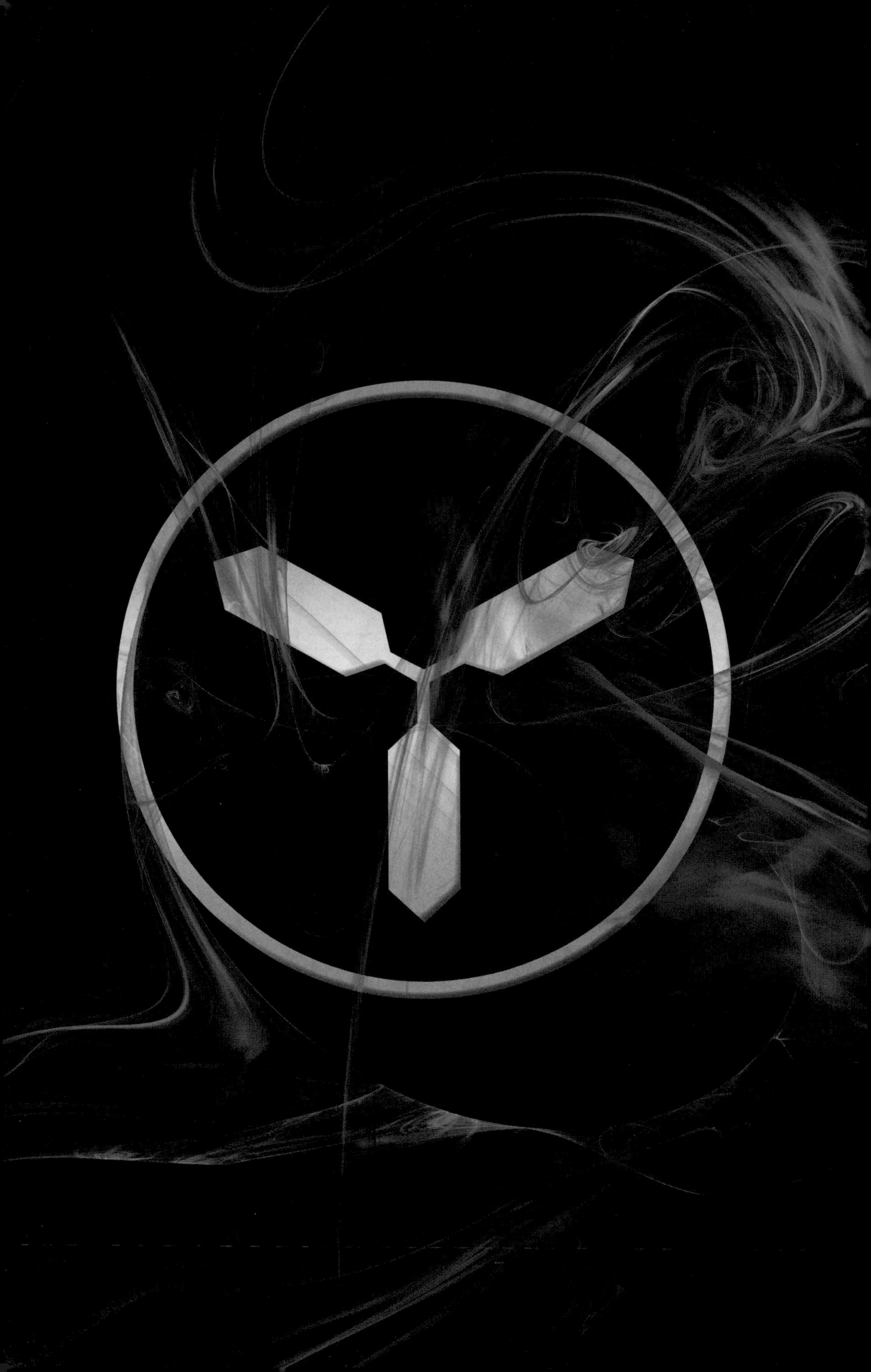

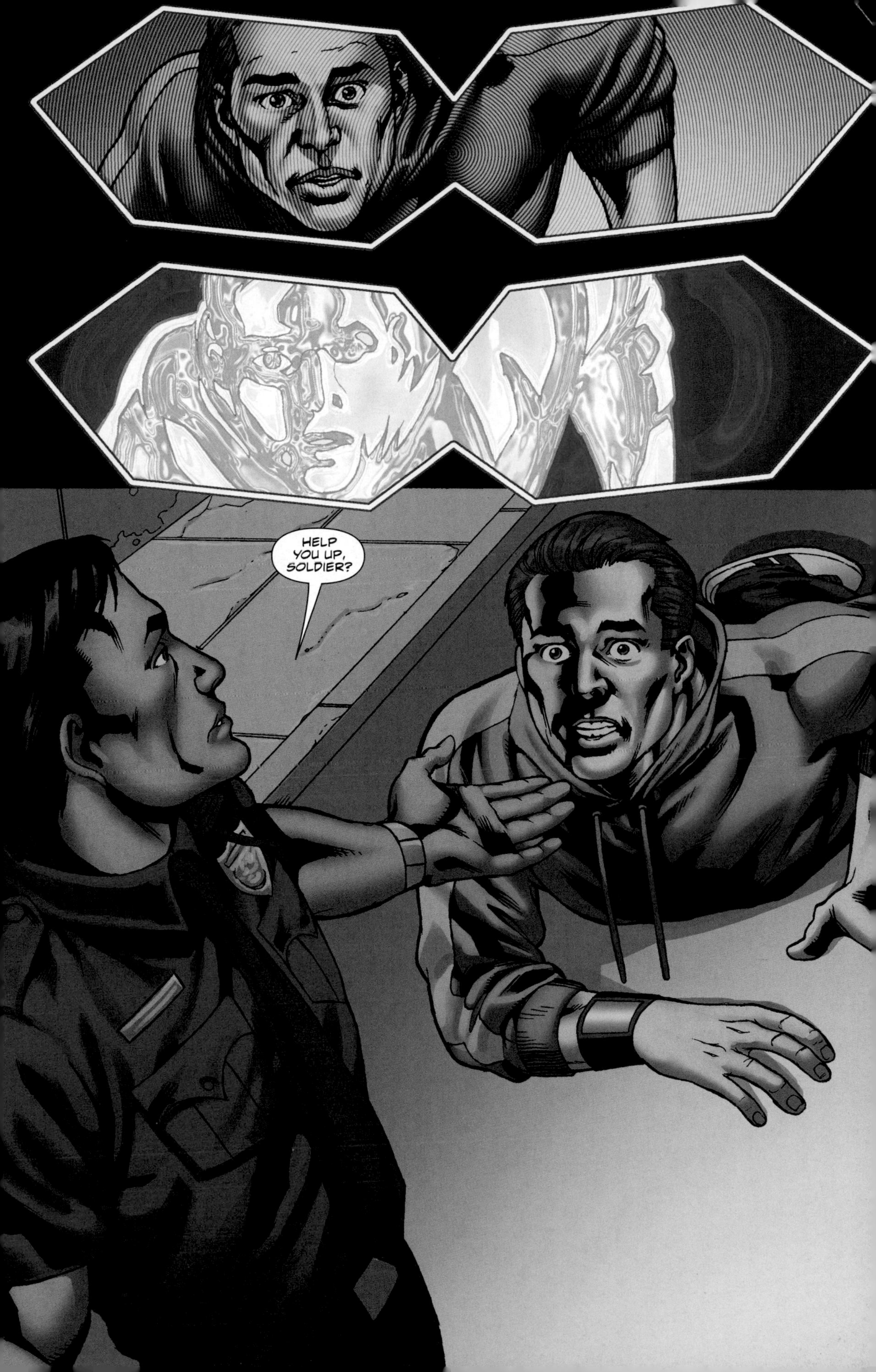
HELP YOU UP, SOLDIER?

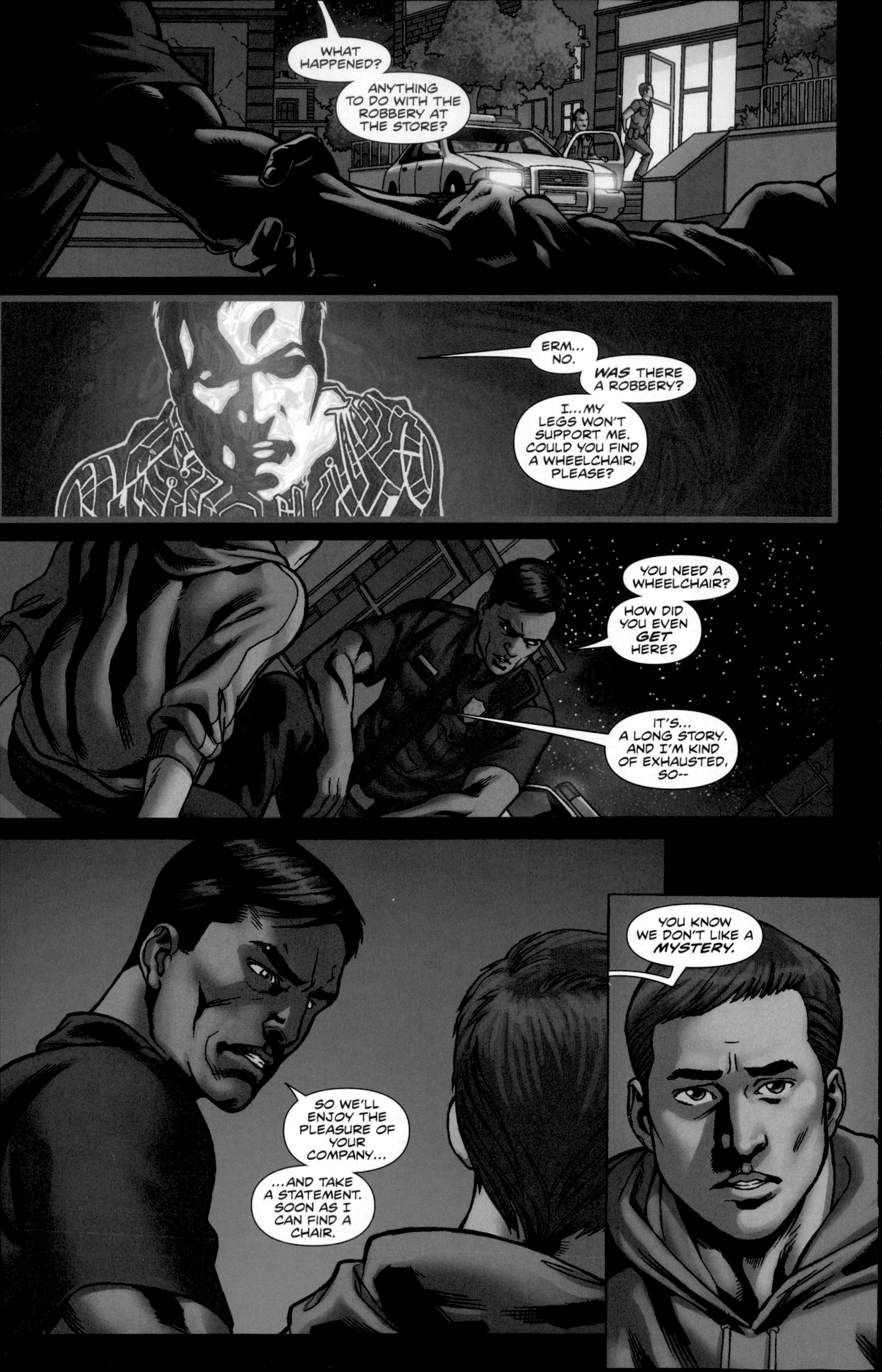
WHAT HAPPENED?
ANYTHING TO DO WITH THE ROBBERY AT THE STORE?
ERM... NO.
WAS THERE A ROBBERY?
I...MY LEGS WON'T SUPPORT ME. COULD YOU FIND A WHEELCHAIR, PLEASE?
YOU NEED A WHEELCHAIR?
HOW DID YOU EVEN GET HERE?
IT'S... A LONG STORY. AND I'M KIND OF EXHAUSTED, SO--
YOU KNOW WE DON'T LIKE A MYSTERY.
SO WE'LL ENJOY THE PLEASURE OF YOUR COMPANY...
...AND TAKE A STATEMENT. SOON AS I CAN FIND A CHAIR.

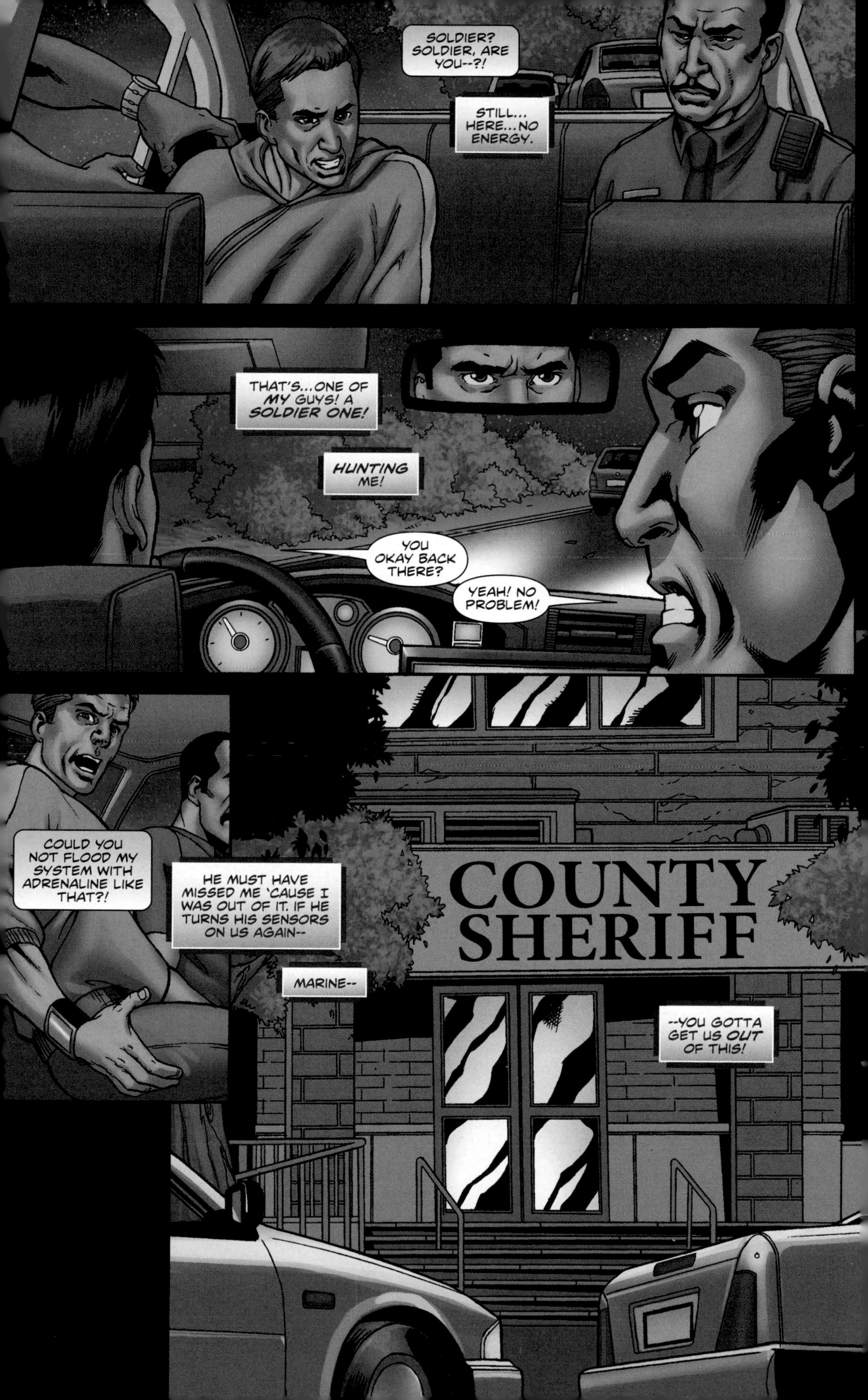
SOLDIER? SOLDIER, ARE YOU--?!
STILL... HERE...NO ENERGY.
THAT'S...ONE OF MY GUYS! A SOLDIER ONE!
HUNTING ME!
YOU OKAY BACK THERE?
YEAH! NO PROBLEM!
COULD YOU NOT FLOOD MY SYSTEM WITH ADRENALINE LIKE THAT?!
HE MUST HAVE MISSED ME 'CAUSE I WAS OUT OF IT. IF HE TURNS HIS SENSORS ON US AGAIN--
MARINE--
COUNTY SHERIFF
--YOU GOTTA GET US OUT OF THIS!

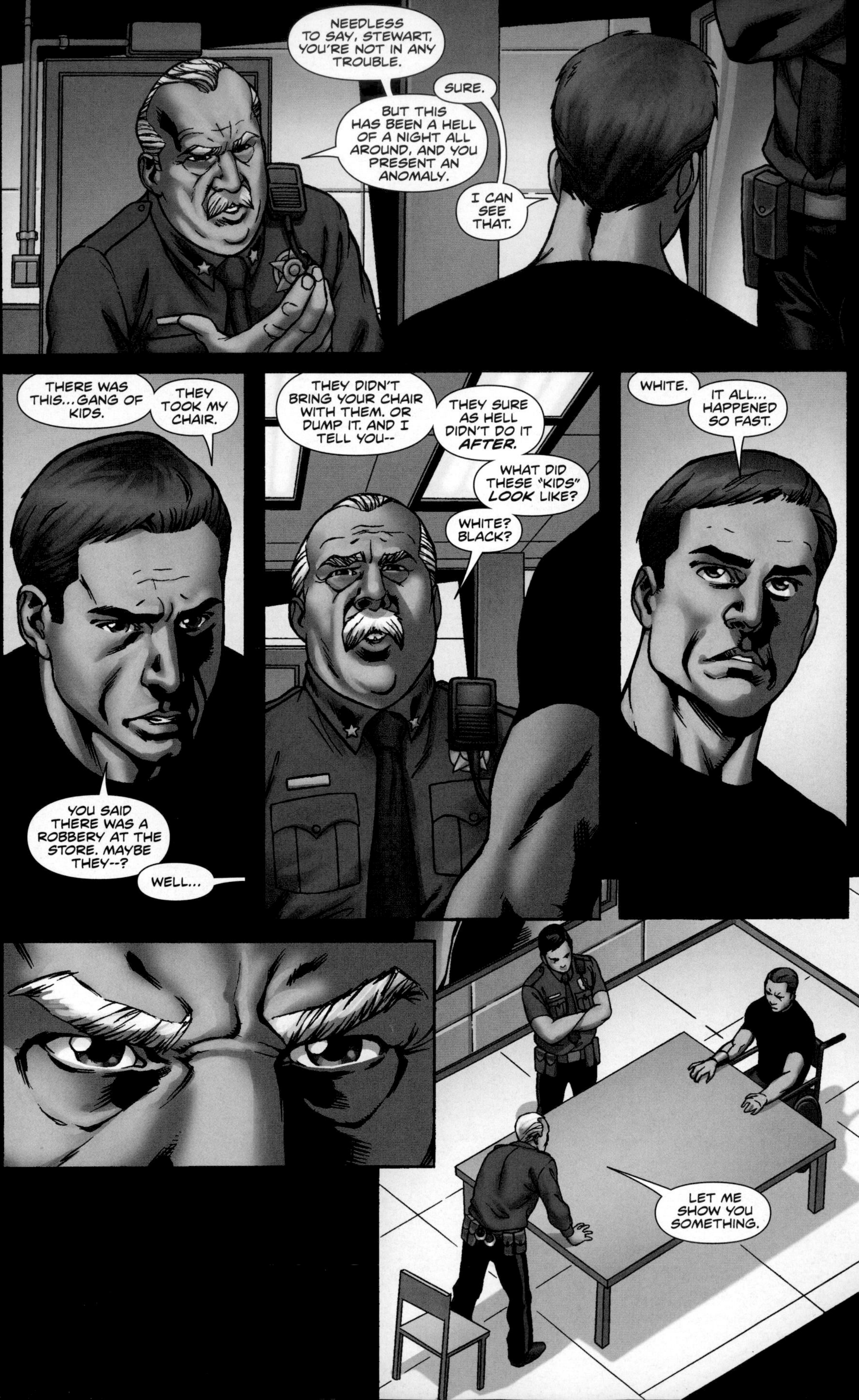
NEEDLESS TO SAY, STEWART, YOU'RE NOT IN ANY TROUBLE.
SURE.
BUT THIS HAS BEEN A HELL OF A NIGHT ALL AROUND, AND YOU PRESENT AN ANOMALY.
I CAN SEE THAT.
THERE WAS THIS...GANG OF KIDS.
THEY TOOK MY CHAIR.
YOU SAID THERE WAS A ROBBERY AT THE STORE. MAYBE THEY--?
WELL...
THEY DIDN'T BRING YOUR CHAIR WITH THEM. OR DUMP IT. AND I TELL YOU--
THEY SURE AS HELL DIDN'T DO IT *AFTER*.
WHAT DID THESE "KIDS" *LOOK* LIKE?
WHITE? BLACK?
WHITE.
IT ALL... HAPPENED SO FAST.
LET ME SHOW YOU SOMETHING.

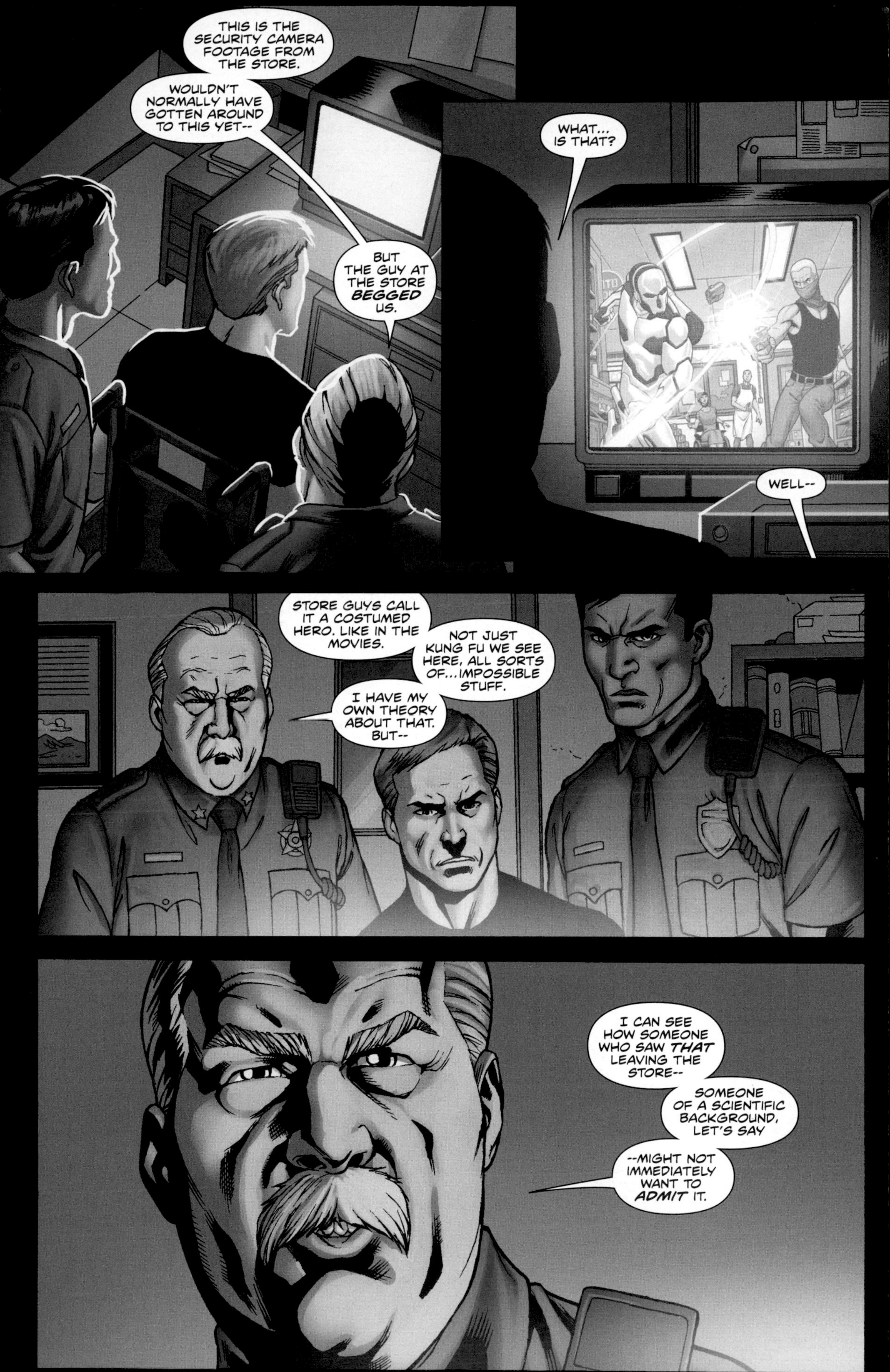
THIS IS THE SECURITY CAMERA FOOTAGE FROM THE STORE.
WOULDN'T NORMALLY HAVE GOTTEN AROUND TO THIS YET--
BUT THE GUY AT THE STORE BEGGED US.
WHAT... IS THAT?
WELL--
STORE GUYS CALL IT A COSTUMED HERO. LIKE IN THE MOVIES.
NOT JUST KUNG FU WE SEE HERE, ALL SORTS OF...IMPOSSIBLE STUFF.
I HAVE MY OWN THEORY ABOUT THAT. BUT--
I CAN SEE HOW SOMEONE WHO SAW THAT LEAVING THE STORE--
SOMEONE OF A SCIENTIFIC BACKGROUND, LET'S SAY
--MIGHT NOT IMMEDIATELY WANT TO ADMIT IT.

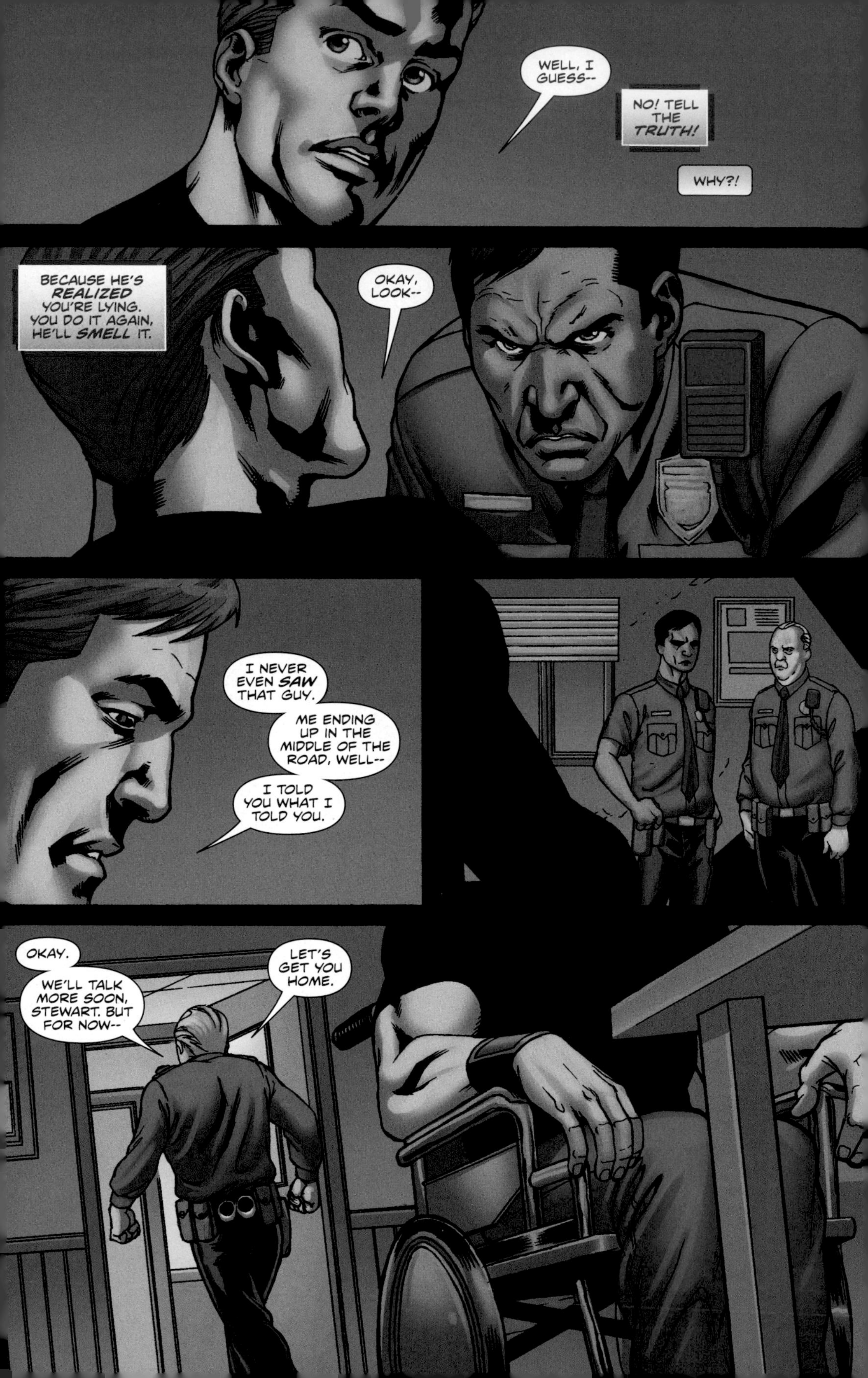
WELL, I GUESS--
NO! TELL THE TRUTH!
WHY?!
BECAUSE HE'S REALIZED YOU'RE LYING. YOU DO IT AGAIN, HE'LL SMELL IT.
OKAY, LOOK--
I NEVER EVEN SAW THAT GUY.
ME ENDING UP IN THE MIDDLE OF THE ROAD, WELL--
I TOLD YOU WHAT I TOLD YOU.
OKAY.
WE'LL TALK MORE SOON, STEWART. BUT FOR NOW--
LET'S GET YOU HOME.

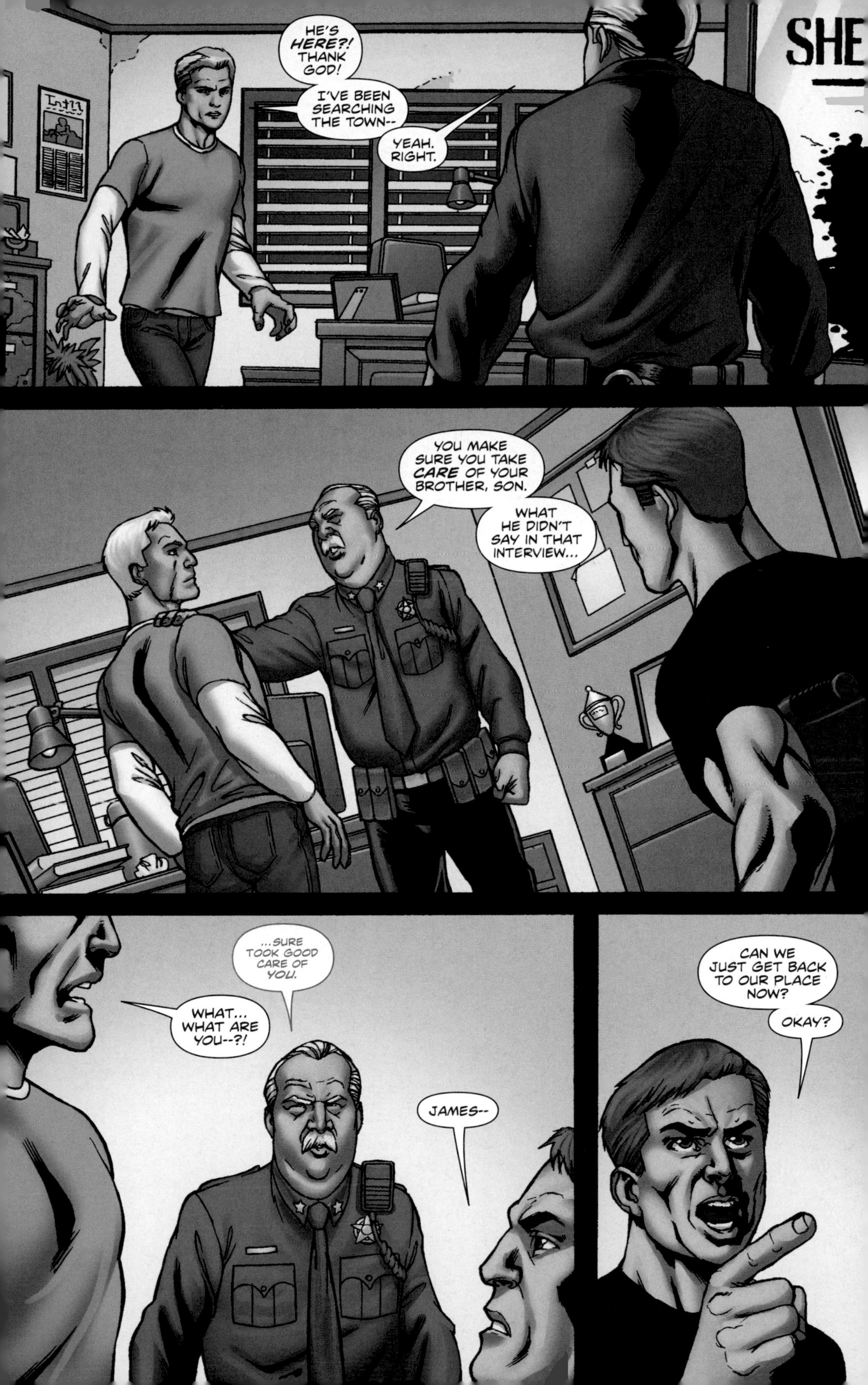
SHE
HE'S *HERE?!* THANK GOD!
I'VE BEEN SEARCHING THE TOWN--
YEAH. RIGHT.
YOU MAKE SURE YOU TAKE *CARE* OF YOUR BROTHER, SON.
WHAT HE DIDN'T SAY IN THAT INTERVIEW...
...SURE TOOK GOOD CARE OF *YOU.*
WHAT... WHAT ARE YOU--?!
JAMES--
CAN WE JUST GET BACK TO OUR PLACE NOW?
OKAY?

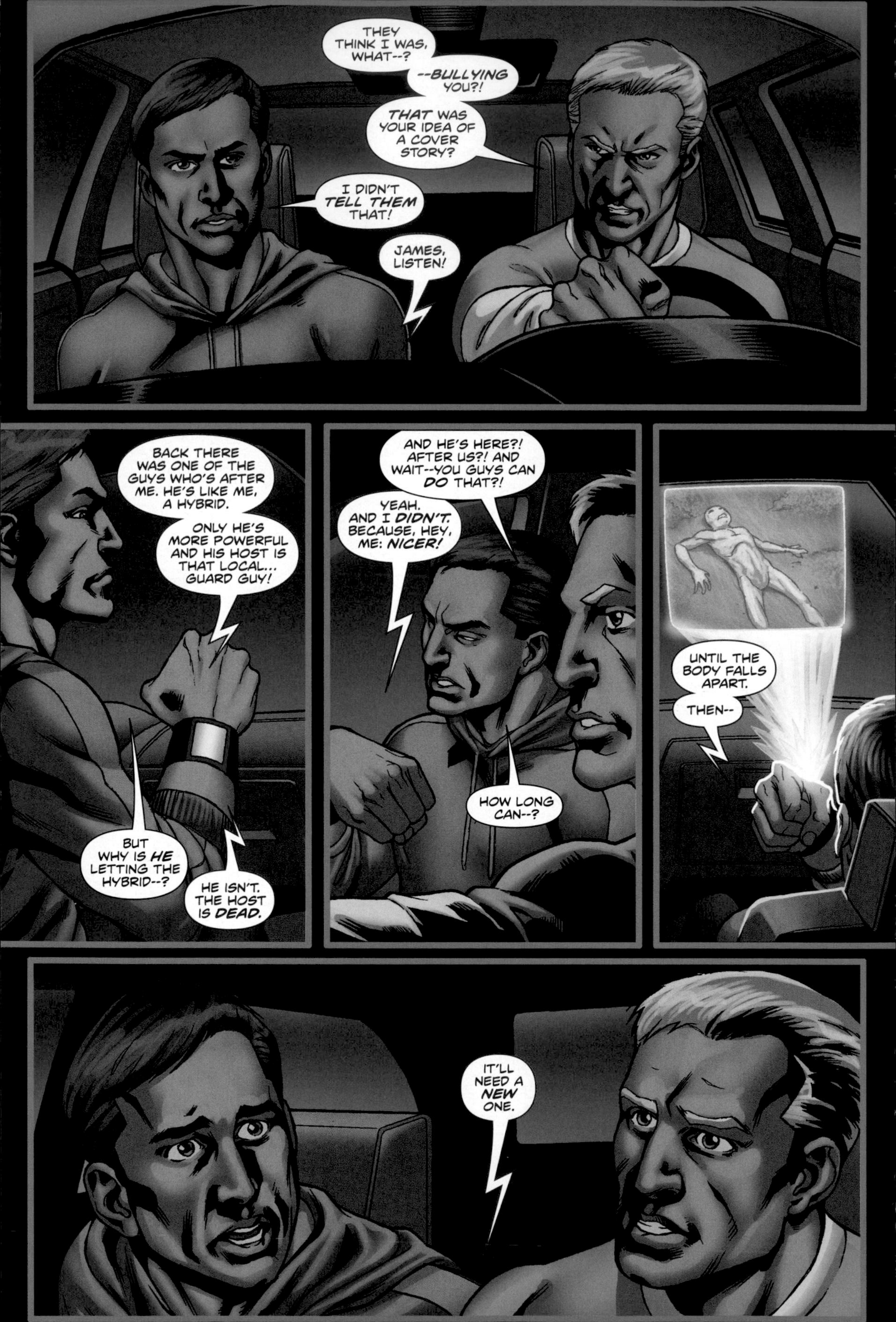
THEY THINK I WAS, WHAT--?
--*BULLYING* YOU?!
THAT WAS YOUR IDEA OF A COVER STORY?
I DIDN'T *TELL THEM* THAT!
JAMES, LISTEN!
BACK THERE WAS ONE OF THE GUYS WHO'S AFTER ME. HE'S LIKE ME, A HYBRID.
ONLY HE'S MORE POWERFUL AND HIS HOST IS THAT LOCAL... GUARD GUY!
BUT WHY IS *HE* LETTING THE HYBRID--?
HE ISN'T. THE HOST IS *DEAD.*
AND HE'S HERE?! AFTER US?! AND WAIT--YOU GUYS CAN *DO* THAT?!
YEAH. AND I *DIDN'T.* BECAUSE, HEY, ME: *NICER!*
HOW LONG CAN--?
UNTIL THE BODY FALLS APART.
THEN--
IT'LL NEED A *NEW* ONE.

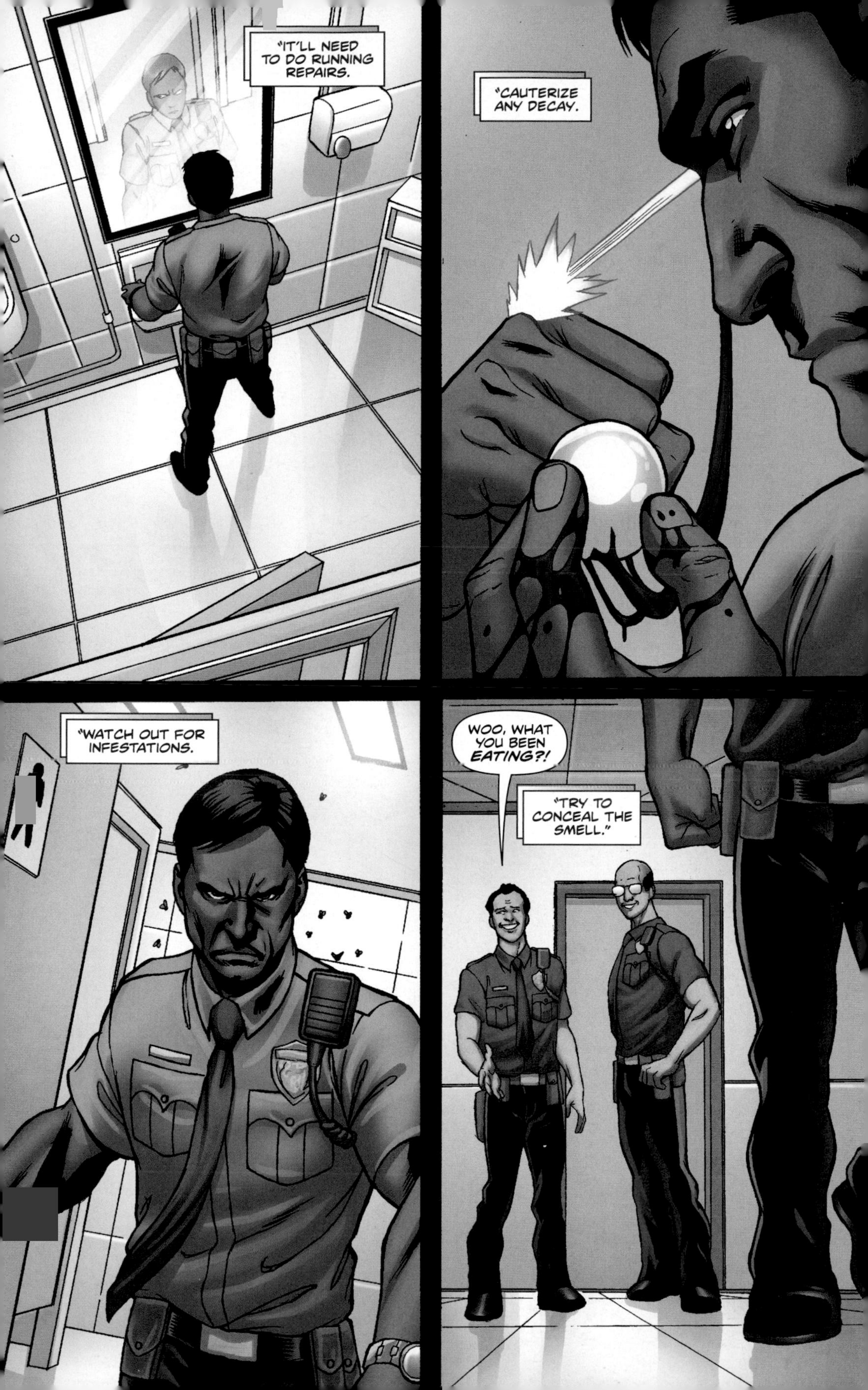
"IT'LL NEED TO DO RUNNING REPAIRS.
"CAUTERIZE ANY DECAY.
"WATCH OUT FOR INFESTATIONS.
WOO, WHAT YOU BEEN *EATING?!*
"TRY TO CONCEAL THE SMELL."

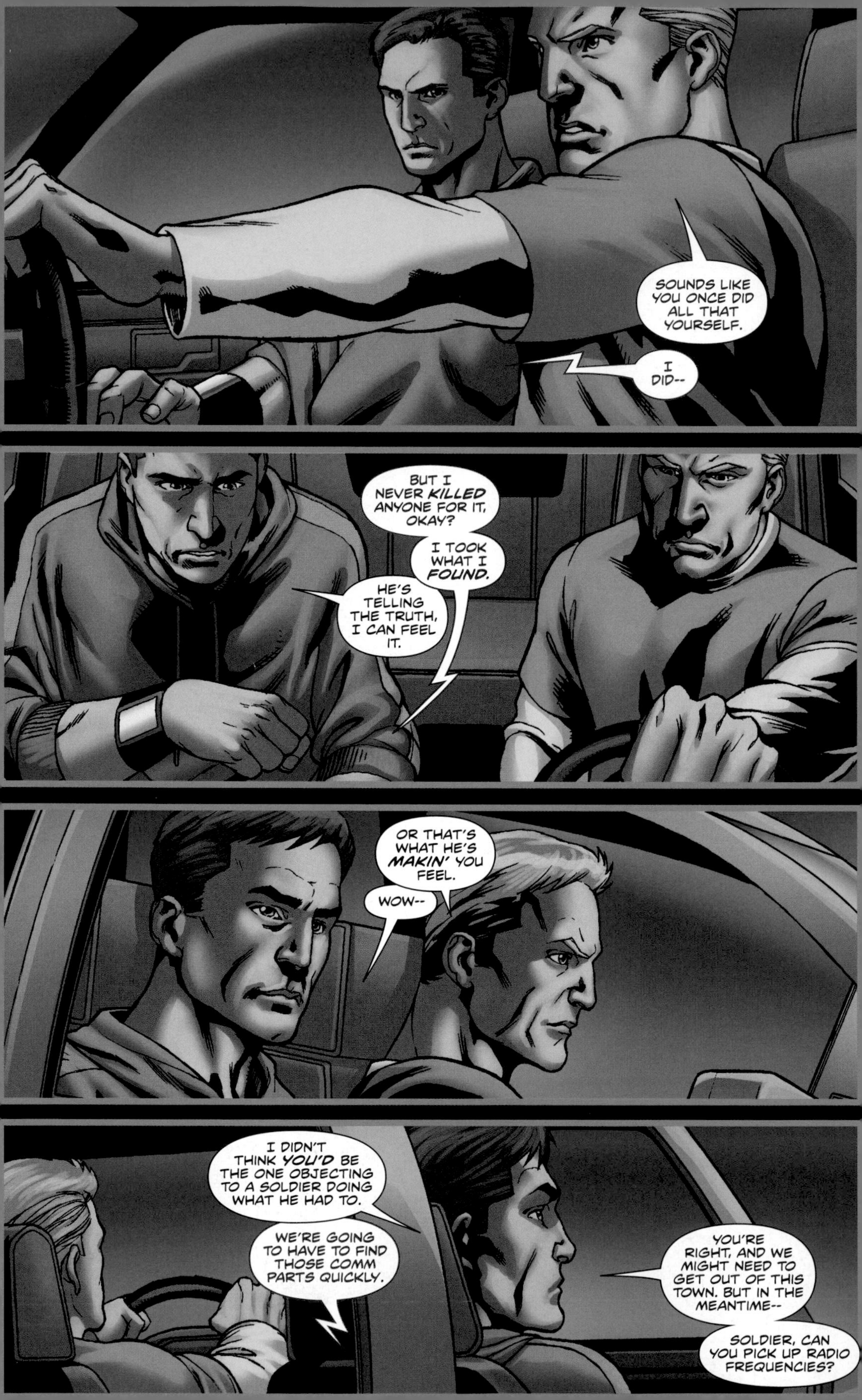
SOUNDS LIKE YOU ONCE DID ALL THAT YOURSELF.
I DID--
BUT I NEVER KILLED ANYONE FOR IT, OKAY?
I TOOK WHAT I FOUND.
HE'S TELLING THE TRUTH, I CAN FEEL IT.
OR THAT'S WHAT HE'S MAKIN' YOU FEEL.
WOW--
I DIDN'T THINK YOU'D BE THE ONE OBJECTING TO A SOLDIER DOING WHAT HE HAD TO.
WE'RE GOING TO HAVE TO FIND THOSE COMM PARTS QUICKLY.
YOU'RE RIGHT, AND WE MIGHT NEED TO GET OUT OF THIS TOWN. BUT IN THE MEANTIME--
SOLDIER, CAN YOU PICK UP RADIO FREQUENCIES?

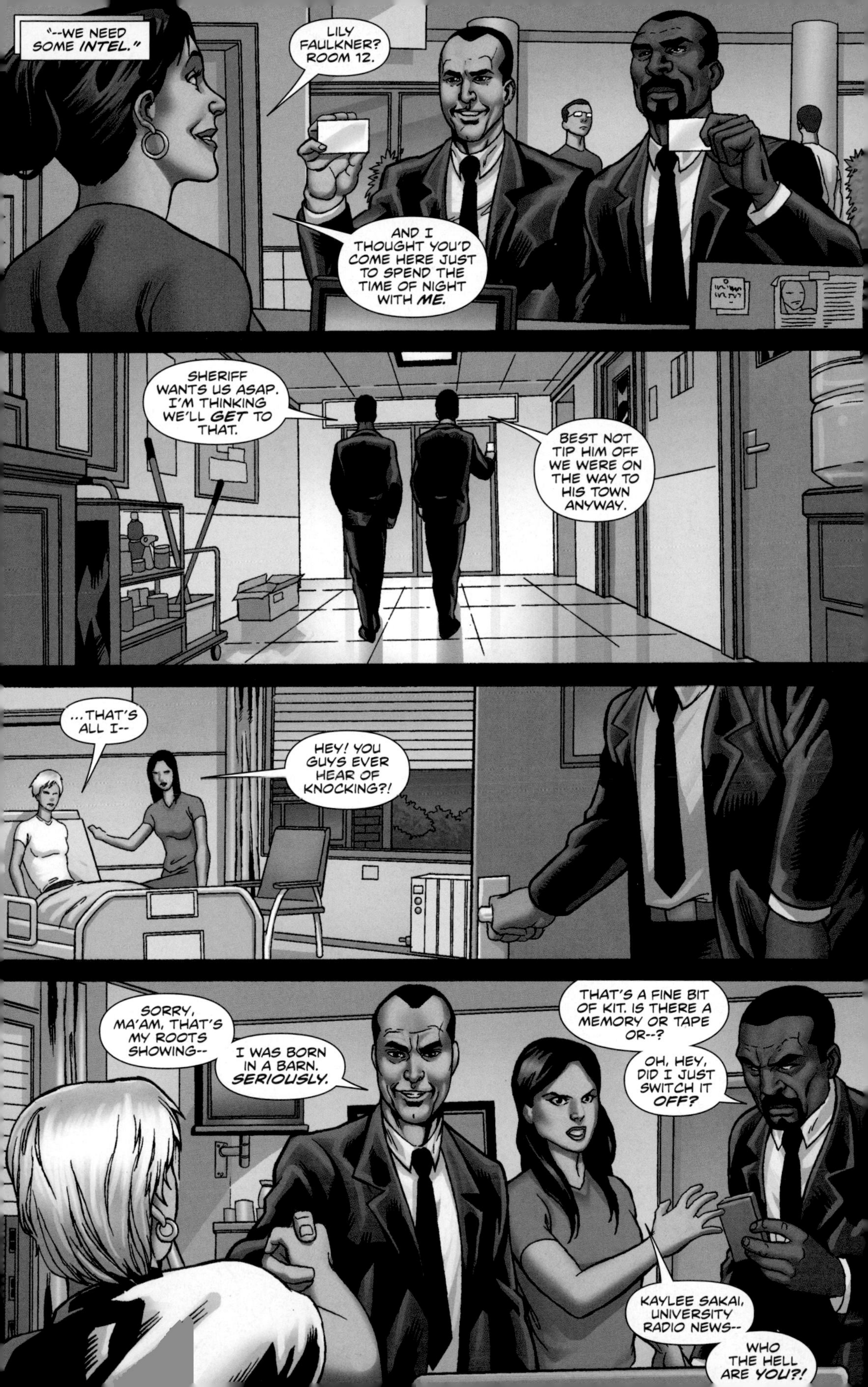
"--WE NEED SOME INTEL."
LILY FAULKNER? ROOM 12.
AND I THOUGHT YOU'D COME HERE JUST TO SPEND THE TIME OF NIGHT WITH ME.
SHERIFF WANTS US ASAP. I'M THINKING WE'LL GET TO THAT.
BEST NOT TIP HIM OFF WE WERE ON THE WAY TO HIS TOWN ANYWAY.
...THAT'S ALL I--
HEY! YOU GUYS EVER HEAR OF KNOCKING?!
SORRY, MA'AM, THAT'S MY ROOTS SHOWING--
I WAS BORN IN A BARN. SERIOUSLY.
THAT'S A FINE BIT OF KIT. IS THERE A MEMORY OR TAPE OR--?
OH, HEY, DID I JUST SWITCH IT OFF?
KAYLEE SAKAI, UNIVERSITY RADIO NEWS--
WHO THE HELL ARE YOU?!

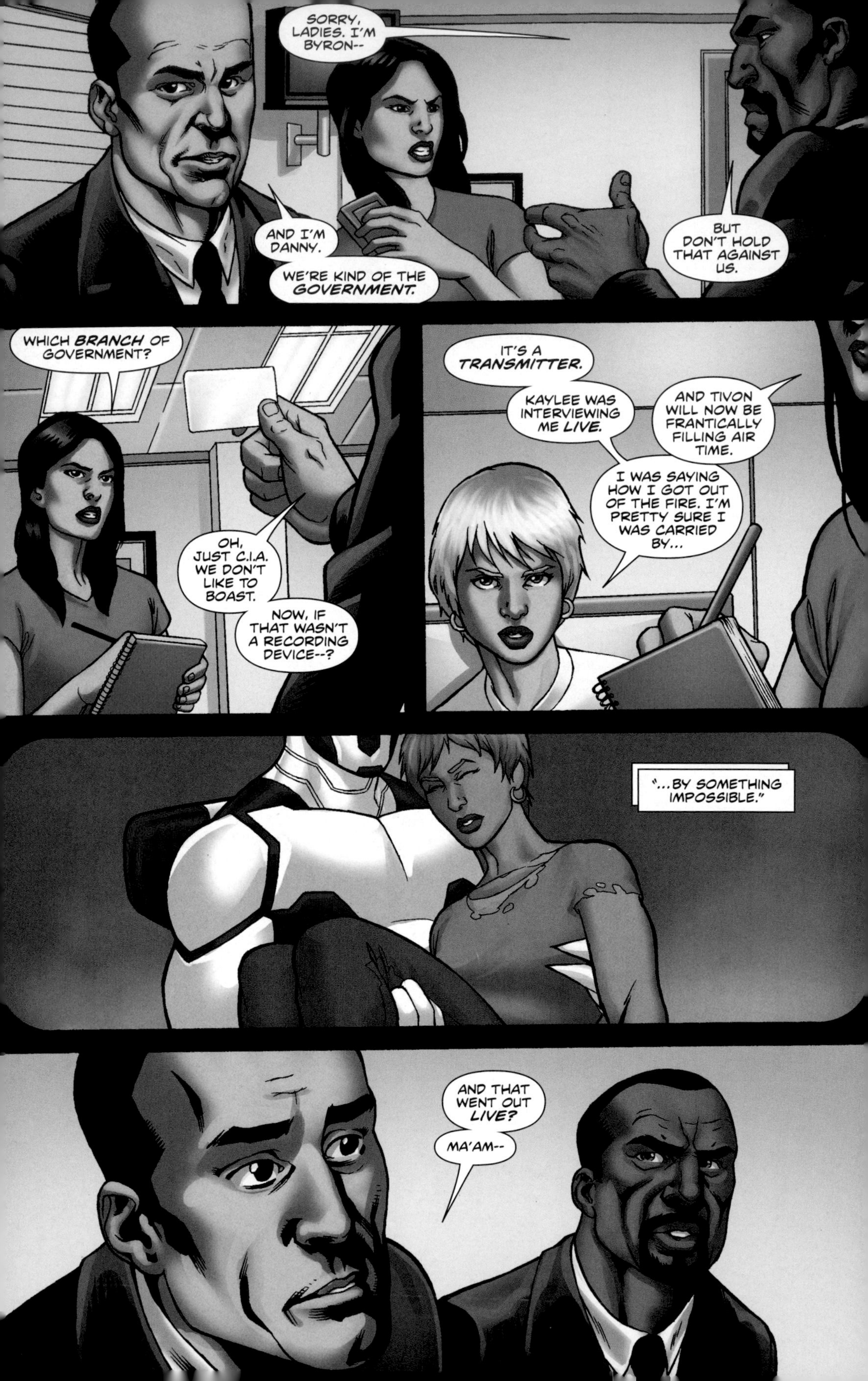
SORRY, LADIES. I'M BYRON--
AND I'M DANNY.
WE'RE KIND OF THE *GOVERNMENT.*
BUT DON'T HOLD THAT AGAINST US.
WHICH *BRANCH* OF GOVERNMENT?
OH, JUST C.I.A. WE DON'T LIKE TO BOAST.
NOW, IF THAT WASN'T A RECORDING DEVICE--?
IT'S A *TRANSMITTER.*
KAYLEE WAS INTERVIEWING ME *LIVE.*
AND TIVON WILL NOW BE FRANTICALLY FILLING AIR TIME.
I WAS SAYING HOW I GOT OUT OF THE FIRE. I'M PRETTY SURE I WAS CARRIED BY...
"...BY SOMETHING IMPOSSIBLE."
AND THAT WENT OUT *LIVE?*
MA'AM--

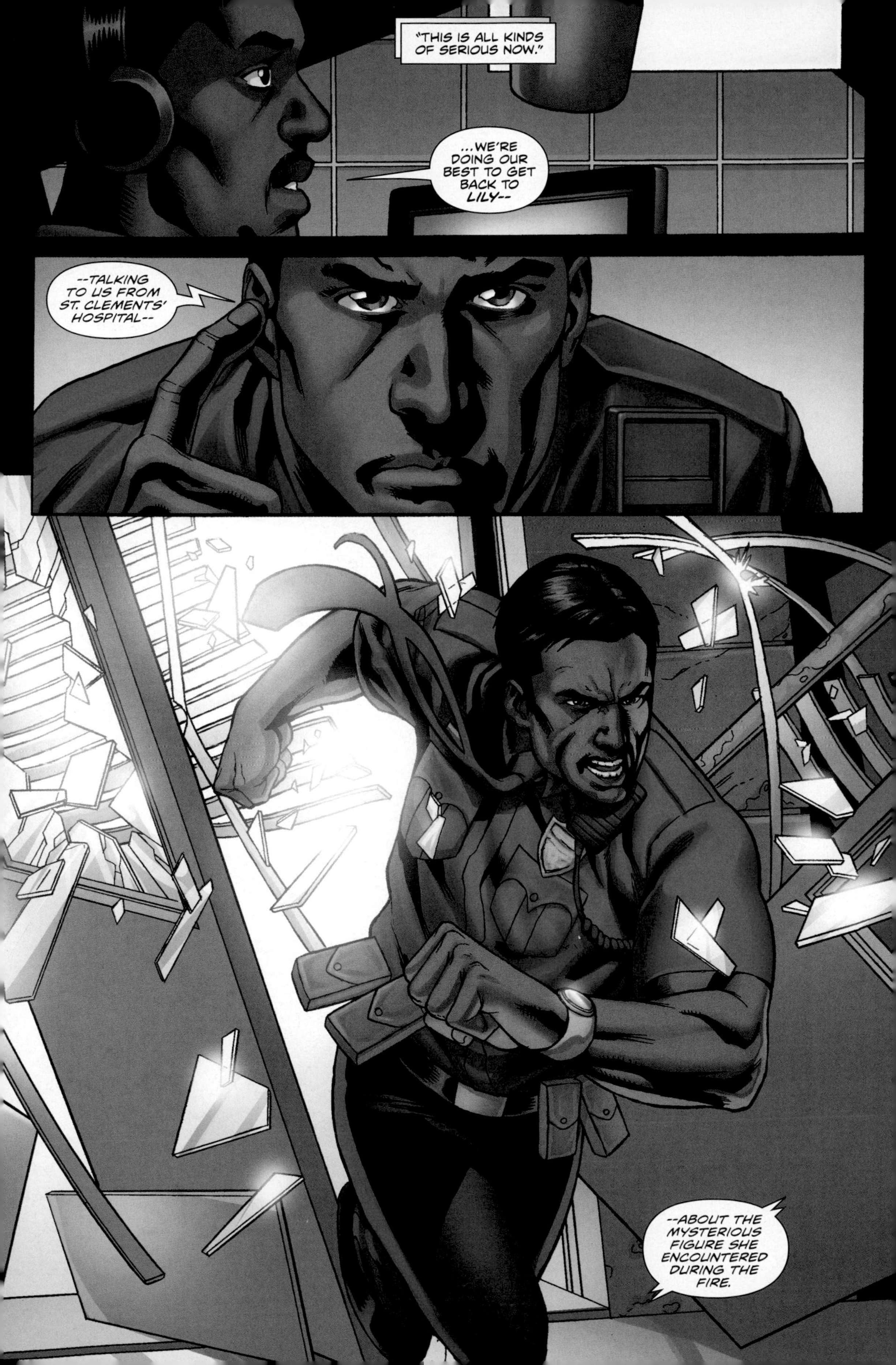
"THIS IS ALL KINDS OF SERIOUS NOW."
...WE'RE DOING OUR BEST TO GET BACK TO LILY--
--TALKING TO US FROM ST. CLEMENTS' HOSPITAL--
--ABOUT THE MYSTERIOUS FIGURE SHE ENCOUNTERED DURING THE FIRE.

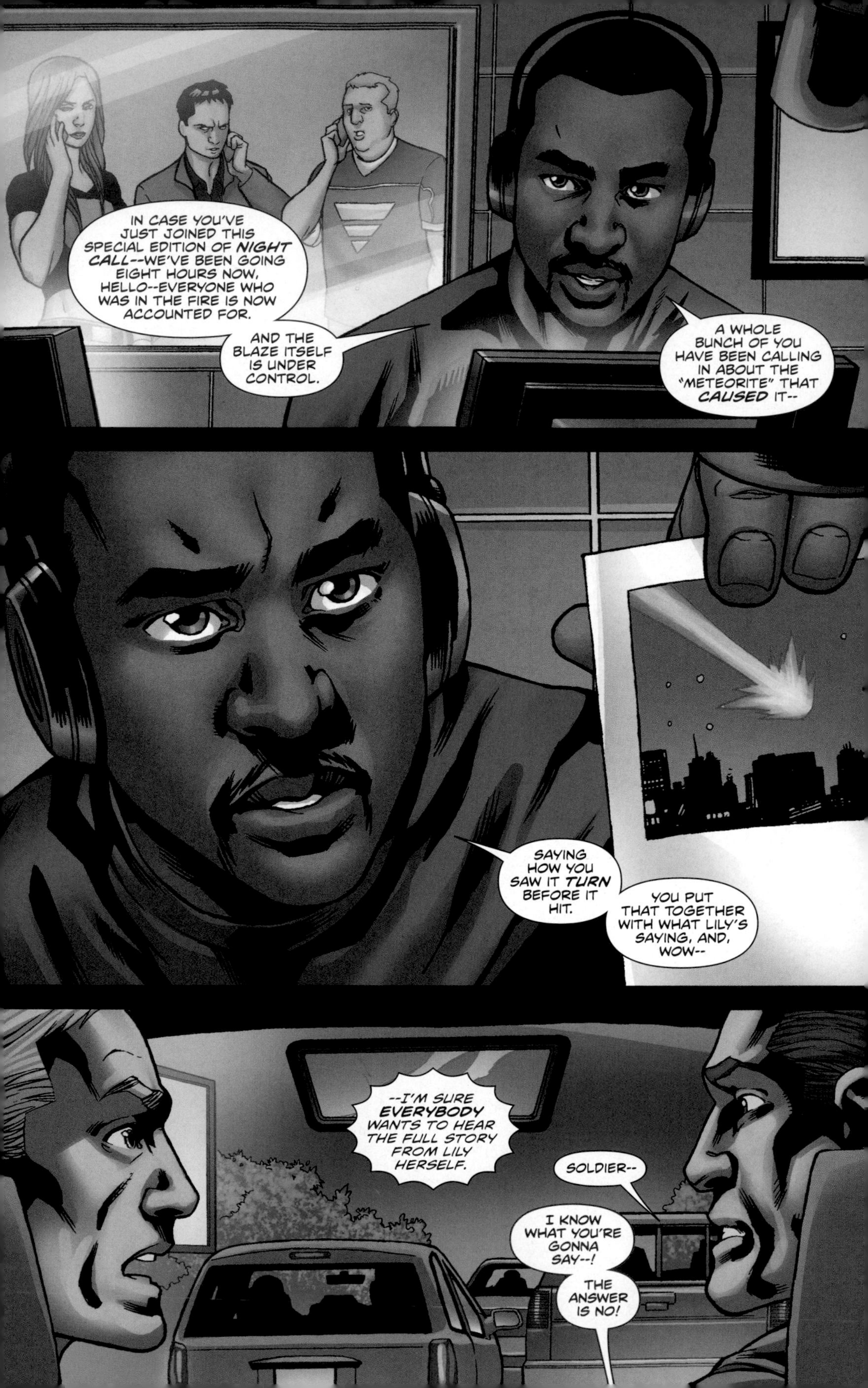
IN CASE YOU'VE JUST JOINED THIS SPECIAL EDITION OF NIGHT CALL--WE'VE BEEN GOING EIGHT HOURS NOW, HELLO--EVERYONE WHO WAS IN THE FIRE IS NOW ACCOUNTED FOR.
AND THE BLAZE ITSELF IS UNDER CONTROL.
A WHOLE BUNCH OF YOU HAVE BEEN CALLING IN ABOUT THE "METEORITE" THAT CAUSED IT--
SAYING HOW YOU SAW IT TURN BEFORE IT HIT.
YOU PUT THAT TOGETHER WITH WHAT LILY'S SAYING, AND, WOW--
--I'M SURE EVERYBODY WANTS TO HEAR THE FULL STORY FROM LILY HERSELF.
SOLDIER--
I KNOW WHAT YOU'RE GONNA SAY--!
THE ANSWER IS NO!

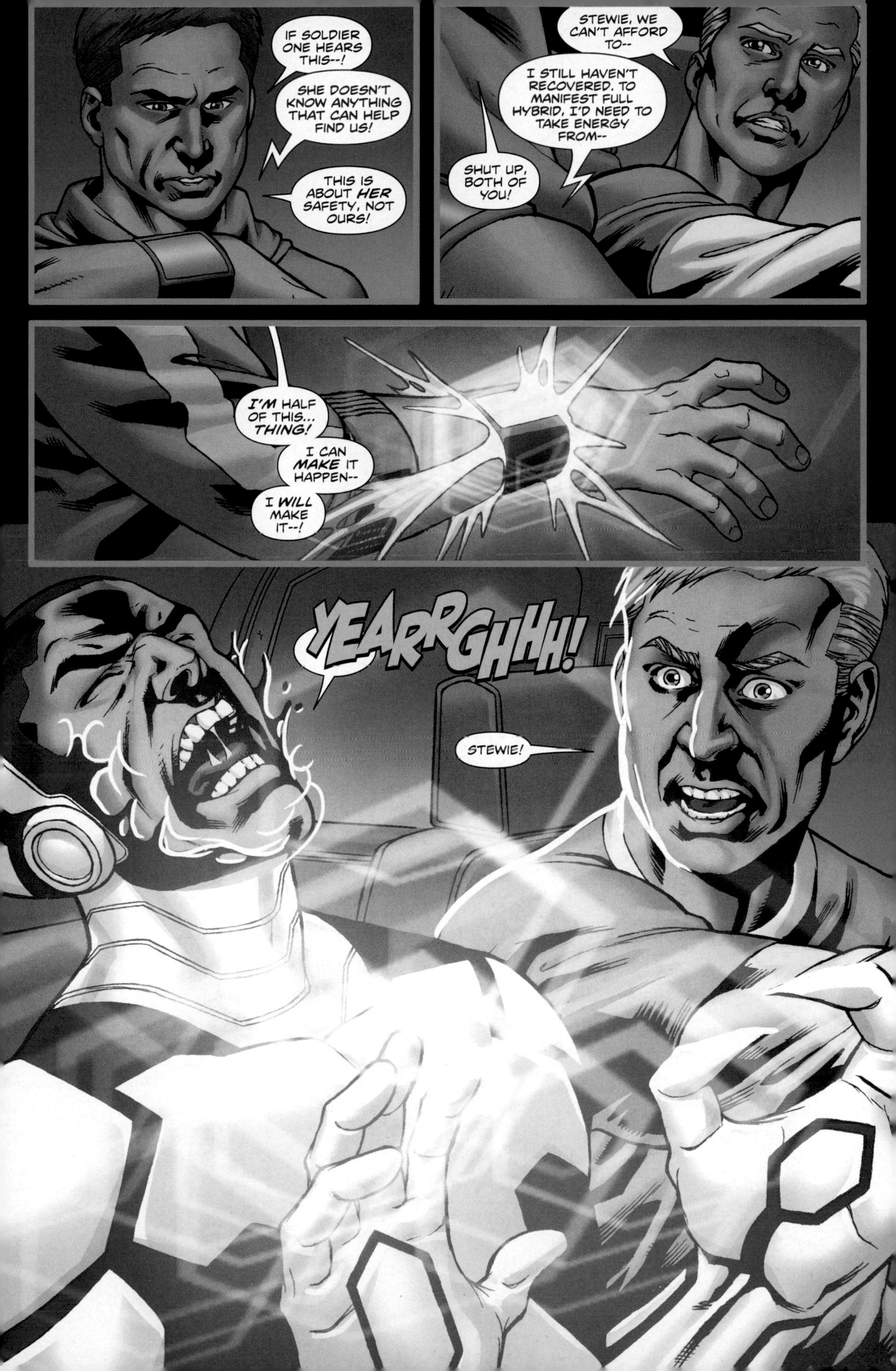
IF SOLDIER ONE HEARS THIS--!
SHE DOESN'T KNOW ANYTHING THAT CAN HELP FIND US!
THIS IS ABOUT HER SAFETY, NOT OURS!
STEWIE, WE CAN'T AFFORD TO--
I STILL HAVEN'T RECOVERED. TO MANIFEST FULL HYBRID, I'D NEED TO TAKE ENERGY FROM--
SHUT UP, BOTH OF YOU!
I'M HALF OF THIS... THING!
I CAN MAKE IT HAPPEN--
I WILL MAKE IT--!
YEARRGHHH!
STEWIE!

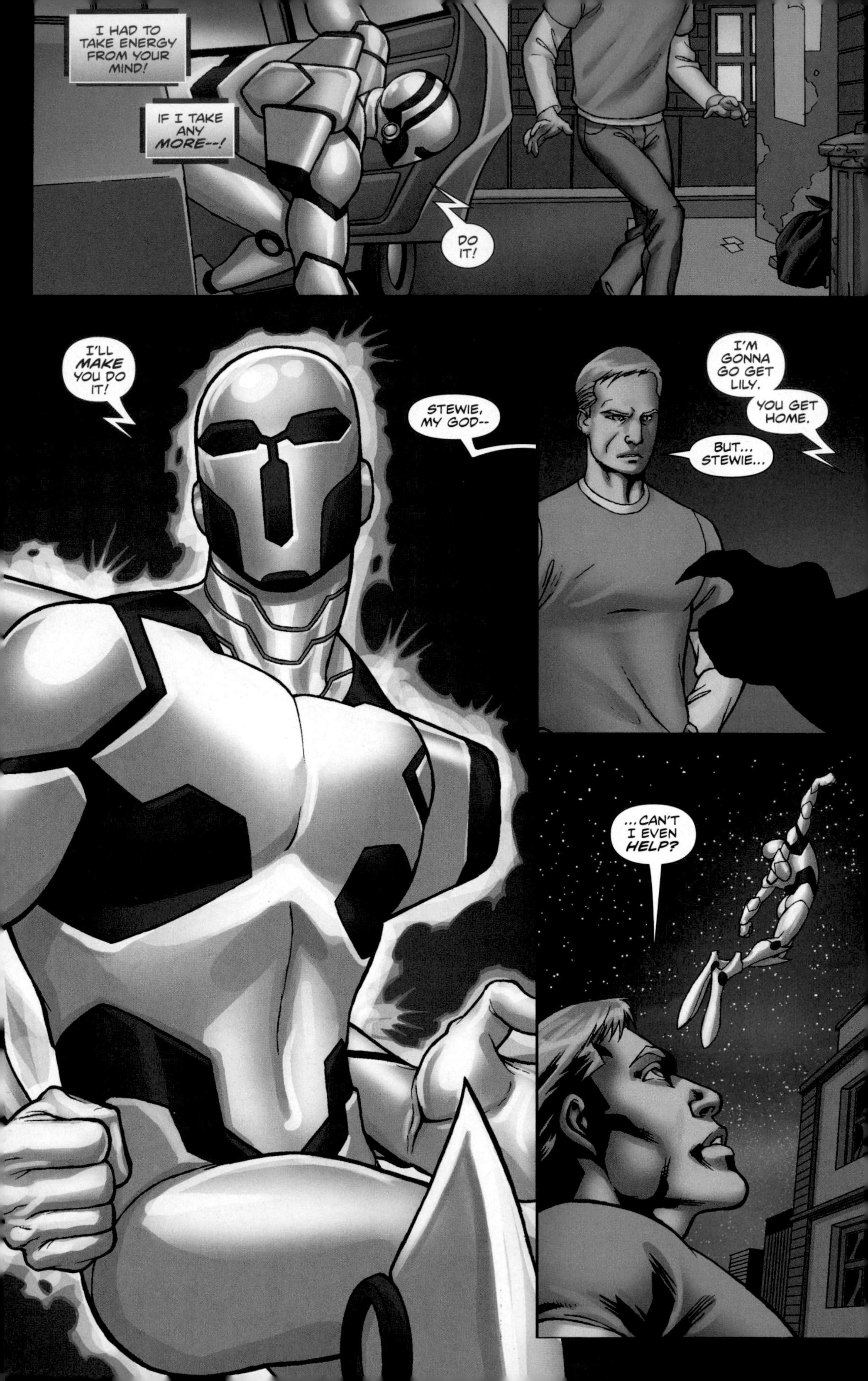
I HAD TO TAKE ENERGY FROM YOUR MIND!
IF I TAKE ANY MORE--!
DO IT!
I'LL MAKE YOU DO IT!
STEWIE, MY GOD--
I'M GONNA GO GET LILY.
YOU GET HOME.
BUT... STEWIE...
...CAN'T I EVEN HELP?

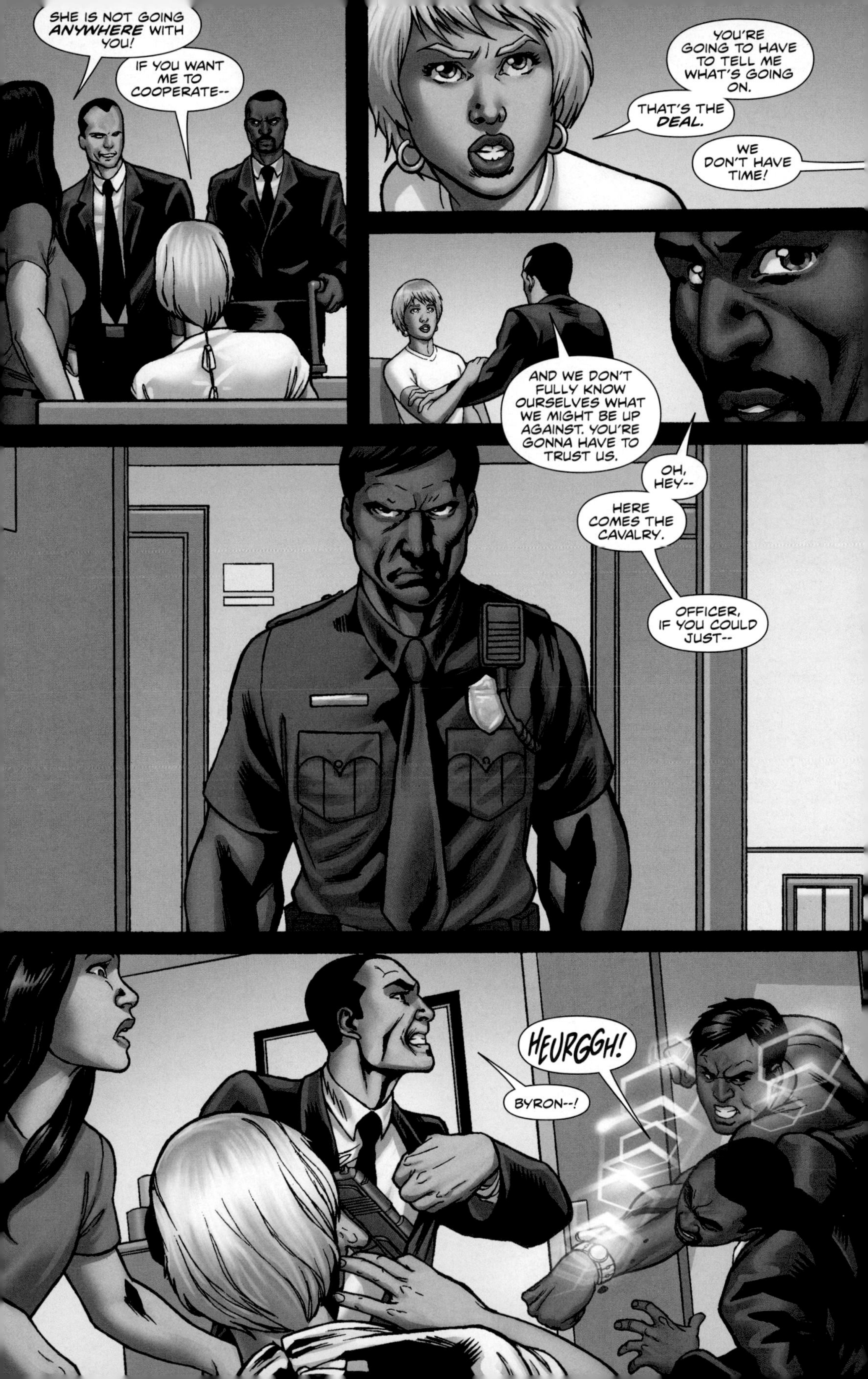
SHE IS NOT GOING ANYWHERE WITH YOU!
IF YOU WANT ME TO COOPERATE--
YOU'RE GOING TO HAVE TO TELL ME WHAT'S GOING ON.
THAT'S THE DEAL.
WE DON'T HAVE TIME!
AND WE DON'T FULLY KNOW OURSELVES WHAT WE MIGHT BE UP AGAINST. YOU'RE GONNA HAVE TO TRUST US.
OH, HEY--
HERE COMES THE CAVALRY.
OFFICER, IF YOU COULD JUST--
HEURGGH!
BYRON--!

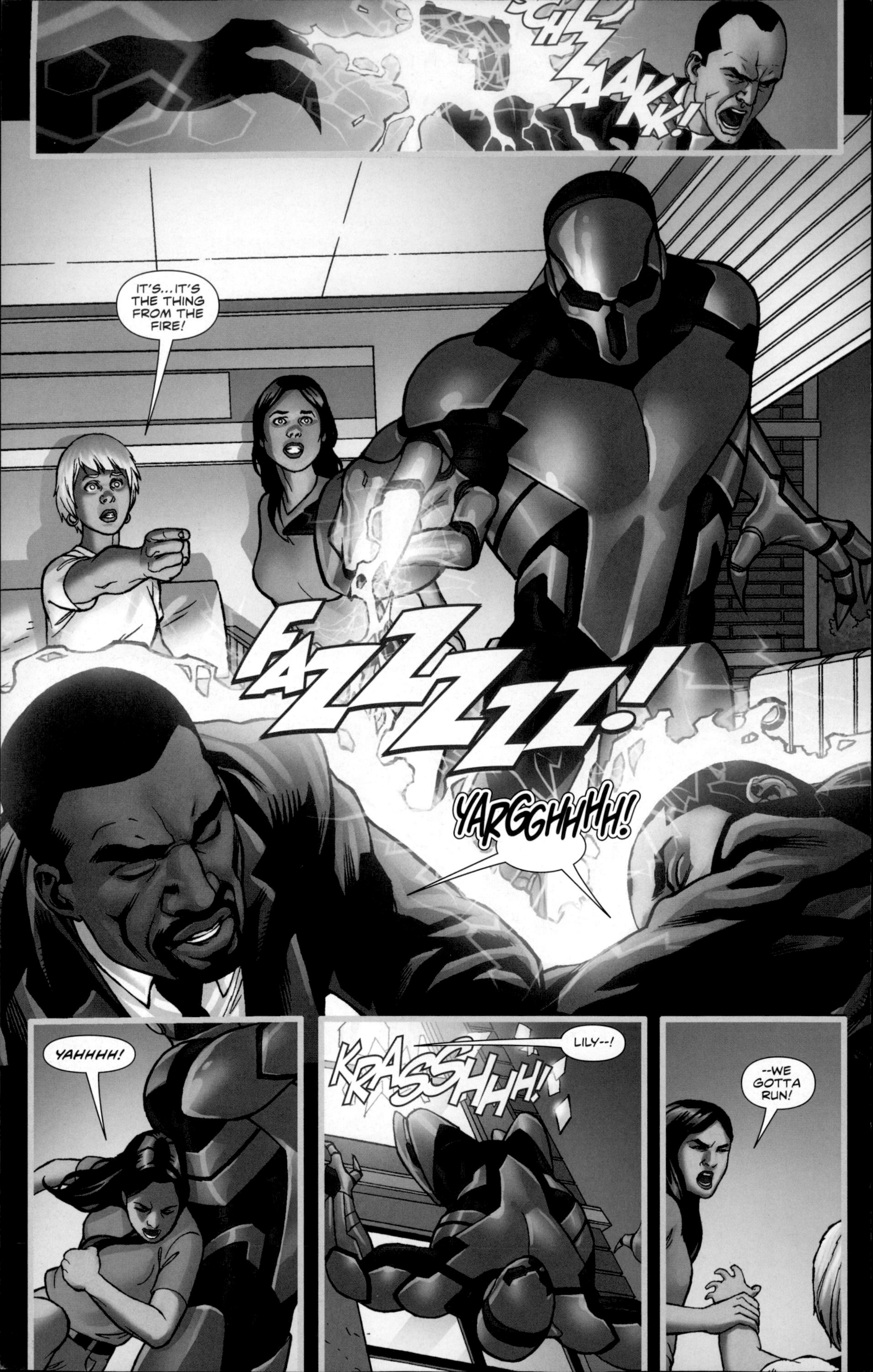
CHZAAKK!
IT'S...IT'S THE THING FROM THE FIRE!
FAZZZZZ!
YARGGHHHH!
YAHHHH!
KRASSHHH!
LILY--!
--WE GOTTA RUN!

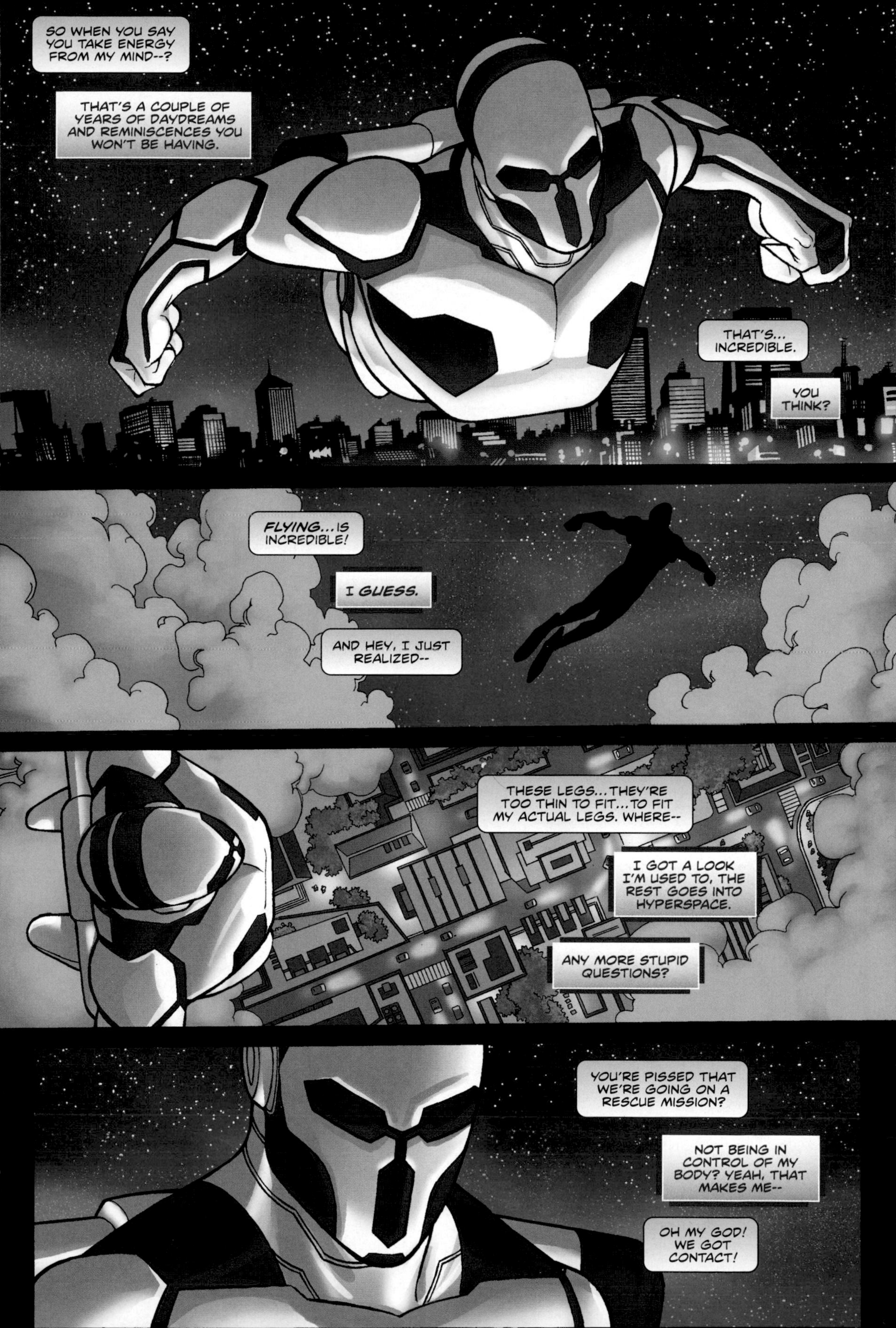
SO WHEN YOU SAY YOU TAKE ENERGY FROM MY MIND--?
THAT'S A COUPLE OF YEARS OF DAYDREAMS AND REMINISCENCES YOU WON'T BE HAVING.
THAT'S... INCREDIBLE.
YOU THINK?
FLYING... IS INCREDIBLE!
I GUESS.
AND HEY, I JUST REALIZED--
THESE LEGS... THEY'RE TOO THIN TO FIT... TO FIT MY ACTUAL LEGS. WHERE--
I GOT A LOOK I'M USED TO, THE REST GOES INTO HYPERSPACE.
ANY MORE STUPID QUESTIONS?
YOU'RE PISSED THAT WE'RE GOING ON A RESCUE MISSION?
NOT BEING IN CONTROL OF MY BODY? YEAH, THAT MAKES ME--
OH MY GOD! WE GOT CONTACT!

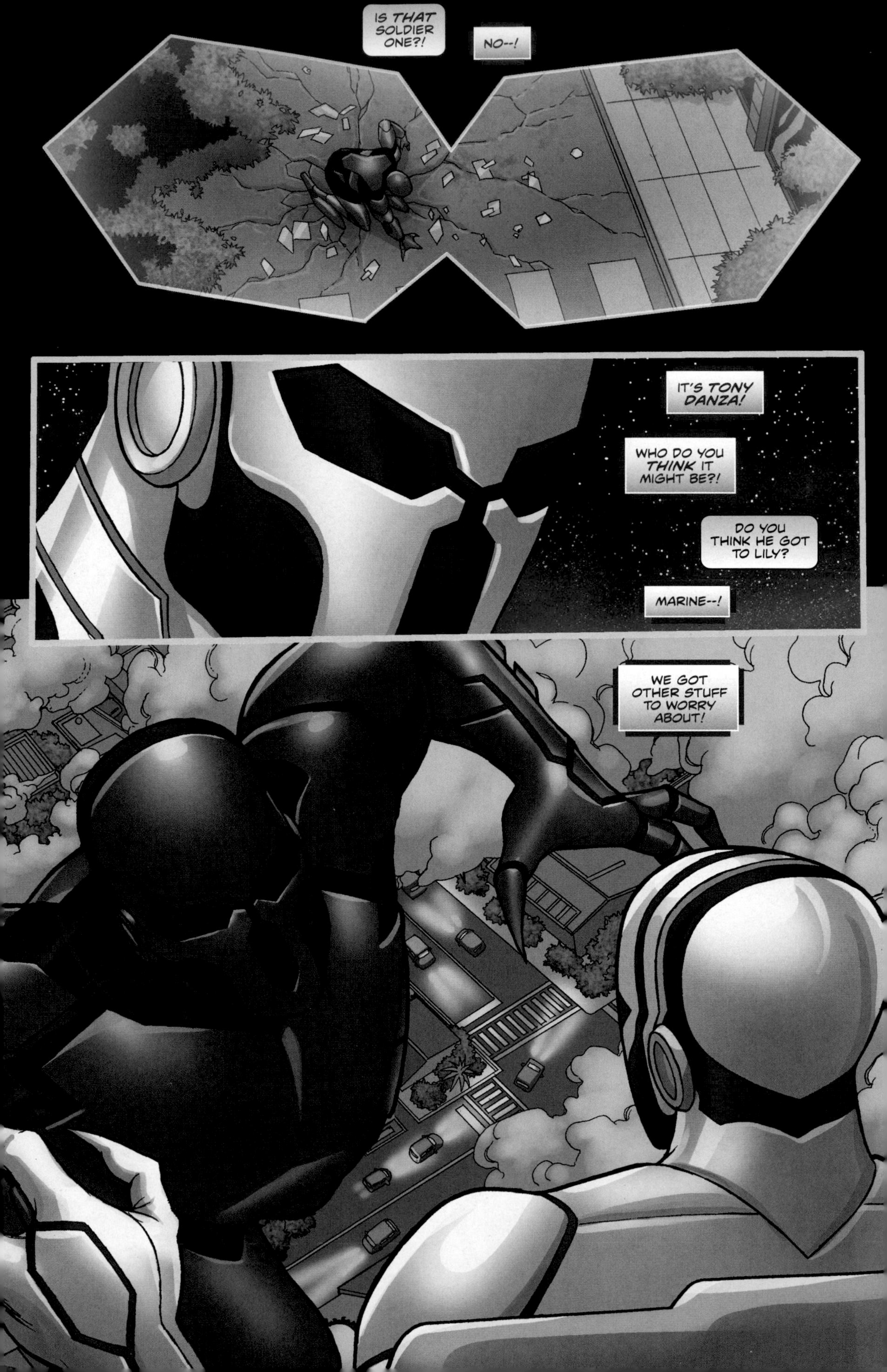
IS THAT SOLDIER ONE?!
NO--!
IT'S TONY DANZA!
WHO DO YOU THINK IT MIGHT BE?!
DO YOU THINK HE GOT TO LILY?
MARINE--!
WE GOT OTHER STUFF TO WORRY ABOUT!

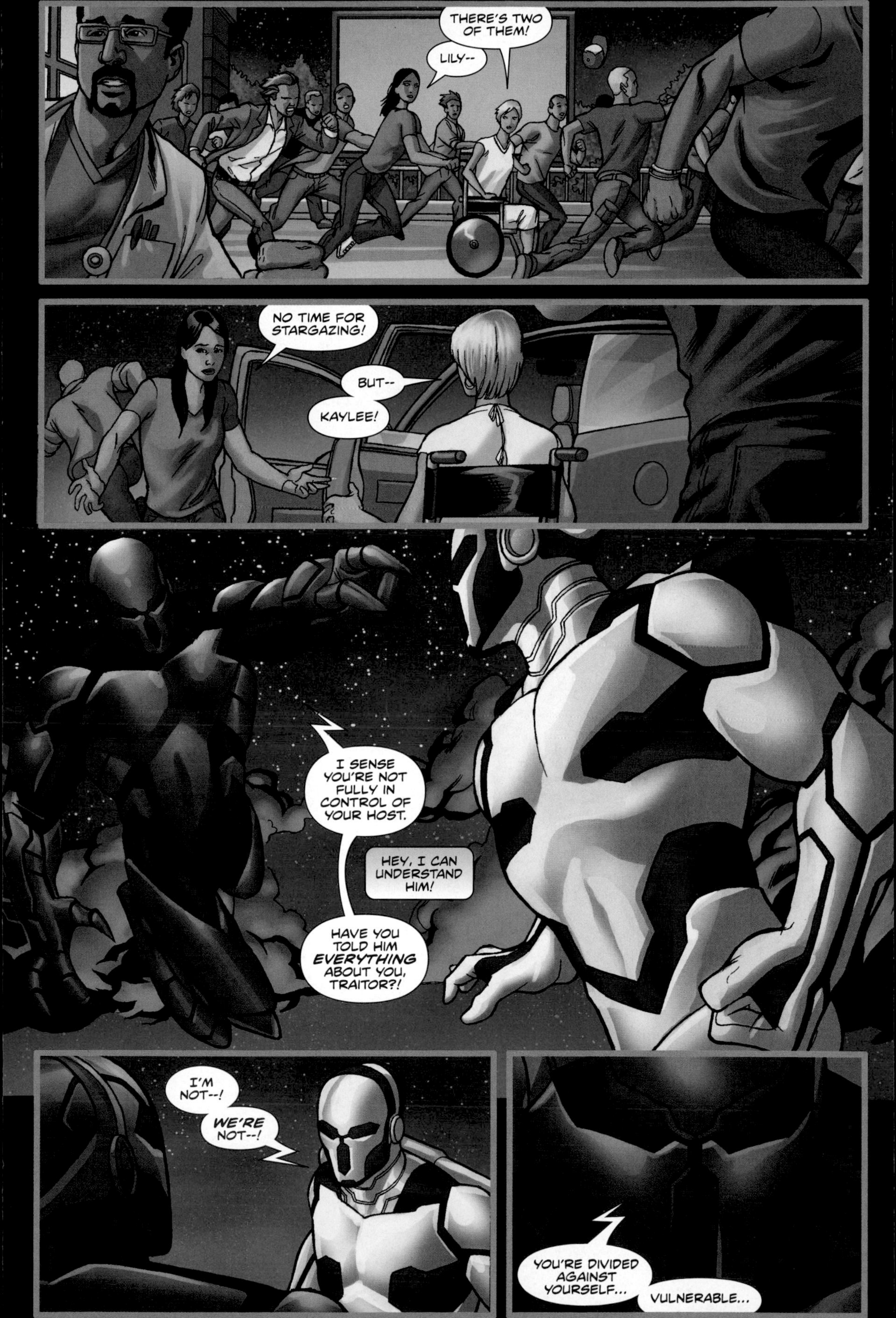
THERE'S TWO OF THEM!
LILY--
NO TIME FOR STARGAZING!
BUT--
KAYLEE!
I SENSE YOU'RE NOT FULLY IN CONTROL OF YOUR HOST.
HEY, I CAN UNDERSTAND HIM!
HAVE YOU TOLD HIM EVERYTHING ABOUT YOU, TRAITOR?!
I'M NOT--!
WE'RE NOT--!
YOU'RE DIVIDED AGAINST YOURSELF...
VULNERABLE...

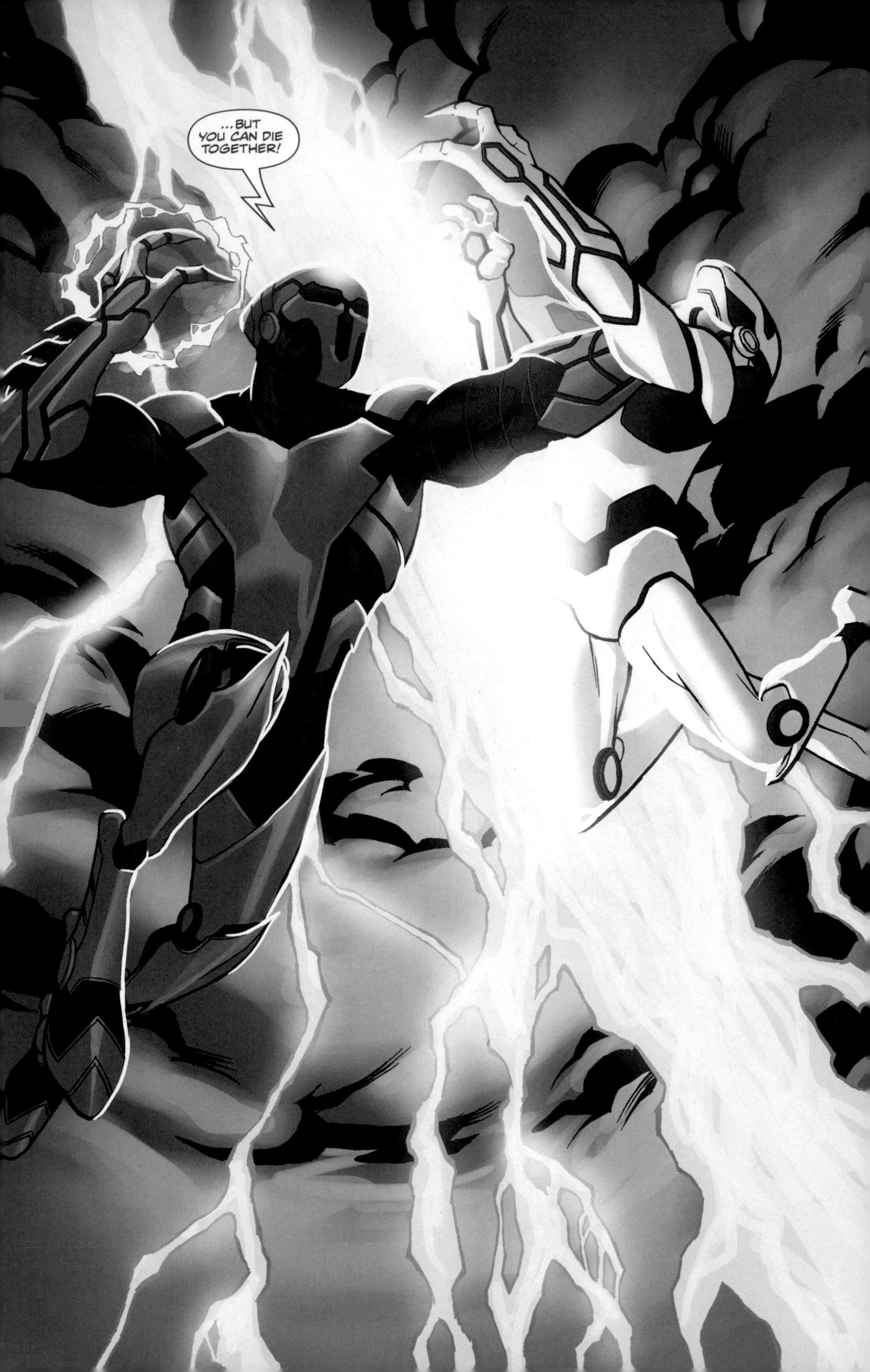
...BUT YOU CAN DIE TOGETHER!

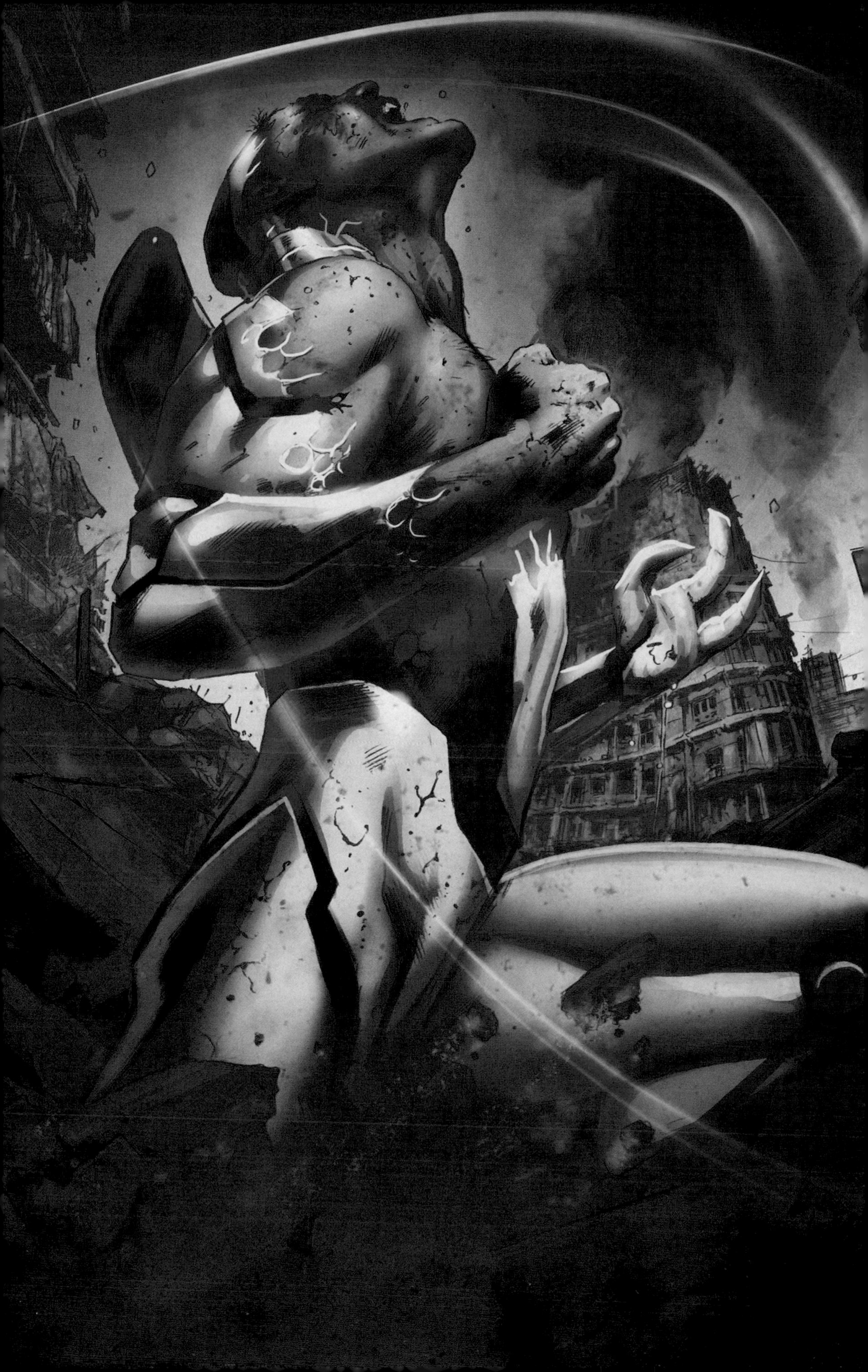

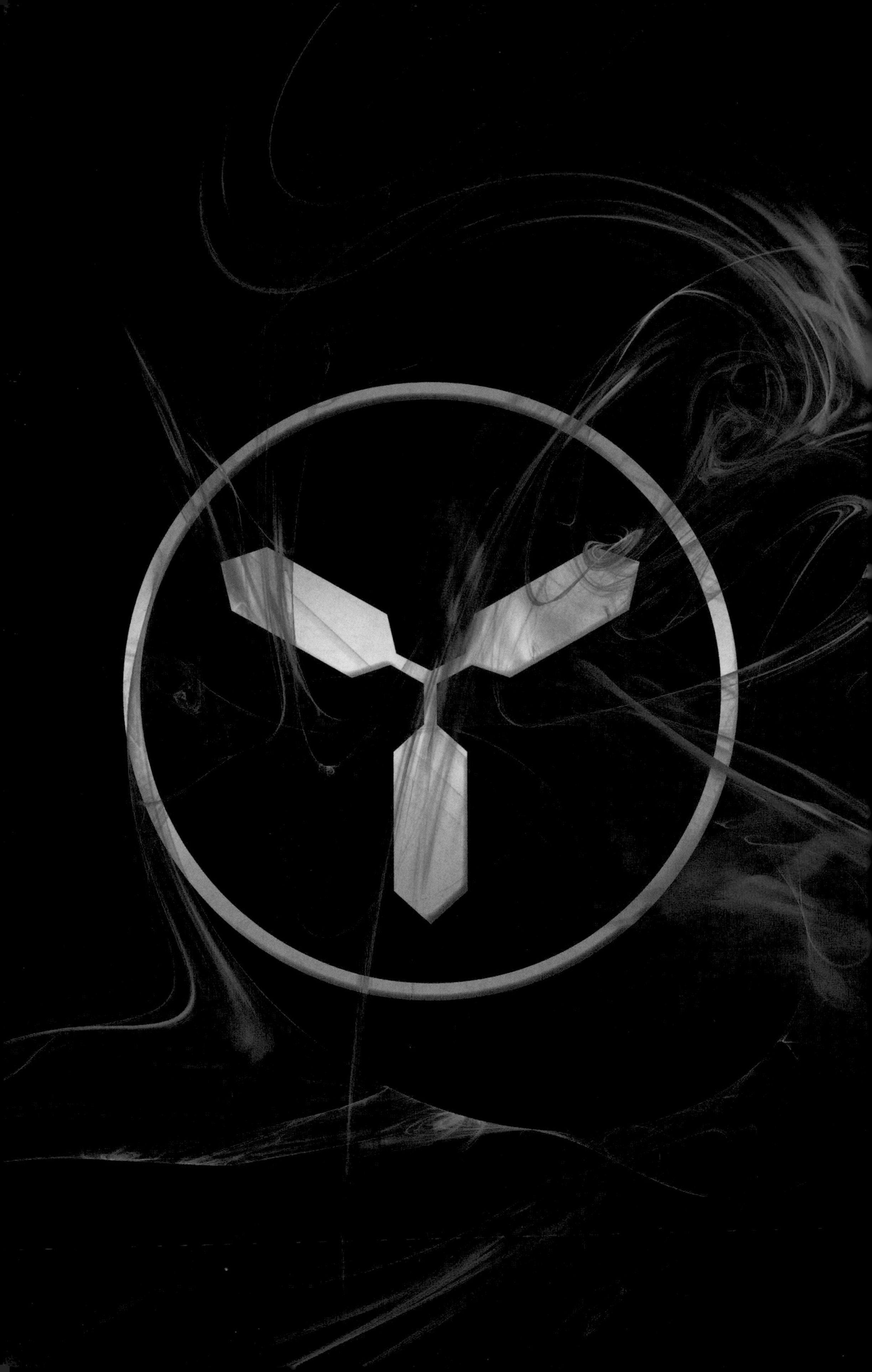

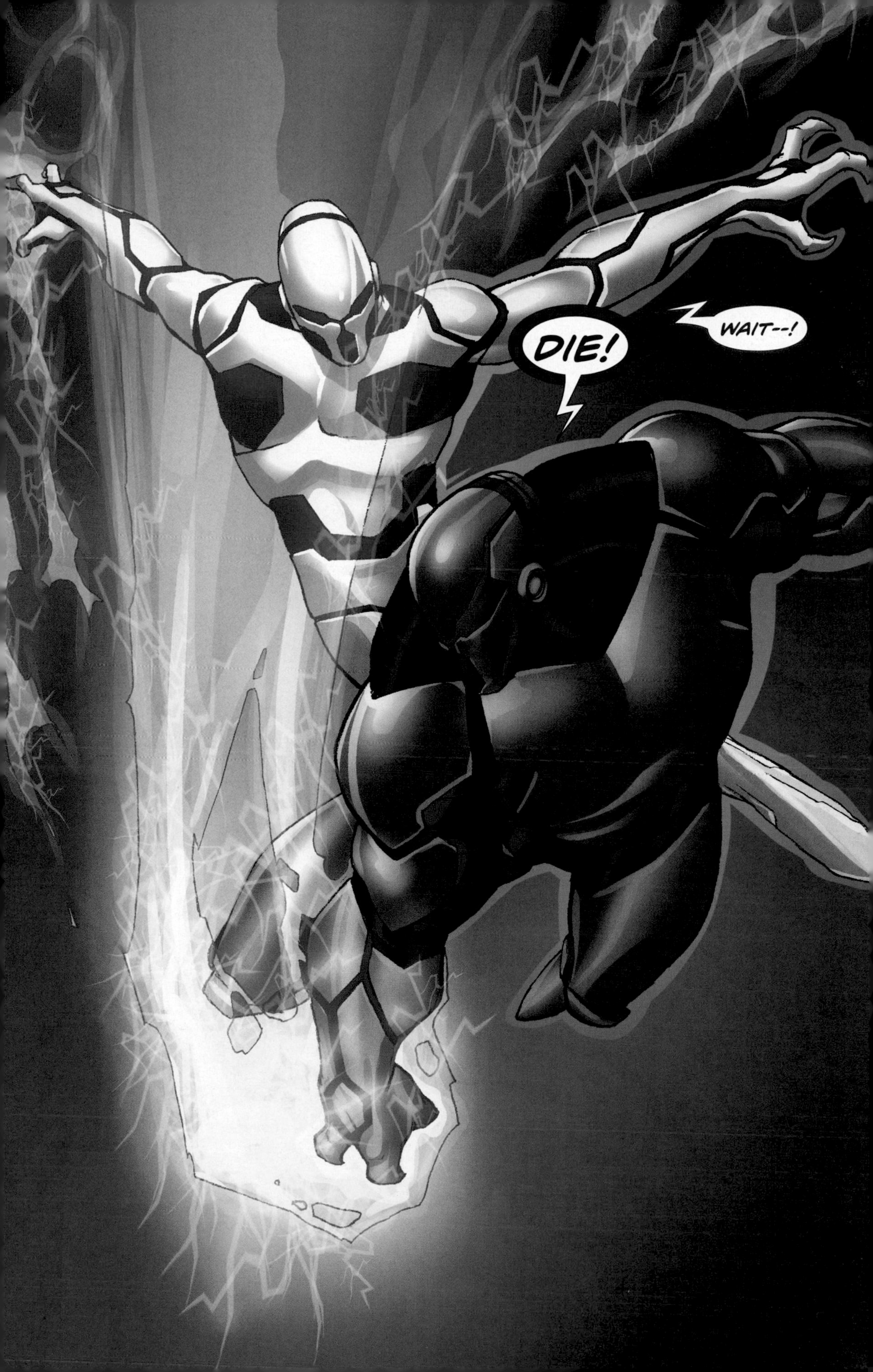
DIE!
WAIT--!

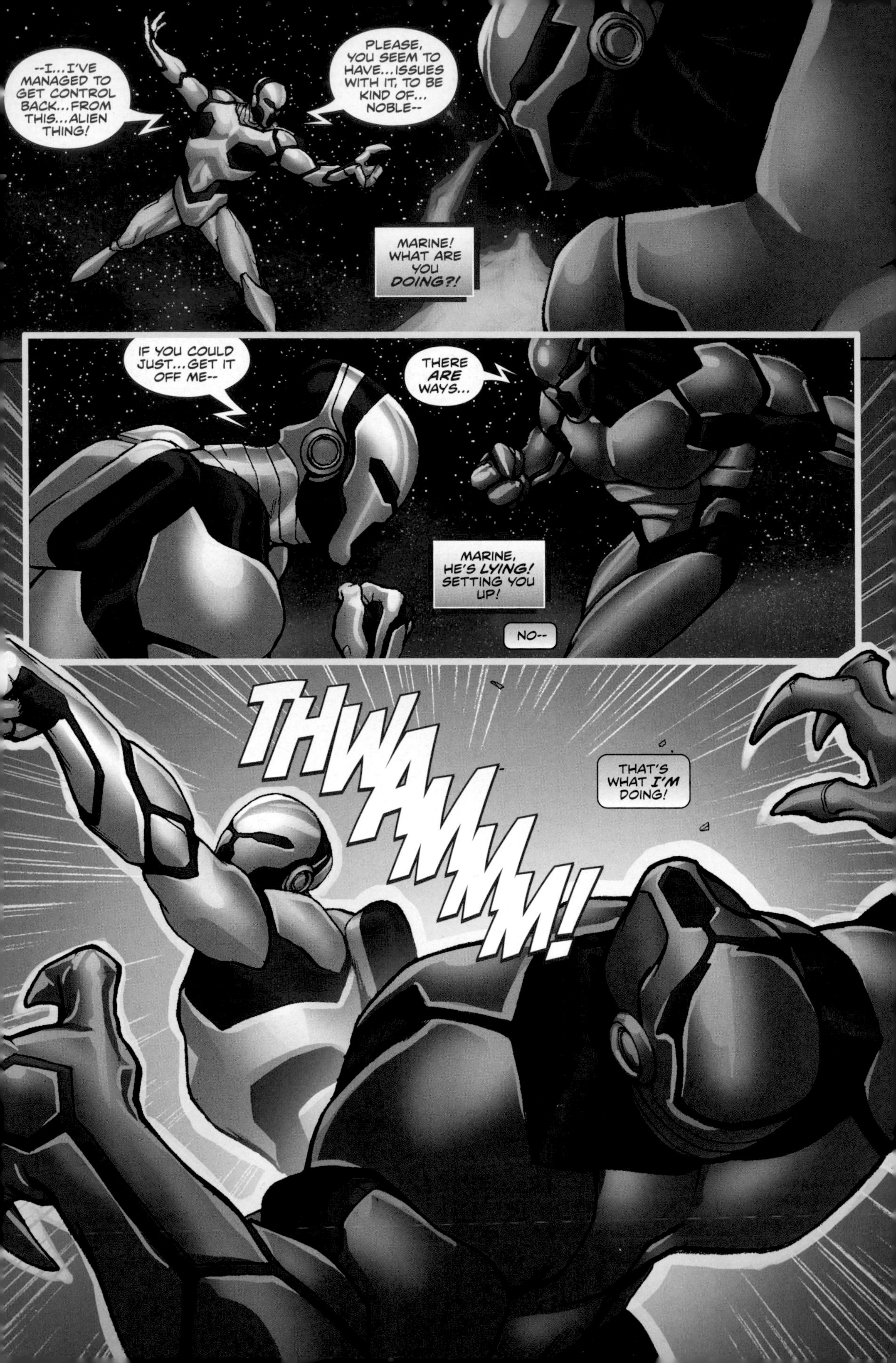
--I...I'VE MANAGED TO GET CONTROL BACK...FROM THIS...ALIEN THING!
PLEASE, YOU SEEM TO HAVE...ISSUES WITH IT, TO BE KIND OF... NOBLE--
MARINE! WHAT ARE YOU *DOING?!*
IF YOU COULD JUST...GET IT OFF ME--
THERE *ARE* WAYS...
MARINE, HE'S *LYING!* SETTING YOU UP!
NO--
THWAMMMM!
THAT'S WHAT *I'M* DOING!

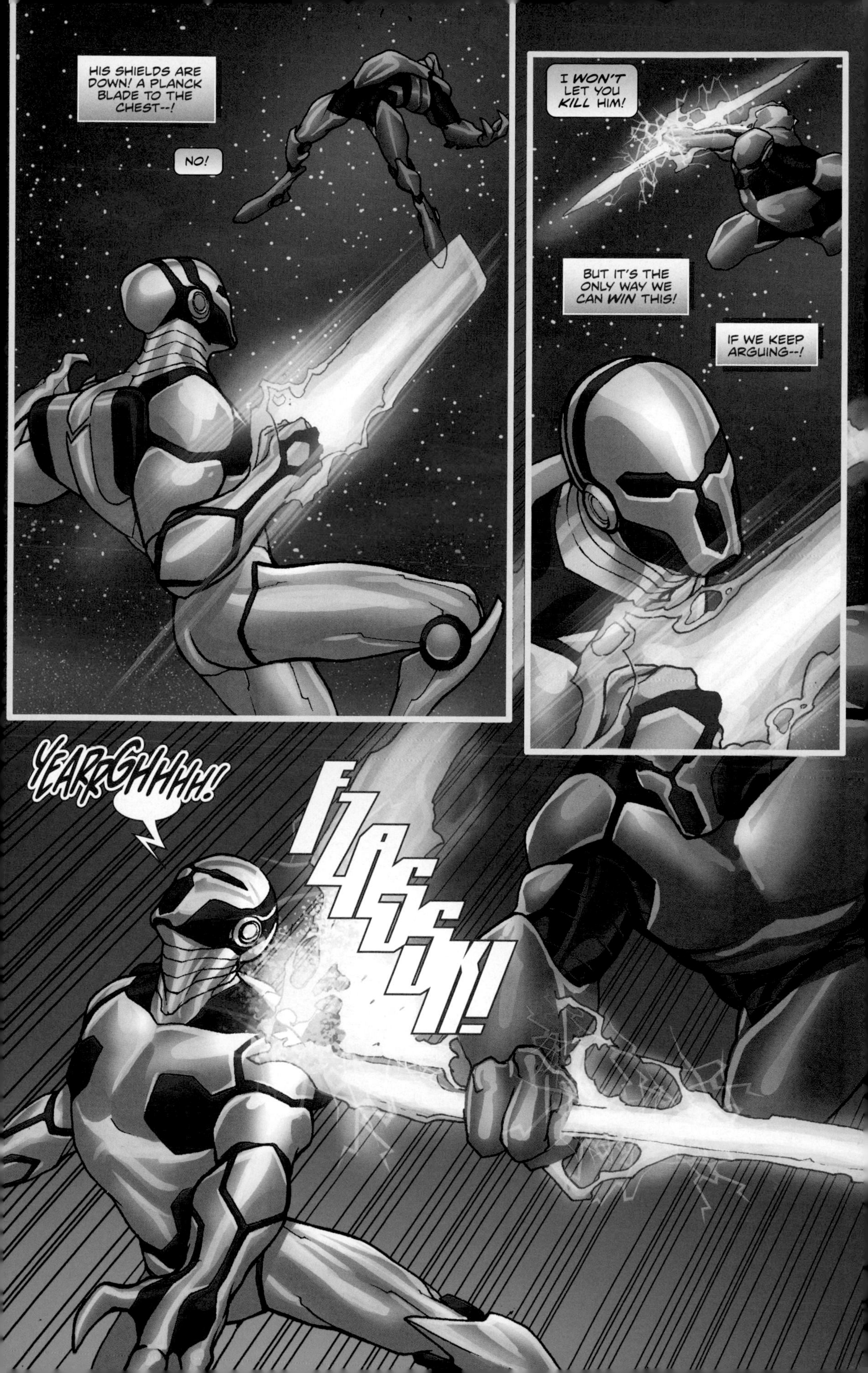
HIS SHIELDS ARE DOWN! A PLANCK BLADE TO THE CHEST--!
NO!
I *WON'T* LET YOU *KILL* HIM!
BUT IT'S THE ONLY WAY WE CAN *WIN* THIS!
IF WE KEEP ARGUING--!
YEARRGHHHH!

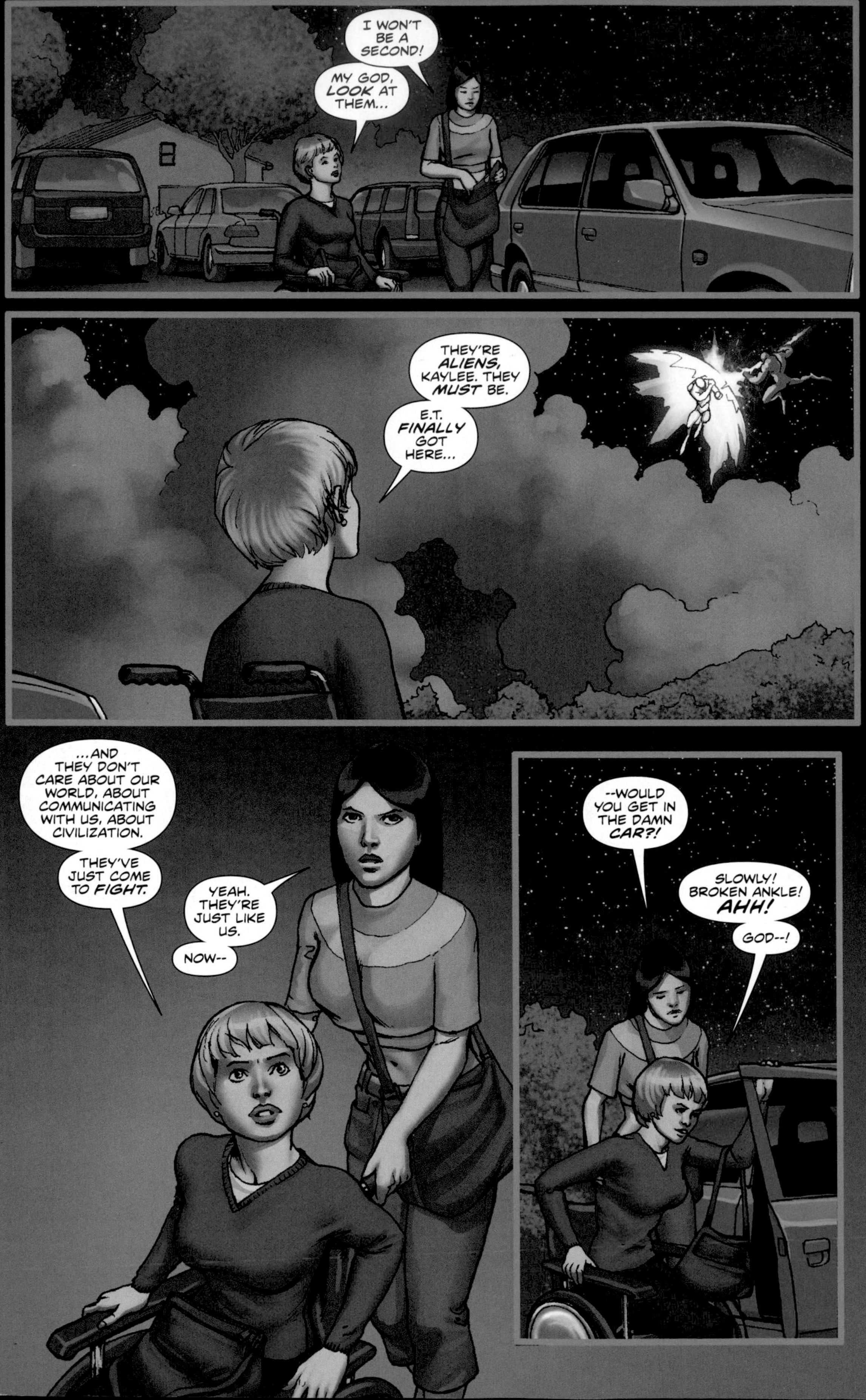
I WON'T BE A SECOND!
MY GOD, LOOK AT THEM...
THEY'RE ALIENS, KAYLEE. THEY MUST BE.
E.T. FINALLY GOT HERE...
...AND THEY DON'T CARE ABOUT OUR WORLD, ABOUT COMMUNICATING WITH US, ABOUT CIVILIZATION.
THEY'VE JUST COME TO FIGHT.
YEAH. THEY'RE JUST LIKE US.
NOW--
--WOULD YOU GET IN THE DAMN CAR?!
SLOWLY! BROKEN ANKLE! AHH!
GOD--!

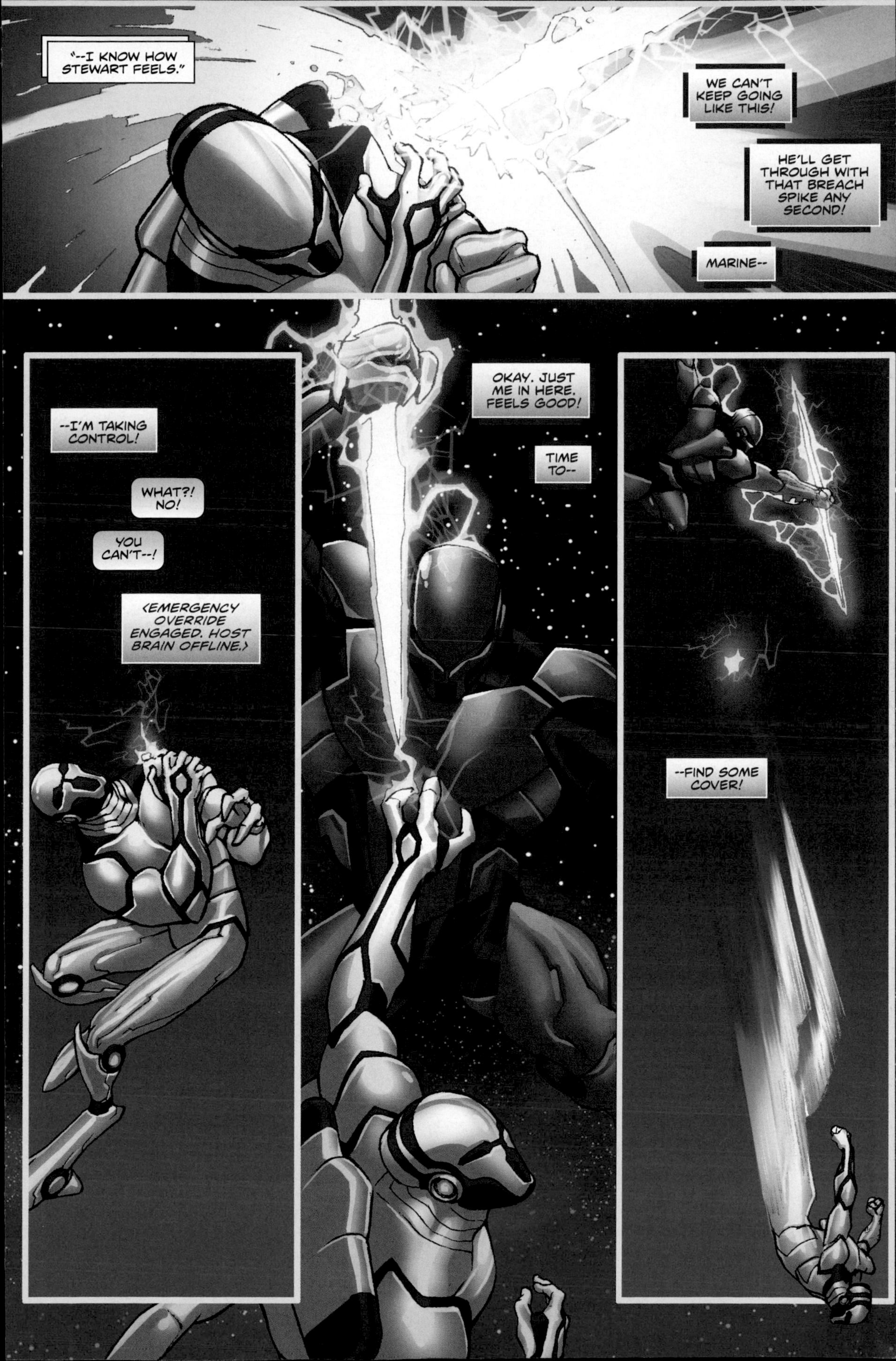
"--I KNOW HOW STEWART FEELS."
WE CAN'T KEEP GOING LIKE THIS!
HE'LL GET THROUGH WITH THAT BREACH SPIKE ANY SECOND!
MARINE--
--I'M TAKING CONTROL!
WHAT?! NO!
YOU CAN'T--!
<EMERGENCY OVERRIDE ENGAGED. HOST BRAIN OFFLINE.>
OKAY. JUST ME IN HERE. FEELS GOOD!
TIME TO--
--FIND SOME COVER!

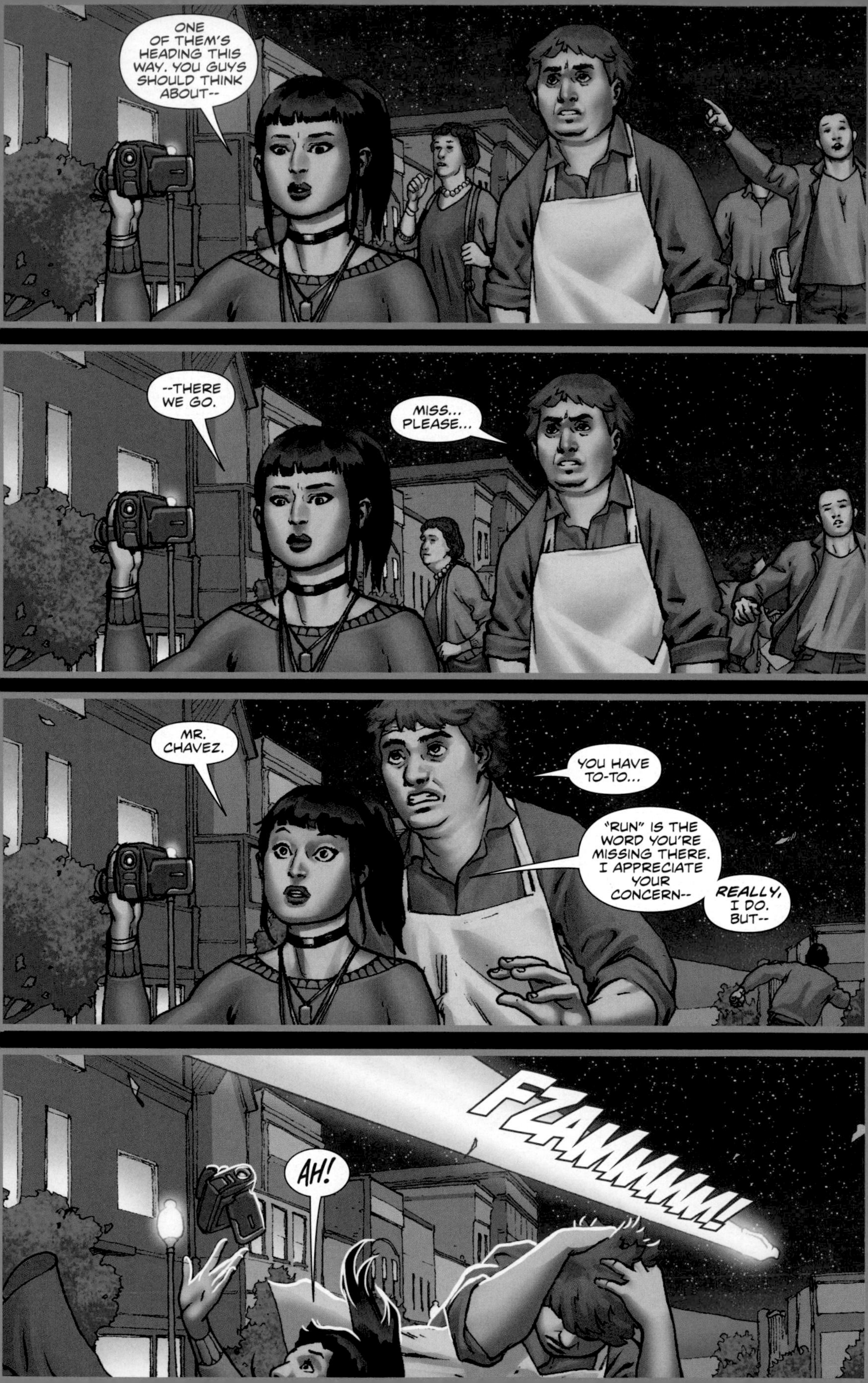
ONE OF THEM'S HEADING THIS WAY. YOU GUYS SHOULD THINK ABOUT--
--THERE WE GO.
MISS... PLEASE...
MR. CHAVEZ.
YOU HAVE TO-TO...
"RUN" IS THE WORD YOU'RE MISSING THERE. I APPRECIATE YOUR CONCERN--
REALLY, I DO. BUT--
FZAMMMMM!
AH!

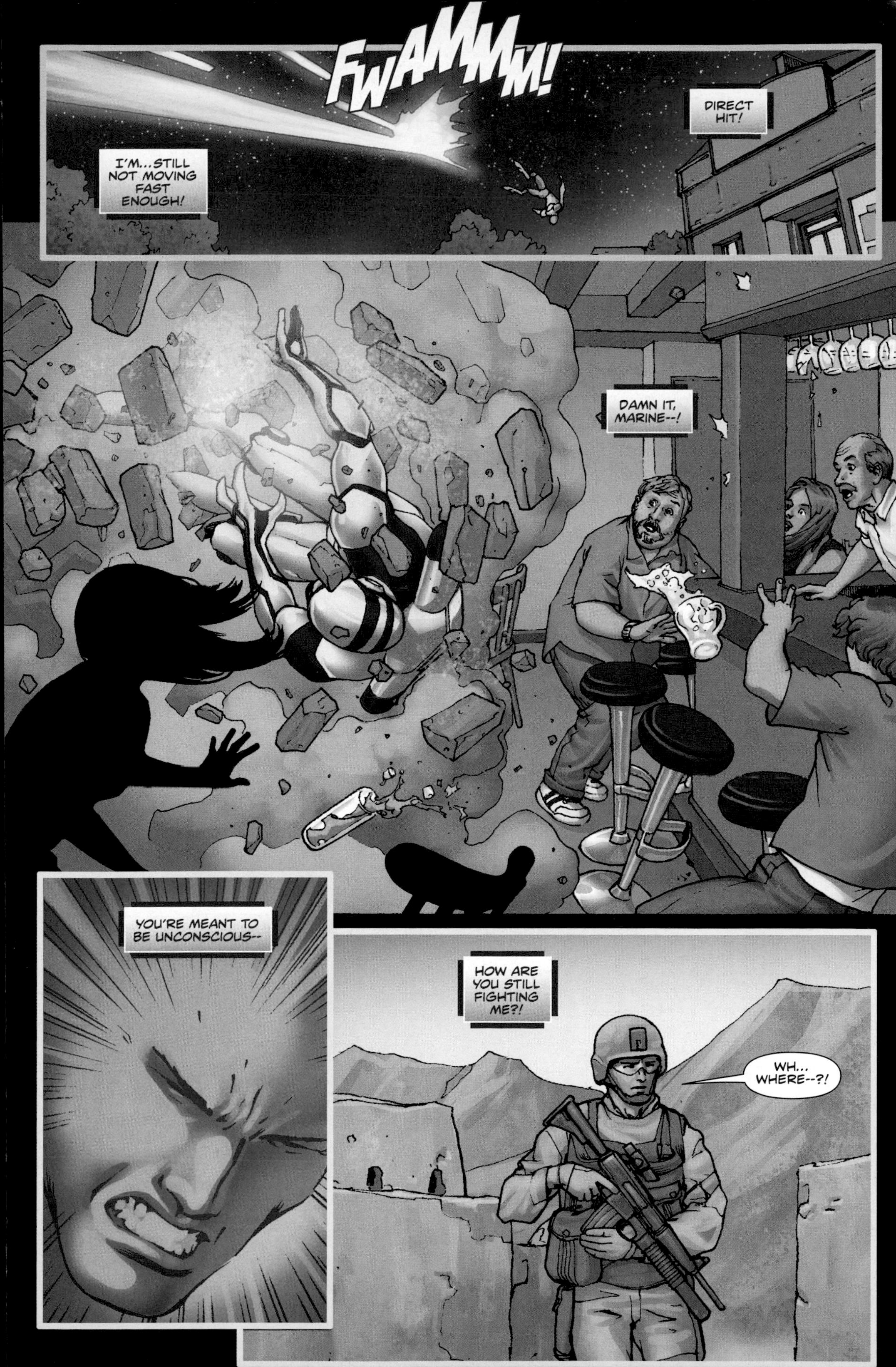
FWAMMM!
I'M...STILL NOT MOVING FAST ENOUGH!
DIRECT HIT!
DAMN IT, MARINE--!
YOU'RE MEANT TO BE UNCONSCIOUS--
HOW ARE YOU STILL FIGHTING ME?!
WH... WHERE--?!

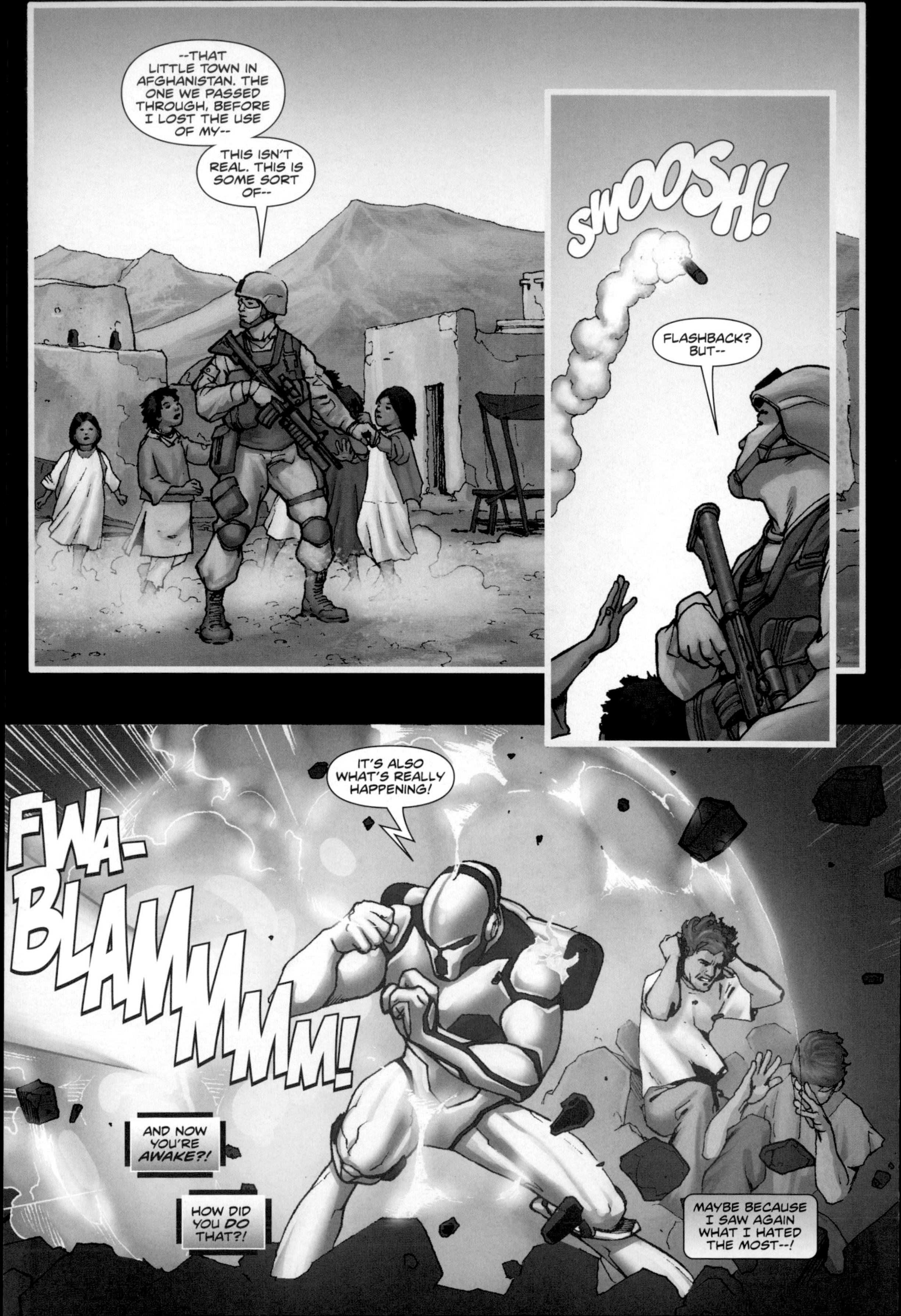
--THAT LITTLE TOWN IN AFGHANISTAN. THE ONE WE PASSED THROUGH, BEFORE I LOST THE USE OF MY--
THIS ISN'T REAL. THIS IS SOME SORT OF--
SWOOSH!
FLASHBACK? BUT--
FWA-BLAMMMM!
IT'S ALSO WHAT'S REALLY HAPPENING!
AND NOW YOU'RE AWAKE?!
HOW DID YOU DO THAT?!
MAYBE BECAUSE I SAW AGAIN WHAT I HATED THE MOST--!

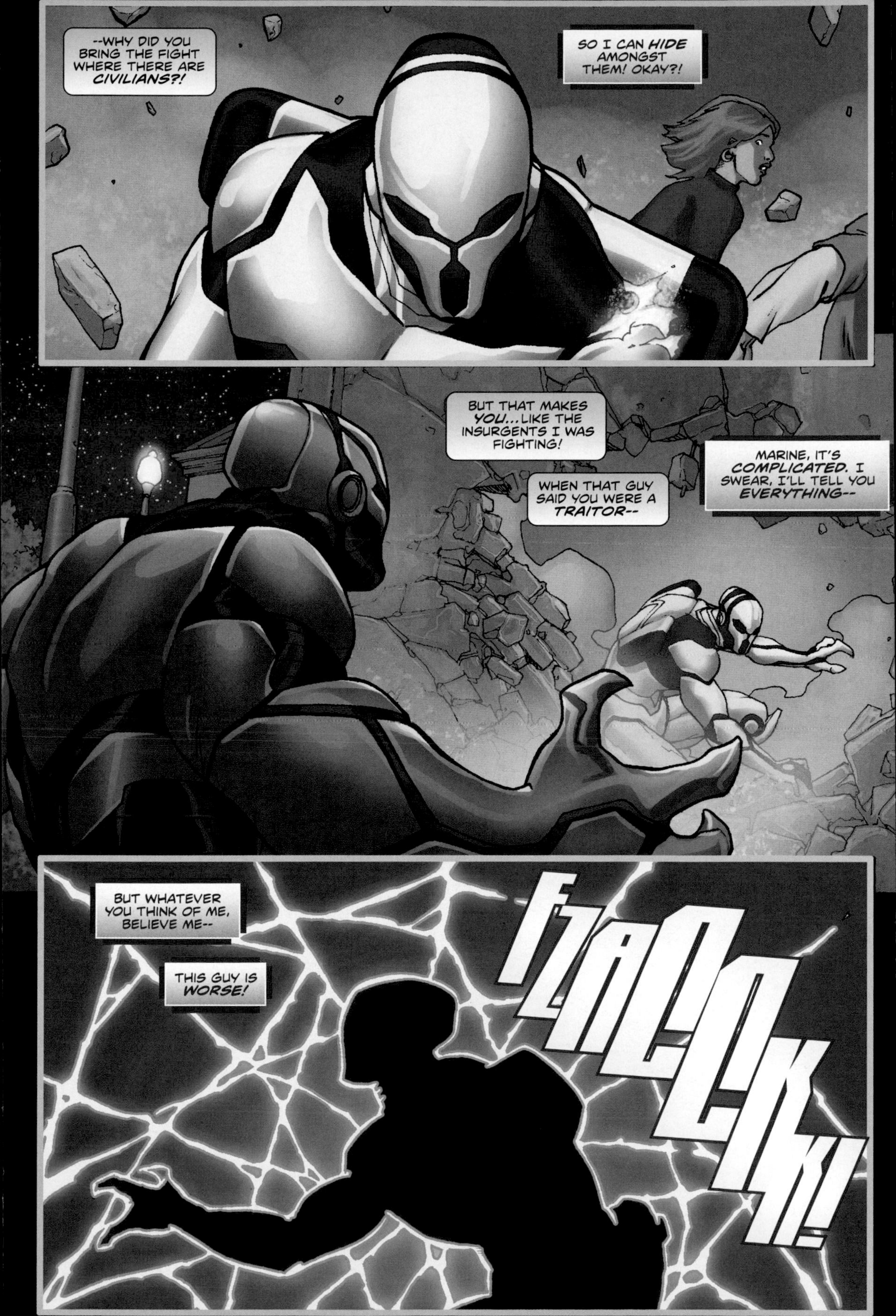
--WHY DID YOU BRING THE FIGHT WHERE THERE ARE *CIVILIANS?!*
SO I CAN *HIDE* AMONGST THEM! OKAY?!
BUT THAT MAKES *YOU*... LIKE THE INSURGENTS I WAS FIGHTING!
WHEN THAT GUY SAID YOU WERE A *TRAITOR*--
MARINE, IT'S **COMPLICATED.** I SWEAR, I'LL TELL YOU *EVERYTHING*--
BUT WHATEVER YOU THINK OF ME, BELIEVE ME--
THIS GUY IS *WORSE!*
FZACCKK!

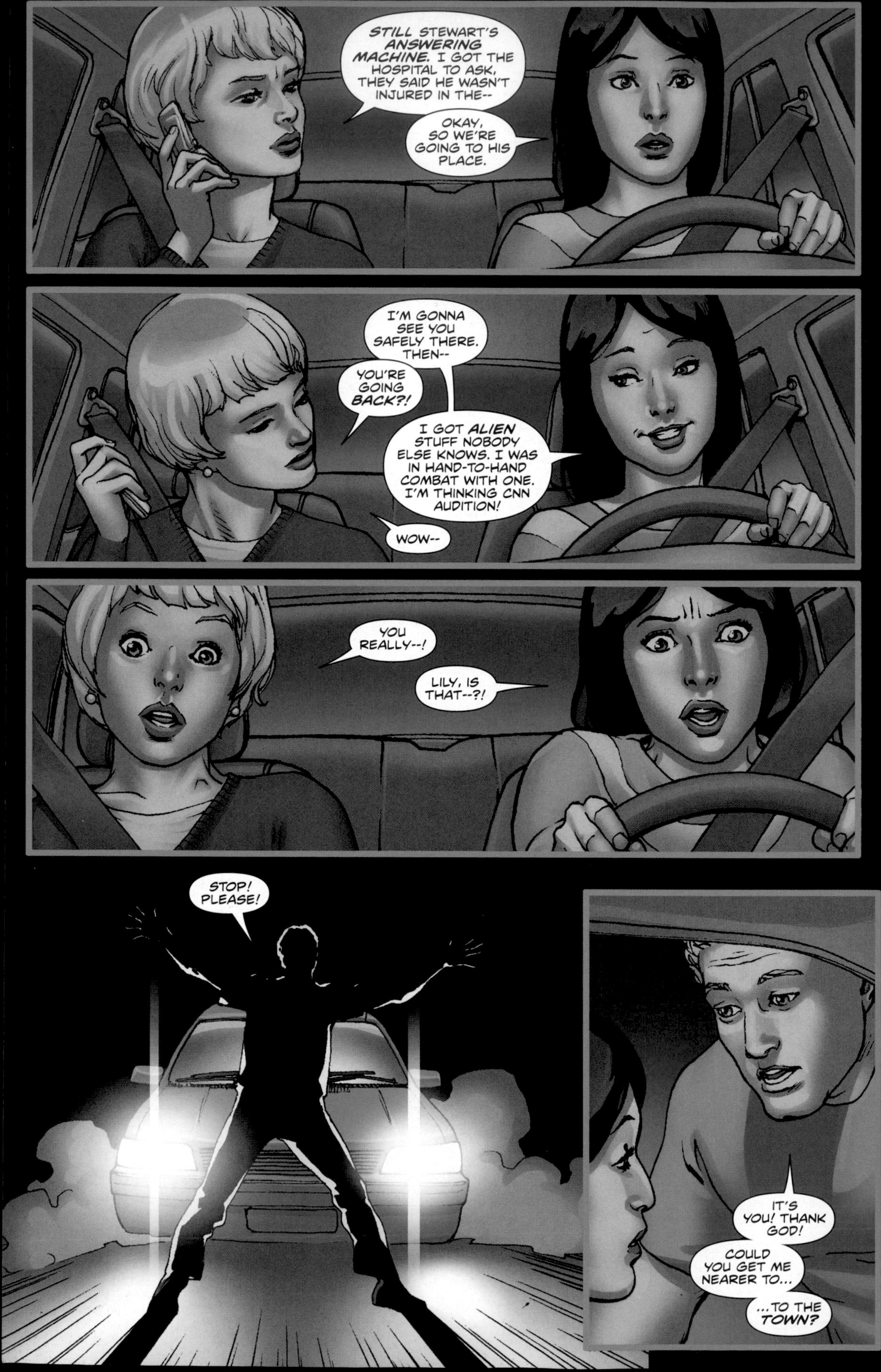
STILL STEWART'S ANSWERING MACHINE. I GOT THE HOSPITAL TO ASK, THEY SAID HE WASN'T INJURED IN THE--
OKAY, SO WE'RE GOING TO HIS PLACE.
I'M GONNA SEE YOU SAFELY THERE. THEN--
YOU'RE GOING BACK?!
I GOT ALIEN STUFF NOBODY ELSE KNOWS. I WAS IN HAND-TO-HAND COMBAT WITH ONE. I'M THINKING CNN AUDITION!
WOW--
YOU REALLY--!
LILY, IS THAT--?!
STOP! PLEASE!
IT'S YOU! THANK GOD!
COULD YOU GET ME NEARER TO...
...TO THE TOWN?

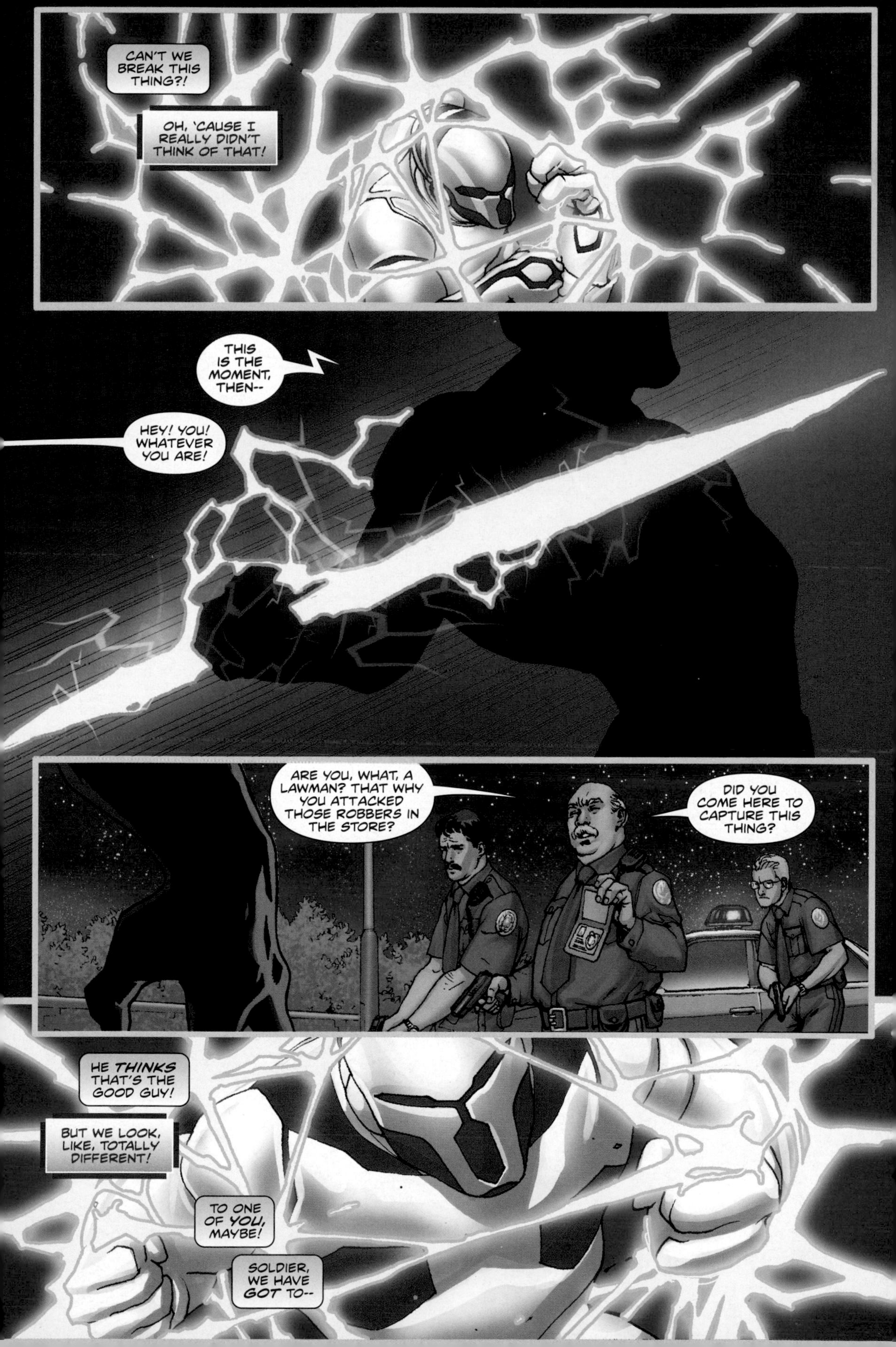

CAN'T WE BREAK THIS THING?!
OH, 'CAUSE I REALLY DIDN'T THINK OF THAT!
THIS IS THE MOMENT, THEN--
HEY! YOU! WHATEVER YOU ARE!
ARE YOU, WHAT, A LAWMAN? THAT WHY YOU ATTACKED THOSE ROBBERS IN THE STORE?
DID YOU COME HERE TO CAPTURE THIS THING?
HE *THINKS* THAT'S THE GOOD GUY!
BUT WE LOOK, LIKE, TOTALLY DIFFERENT!
TO ONE OF *YOU*, MAYBE!
SOLDIER, WE HAVE *GOT* TO--

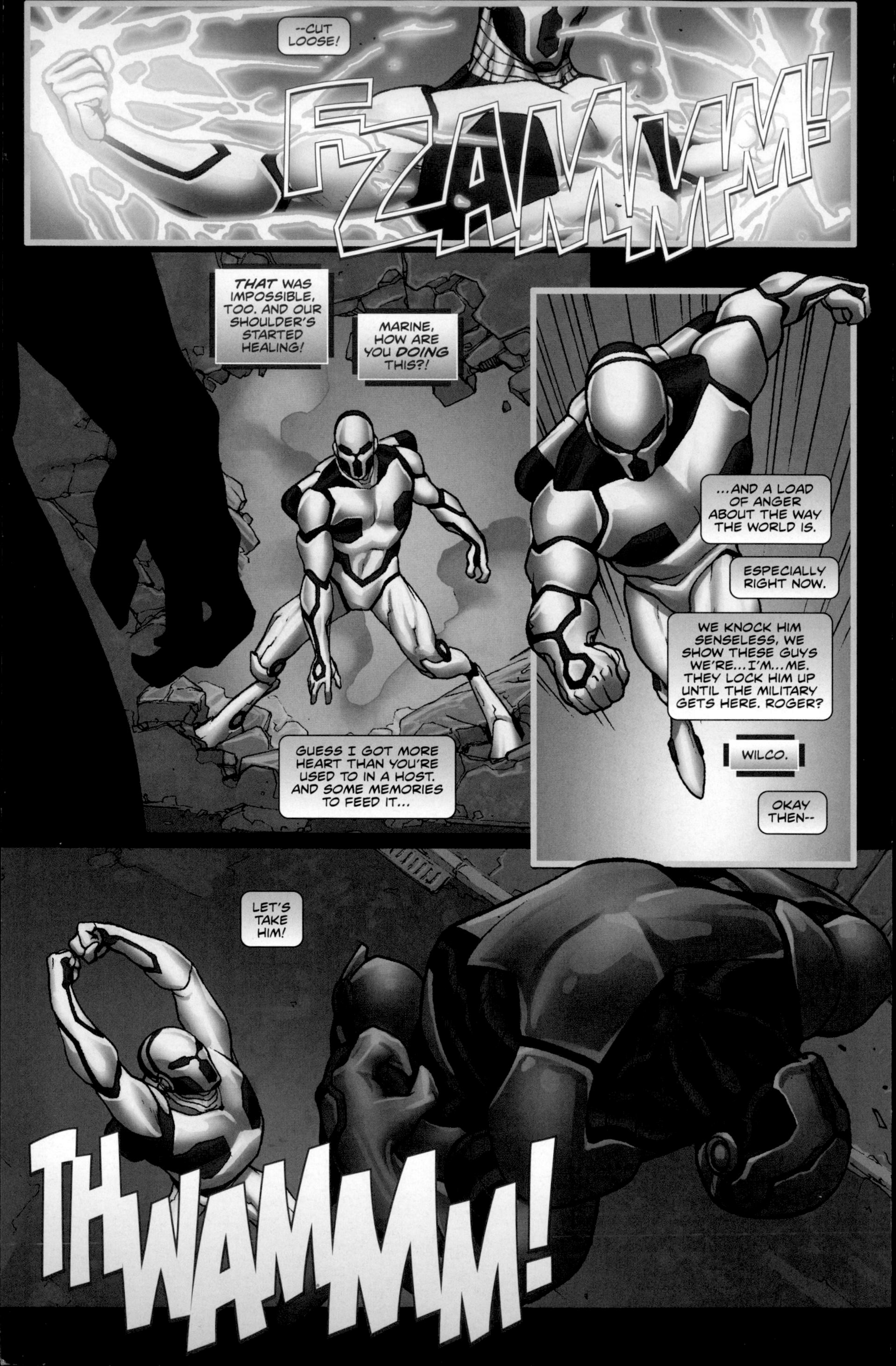
--CUT LOOSE!
FZAMMM!
THAT WAS IMPOSSIBLE, TOO. AND OUR SHOULDER'S STARTED HEALING!
MARINE, HOW ARE YOU DOING THIS?!
GUESS I GOT MORE HEART THAN YOU'RE USED TO IN A HOST. AND SOME MEMORIES TO FEED IT...
...AND A LOAD OF ANGER ABOUT THE WAY THE WORLD IS.
ESPECIALLY RIGHT NOW.
WE KNOCK HIM SENSELESS, WE SHOW THESE GUYS WE'RE... I'M... ME. THEY LOCK HIM UP UNTIL THE MILITARY GETS HERE. ROGER?
WILCO.
OKAY THEN--
LET'S TAKE HIM!
THWAMMM!

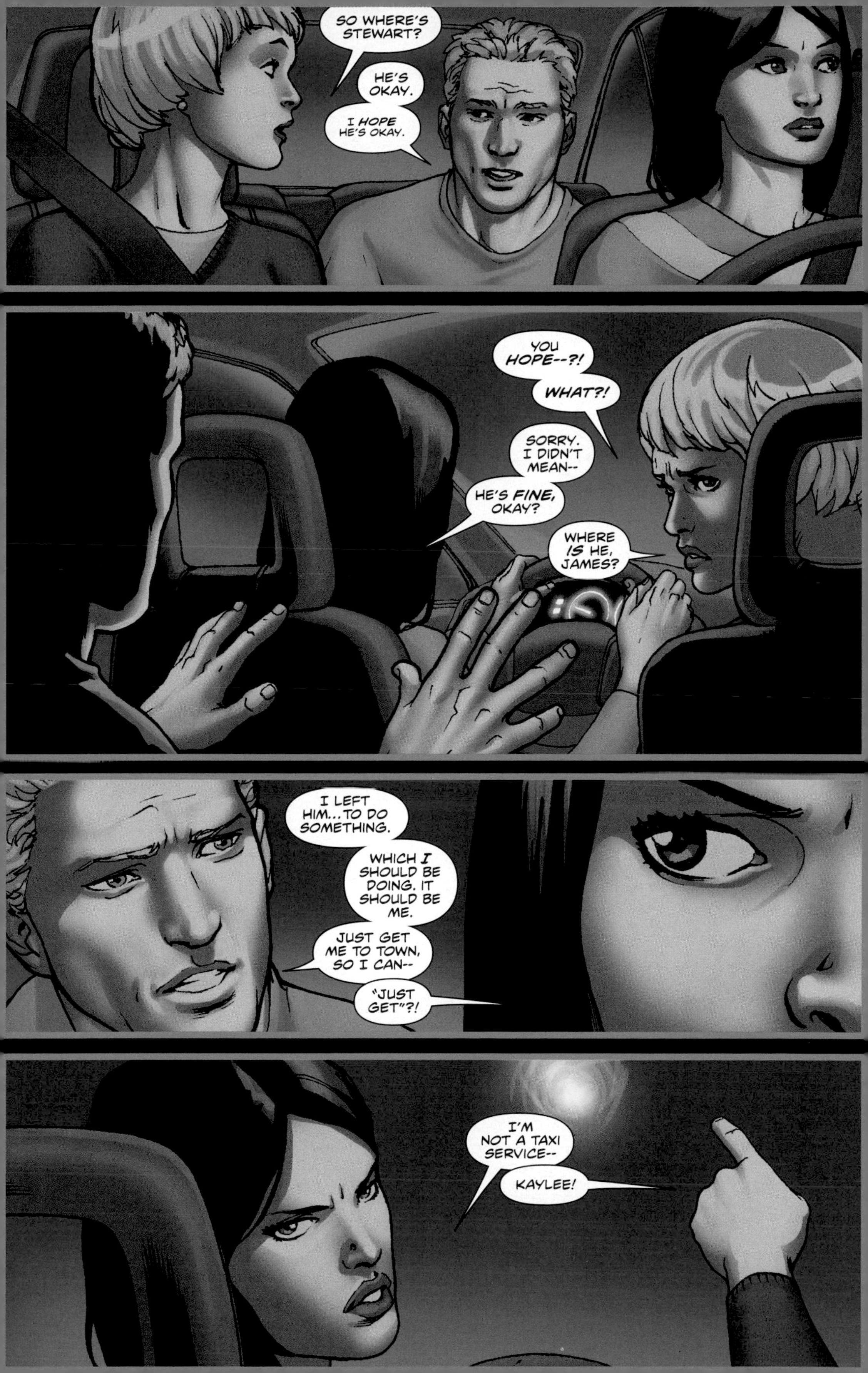
SO WHERE'S STEWART?
HE'S OKAY.
I HOPE HE'S OKAY.
YOU HOPE--?!
WHAT?!
SORRY. I DIDN'T MEAN--
HE'S FINE, OKAY?
WHERE IS HE, JAMES?
I LEFT HIM...TO DO SOMETHING.
WHICH I SHOULD BE DOING. IT SHOULD BE ME.
JUST GET ME TO TOWN, SO I CAN--
"JUST GET"?!
I'M NOT A TAXI SERVICE--
KAYLEE!

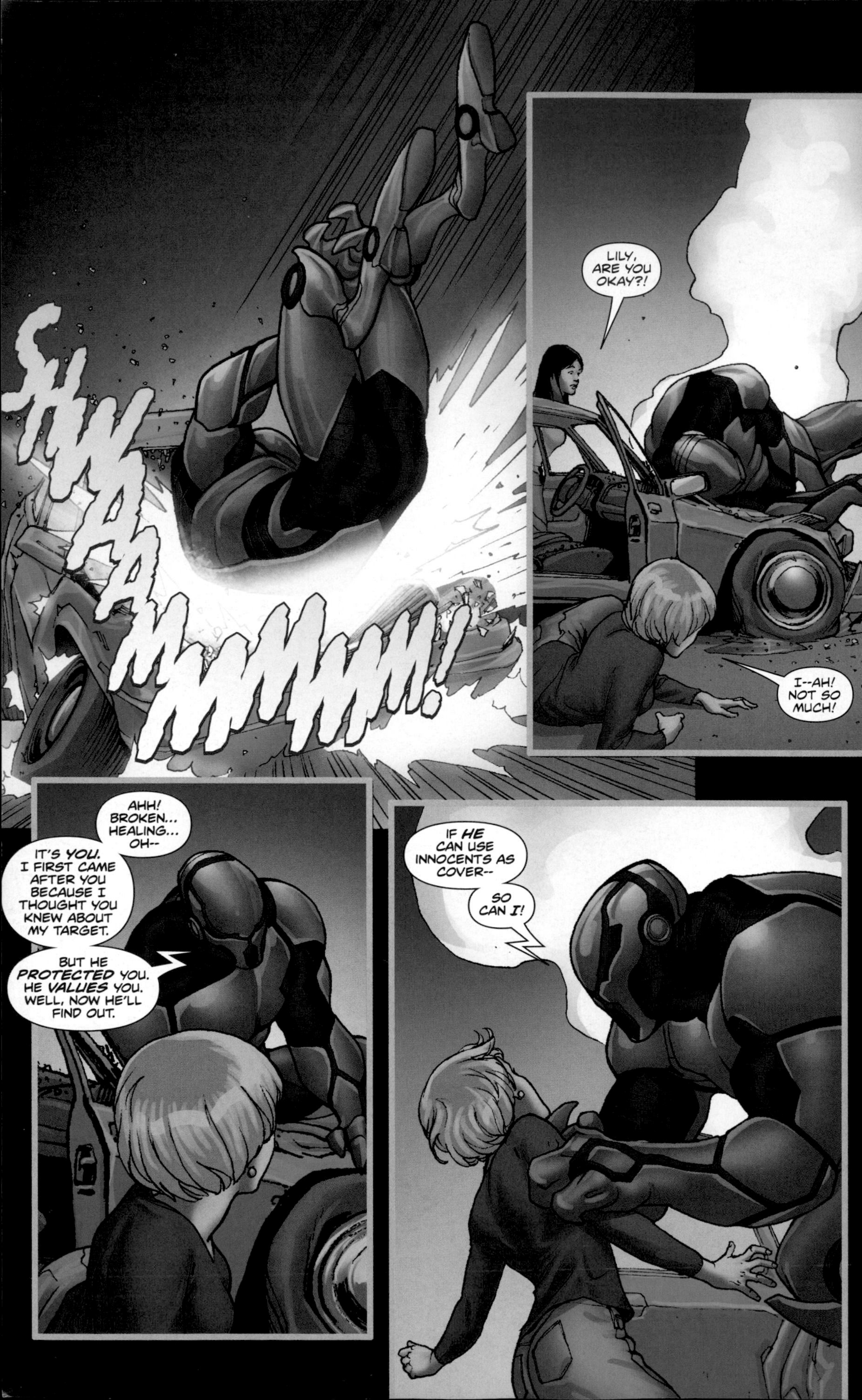
SHWAMMMMMM!
LILY, ARE YOU OKAY?!
I--AH! NOT SO MUCH!
AHH! BROKEN... HEALING... OH--
IT'S YOU. I FIRST CAME AFTER YOU BECAUSE I THOUGHT YOU KNEW ABOUT MY TARGET.
BUT HE PROTECTED YOU. HE VALUES YOU. WELL, NOW HE'LL FIND OUT.
IF HE CAN USE INNOCENTS AS COVER--
SO CAN I!

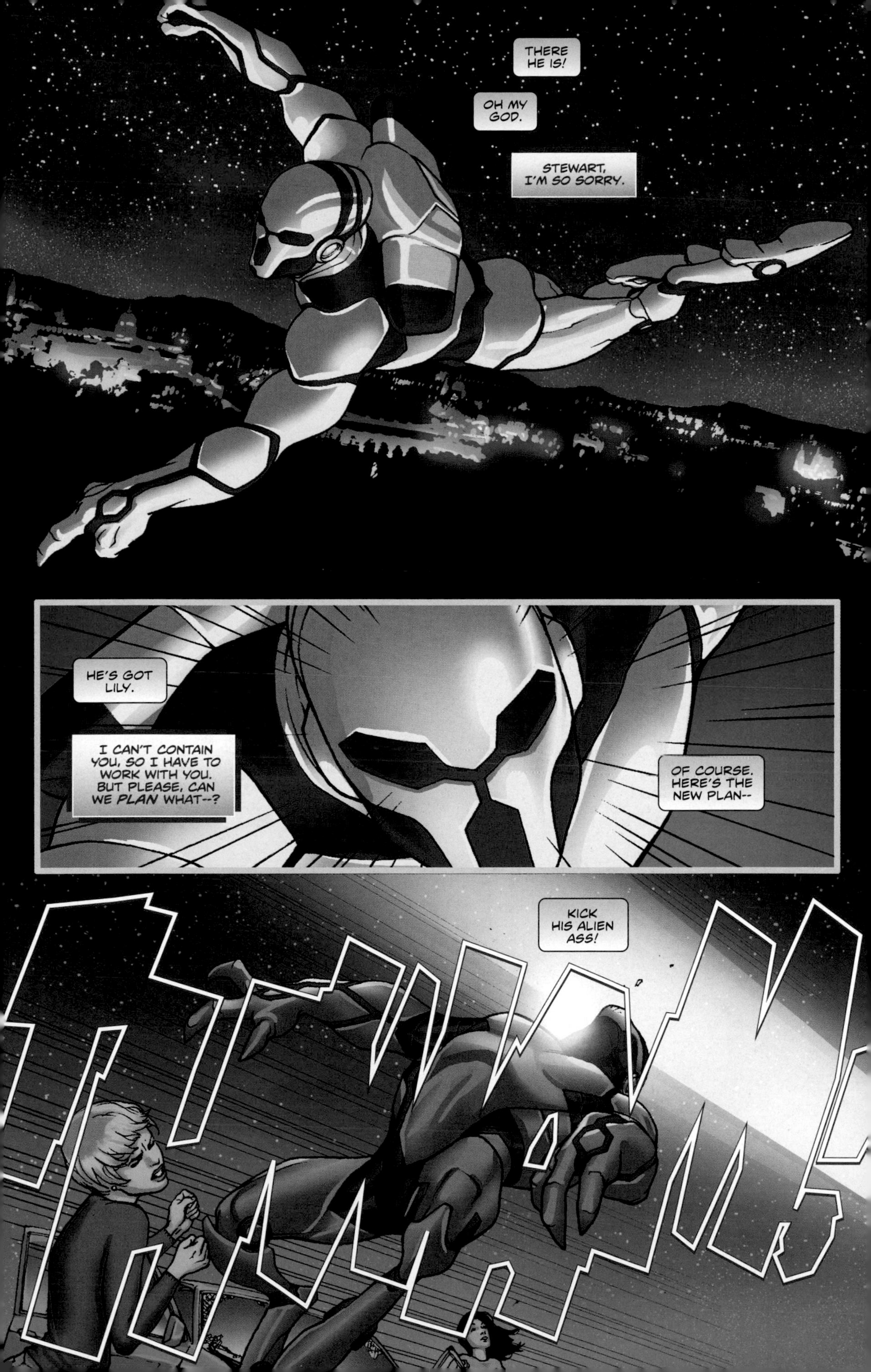
THERE HE IS!
OH MY GOD.
STEWART, I'M SO SORRY.
HE'S GOT LILY.
I CAN'T CONTAIN YOU, SO I HAVE TO WORK WITH YOU. BUT PLEASE, CAN WE *PLAN* WHAT--?
OF COURSE. HERE'S THE NEW PLAN--
KICK HIS ALIEN ASS!

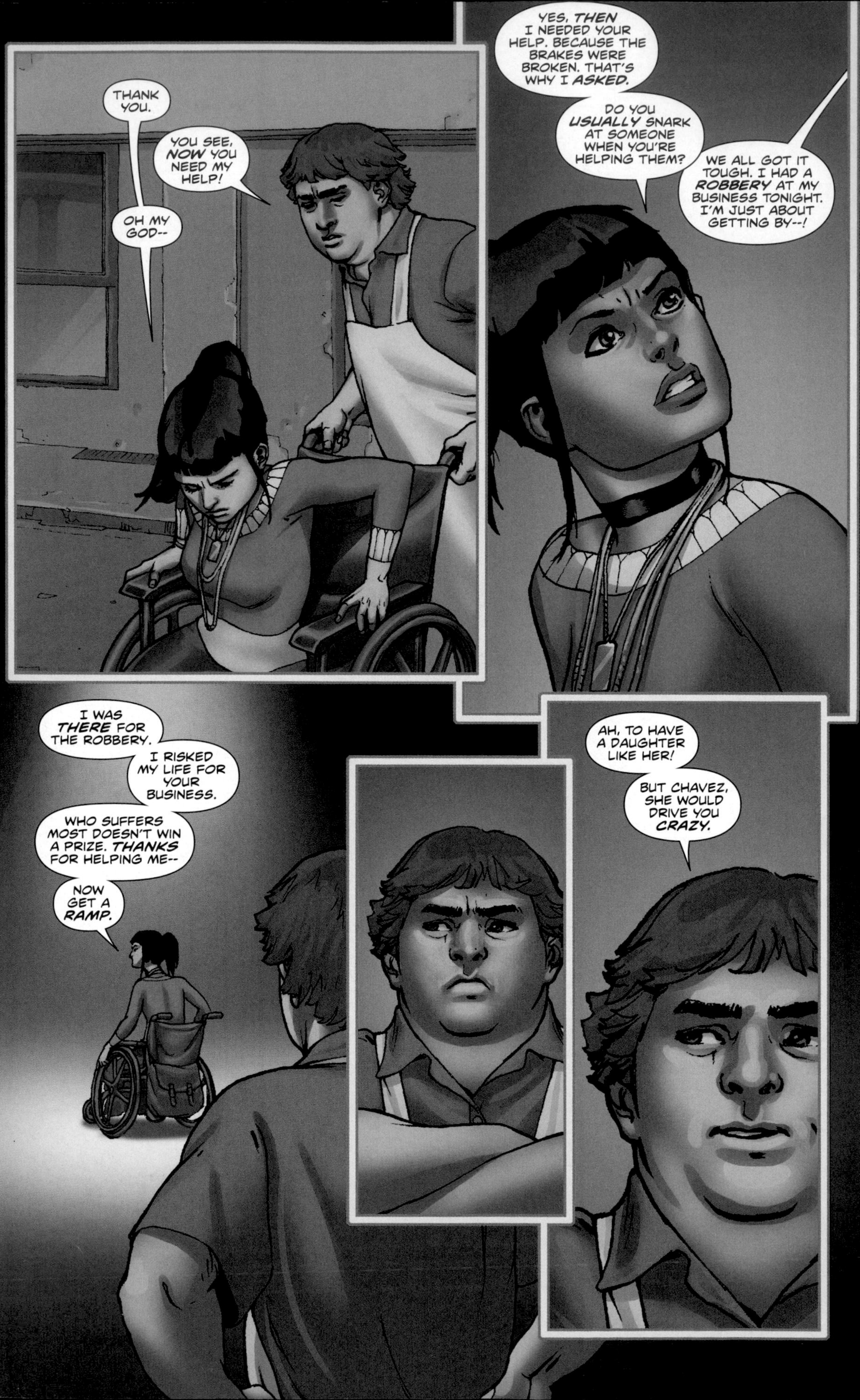
THANK YOU.
YOU SEE, NOW YOU NEED MY HELP!
OH MY GOD--
YES, THEN I NEEDED YOUR HELP. BECAUSE THE BRAKES WERE BROKEN. THAT'S WHY I ASKED.
DO YOU USUALLY SNARK AT SOMEONE WHEN YOU'RE HELPING THEM?
WE ALL GOT IT TOUGH. I HAD A ROBBERY AT MY BUSINESS TONIGHT. I'M JUST ABOUT GETTING BY--!
I WAS THERE FOR THE ROBBERY.
I RISKED MY LIFE FOR YOUR BUSINESS.
WHO SUFFERS MOST DOESN'T WIN A PRIZE. THANKS FOR HELPING ME--
NOW GET A RAMP.
AH, TO HAVE A DAUGHTER LIKE HER!
BUT CHAVEZ, SHE WOULD DRIVE YOU CRAZY.

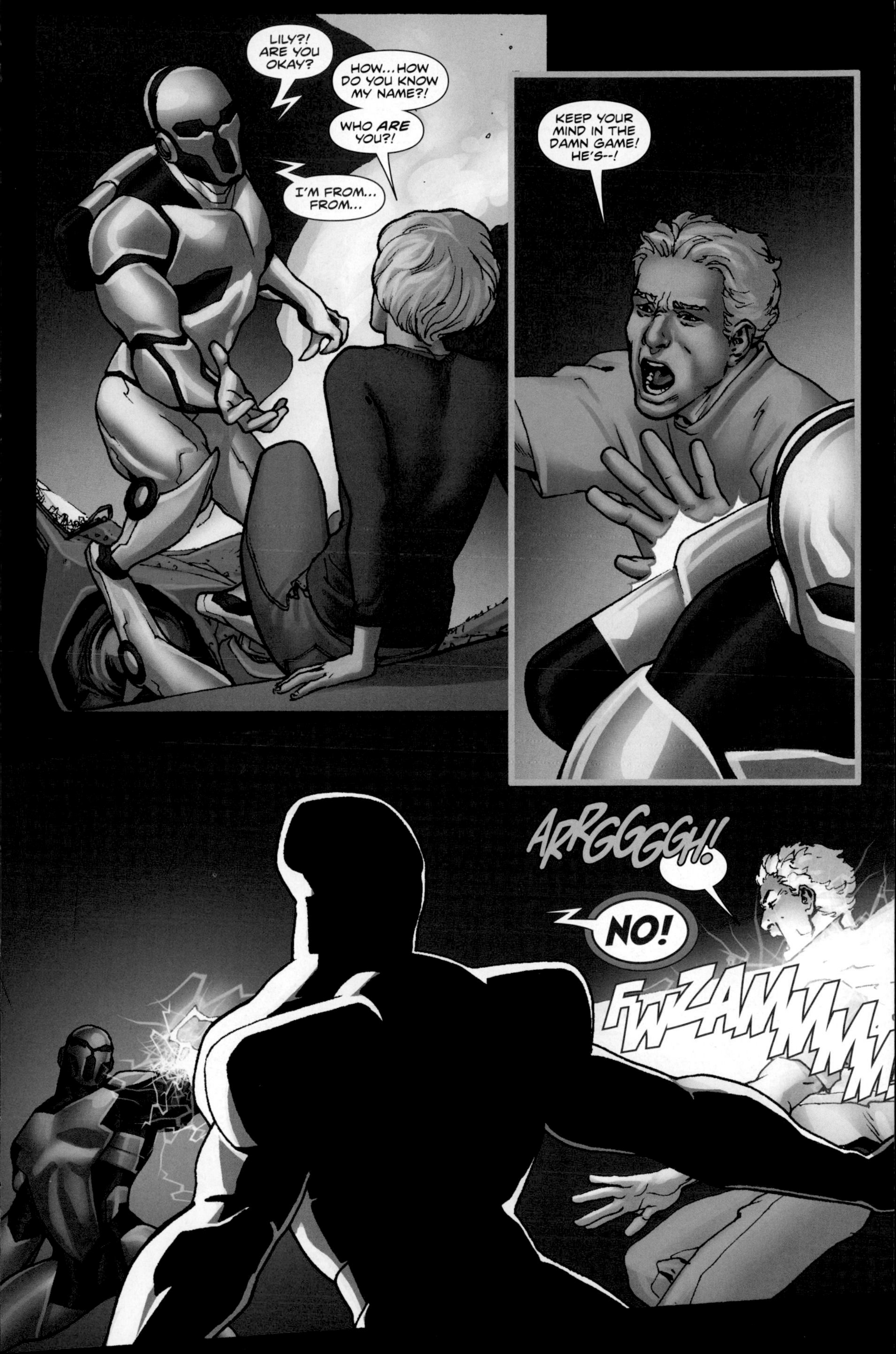
LILY?! ARE YOU OKAY?
HOW...HOW DO YOU KNOW MY NAME?!
WHO ARE YOU?!
I'M FROM... FROM...
KEEP YOUR MIND IN THE DAMN GAME! HE'S--!
ARRGGGGH!
NO!
FWZAMMMMM

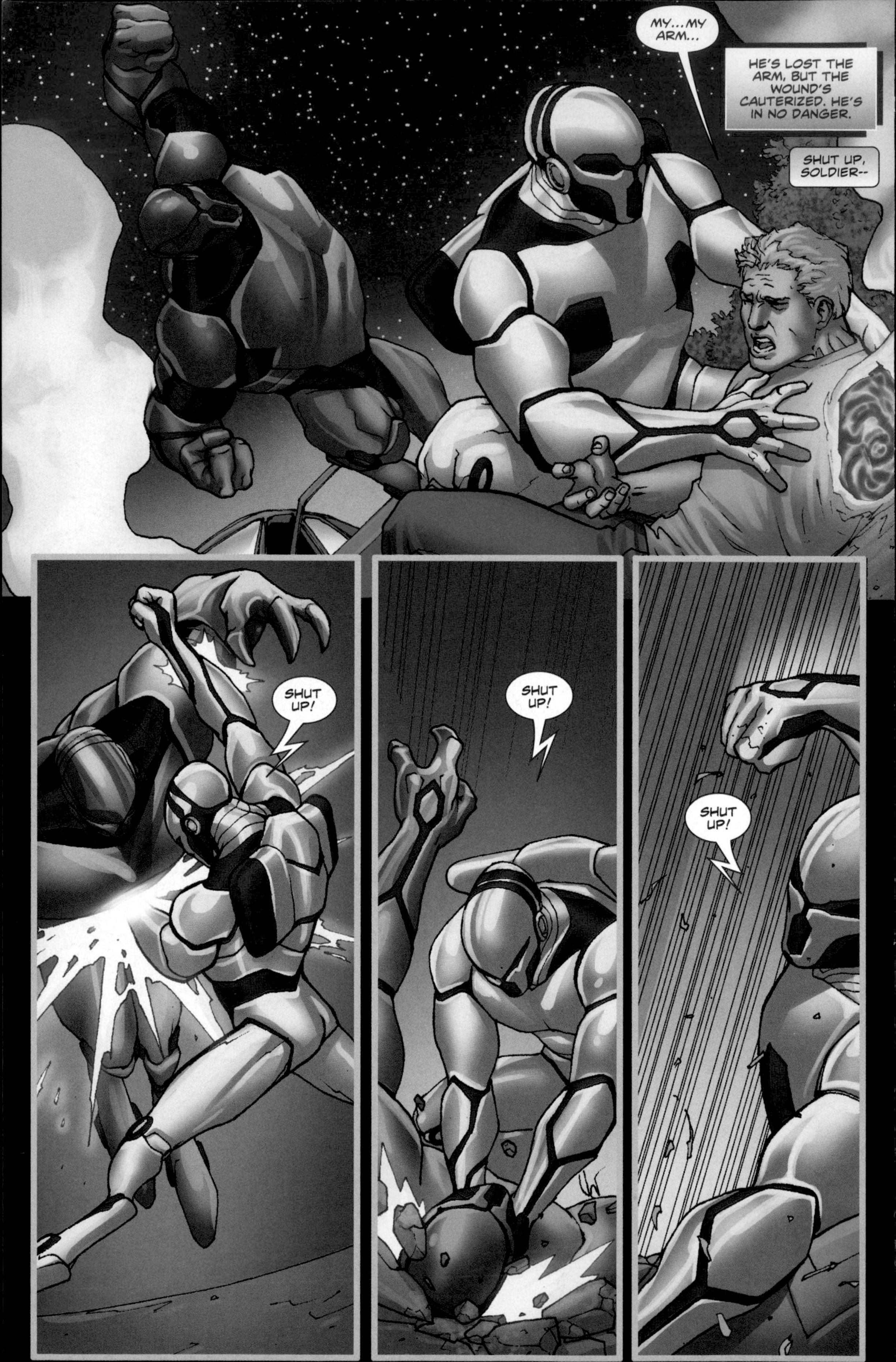
MY...MY ARM...
HE'S LOST THE ARM, BUT THE WOUND'S CAUTERIZED. HE'S IN NO DANGER.
SHUT UP, SOLDIER--
SHUT UP!
SHUT UP!
SHUT UP!

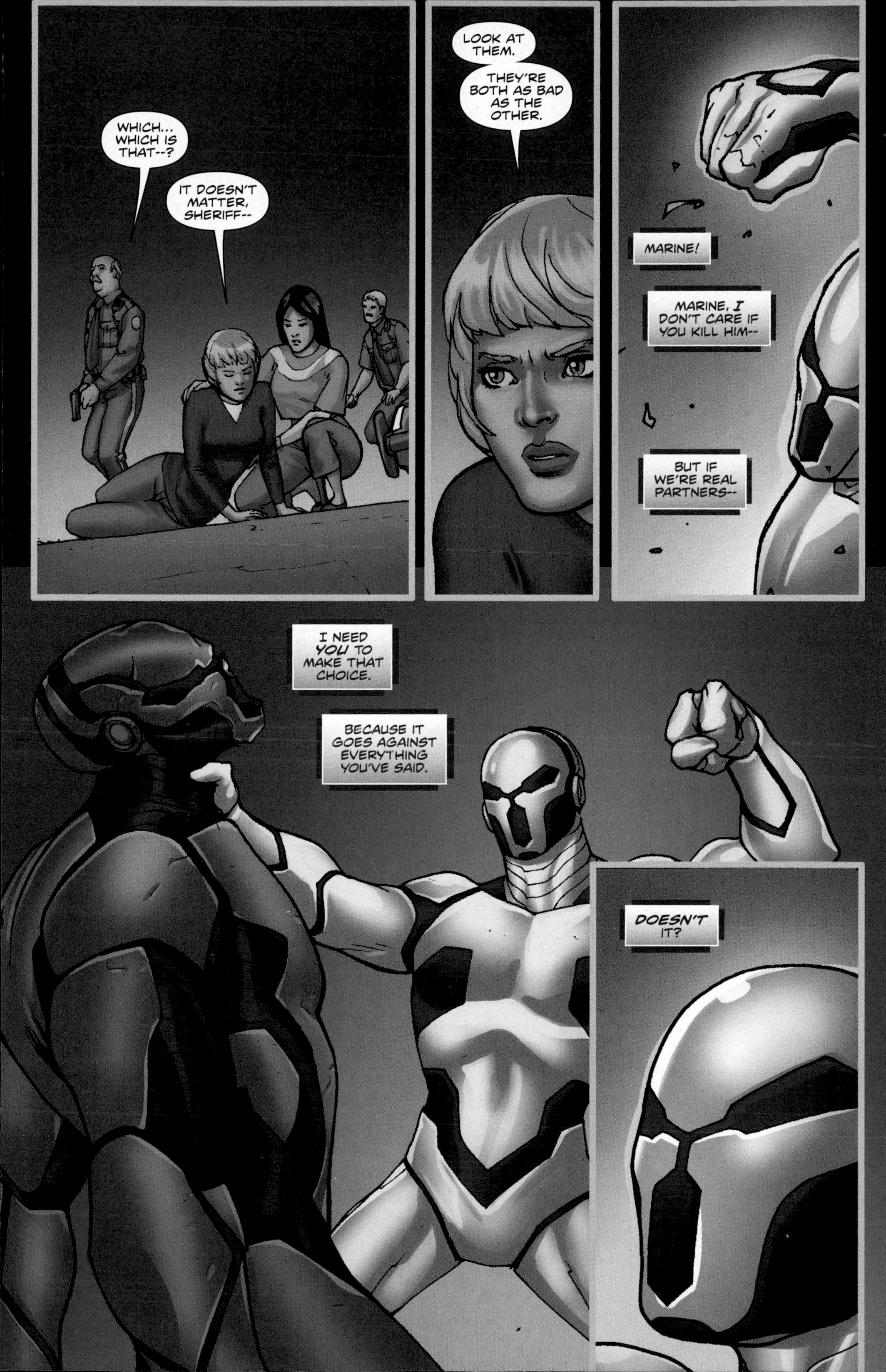
WHICH... WHICH IS THAT--?
IT DOESN'T MATTER, SHERIFF--
LOOK AT THEM.
THEY'RE BOTH AS BAD AS THE OTHER.
MARINE!
MARINE, I DON'T CARE IF YOU KILL HIM--
BUT IF WE'RE REAL PARTNERS--
I NEED YOU TO MAKE THAT CHOICE.
BECAUSE IT GOES AGAINST EVERYTHING YOU'VE SAID.
DOESN'T IT?

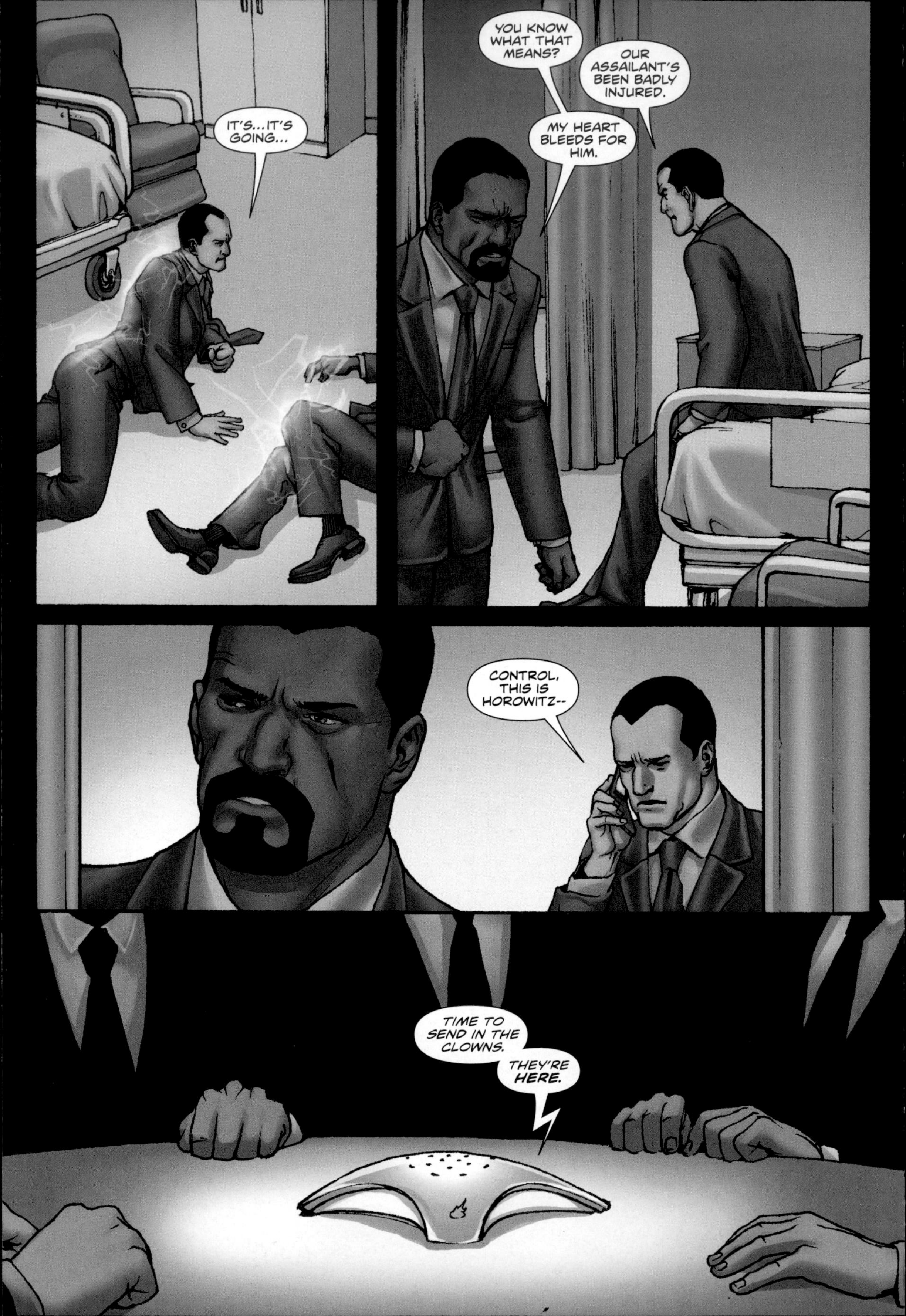
IT'S...IT'S GOING...
YOU KNOW WHAT THAT MEANS?
OUR ASSAILANT'S BEEN BADLY INJURED.
MY HEART BLEEDS FOR HIM.
CONTROL, THIS IS HOROWITZ--
TIME TO SEND IN THE CLOWNS.
THEY'RE HERE.

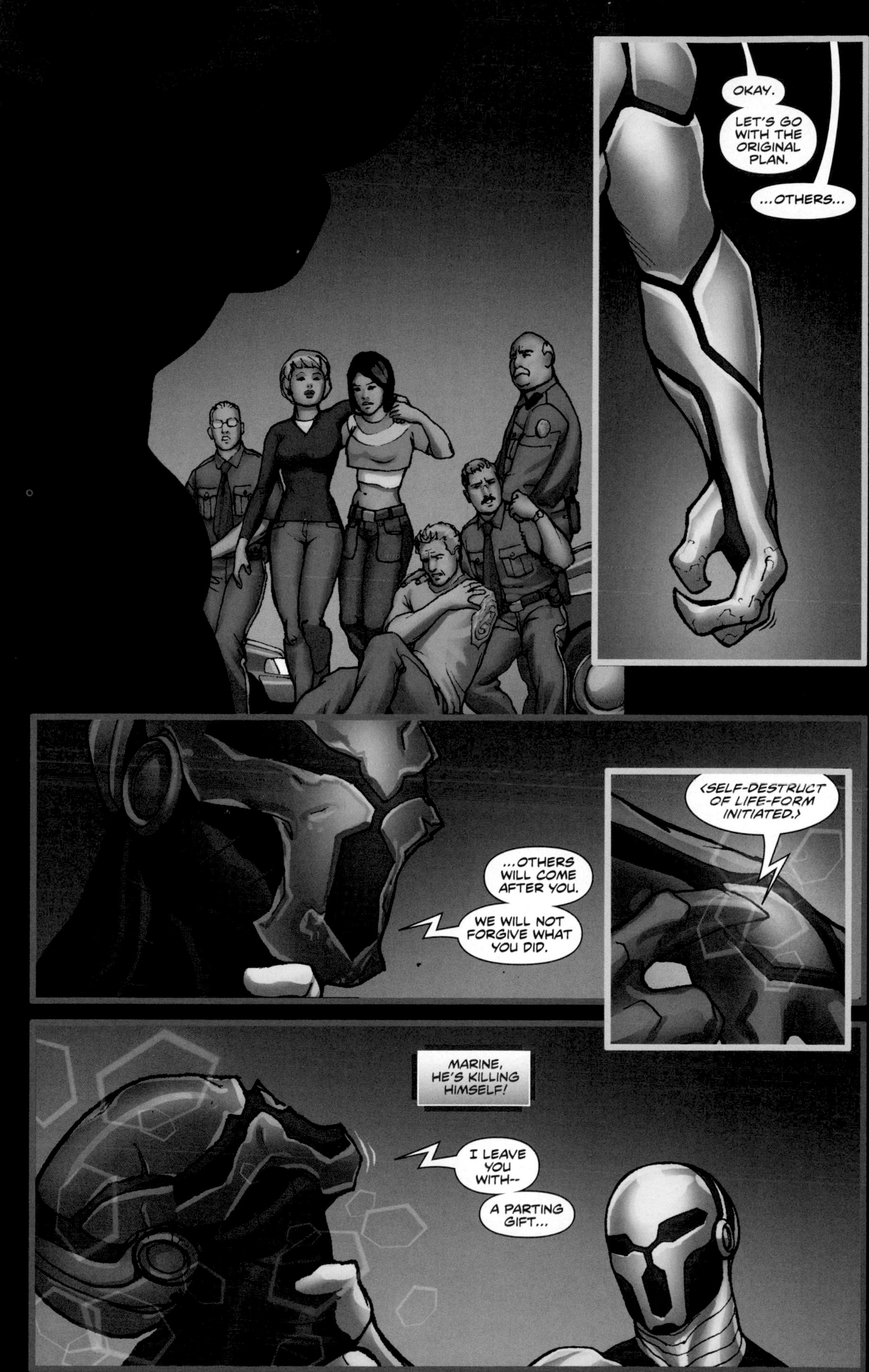
OKAY.
LET'S GO WITH THE ORIGINAL PLAN.
...OTHERS...
...OTHERS WILL COME AFTER YOU.
WE WILL NOT FORGIVE WHAT YOU DID.
<SELF-DESTRUCT OF LIFE-FORM INITIATED.>
MARINE, HE'S KILLING HIMSELF!
I LEAVE YOU WITH--
A PARTING GIFT...

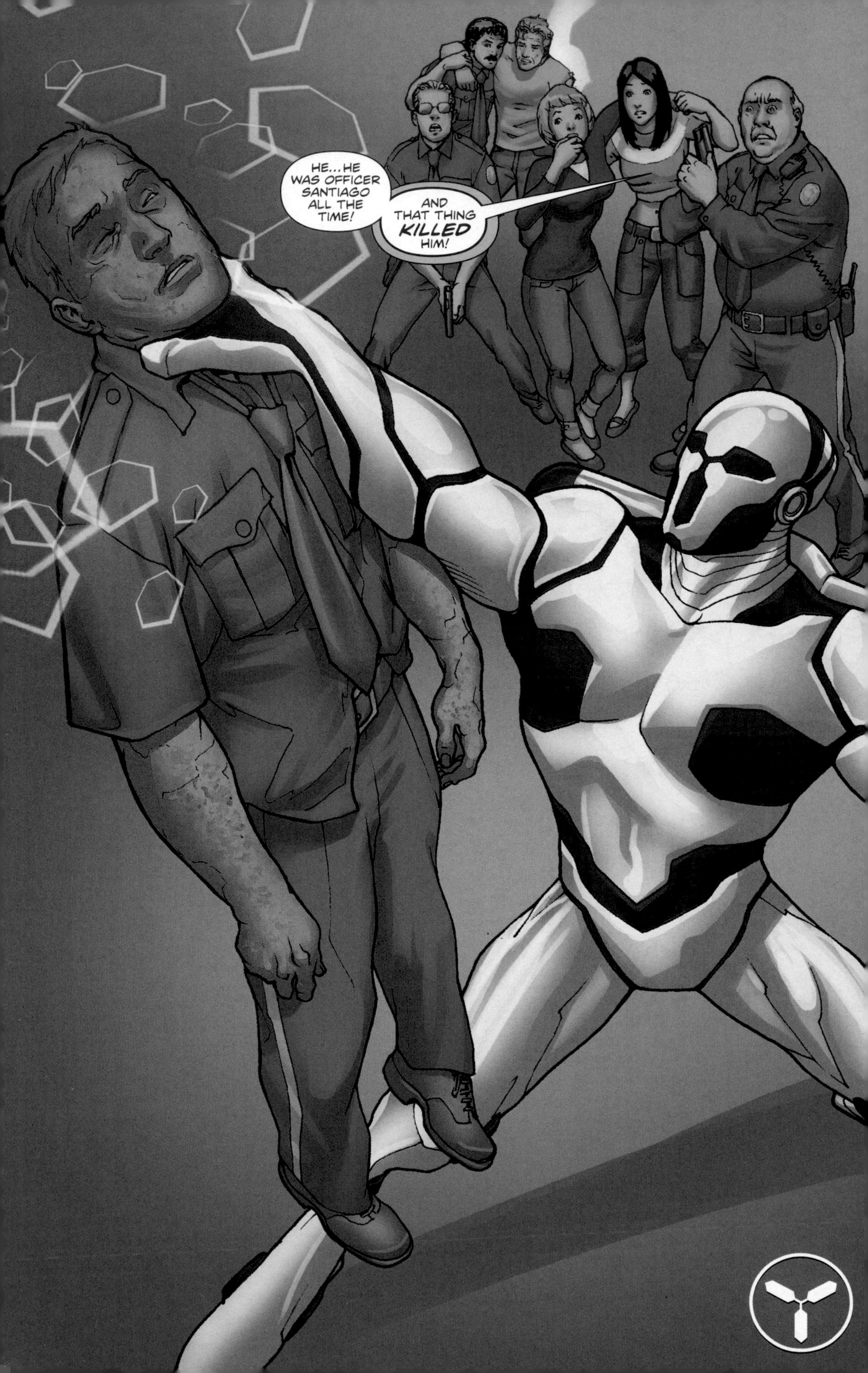
HE...HE WAS OFFICER SANTIAGO ALL THE TIME!
AND THAT THING KILLED HIM!

COMING SOON

CODE ICARUS

STAN LEE

SOLDIER ZERO

DAN ABNETT

ANDY LANNING

JAVIER PINA

VOLUME TWO

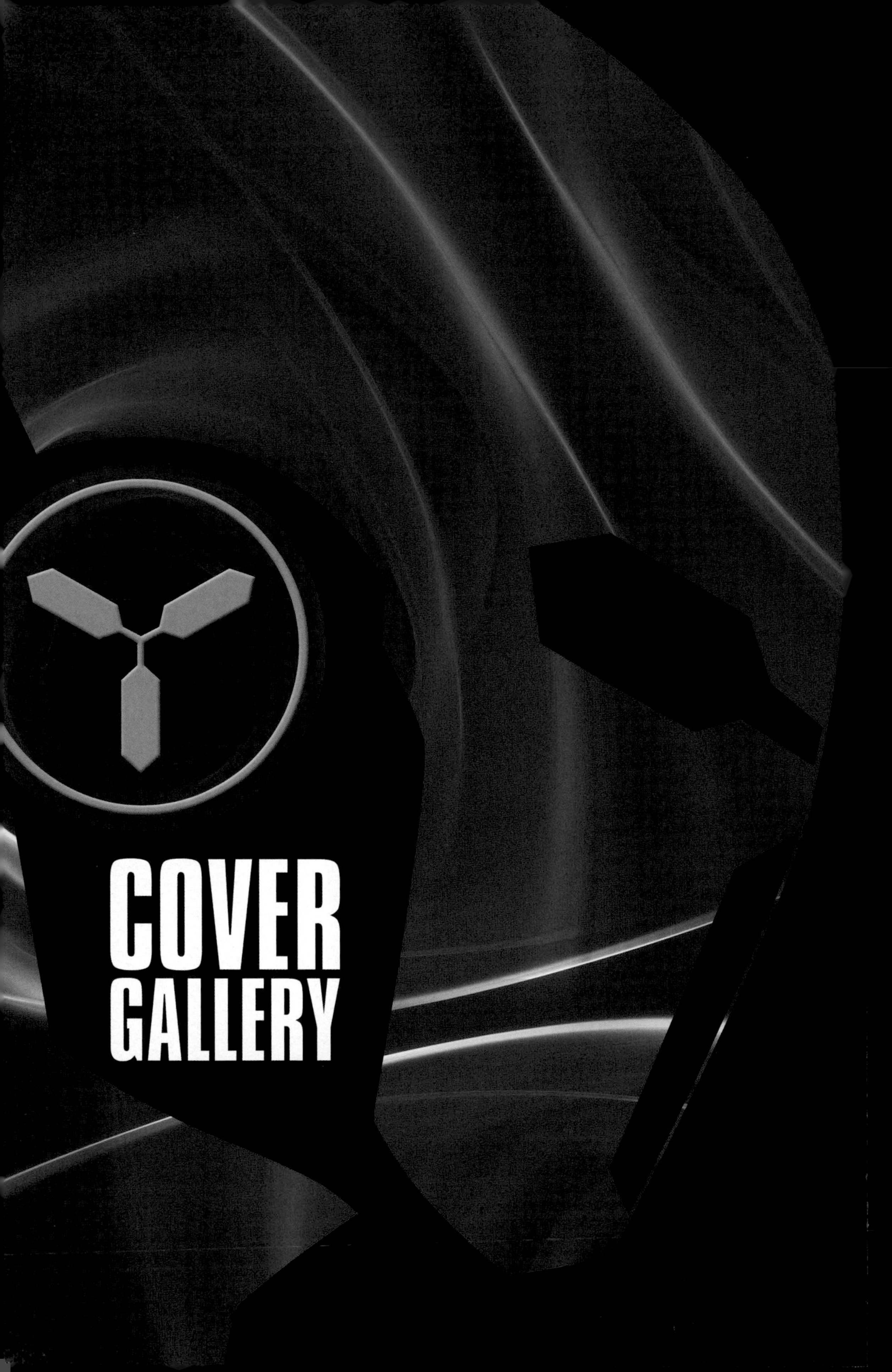
COVER
GALLERY

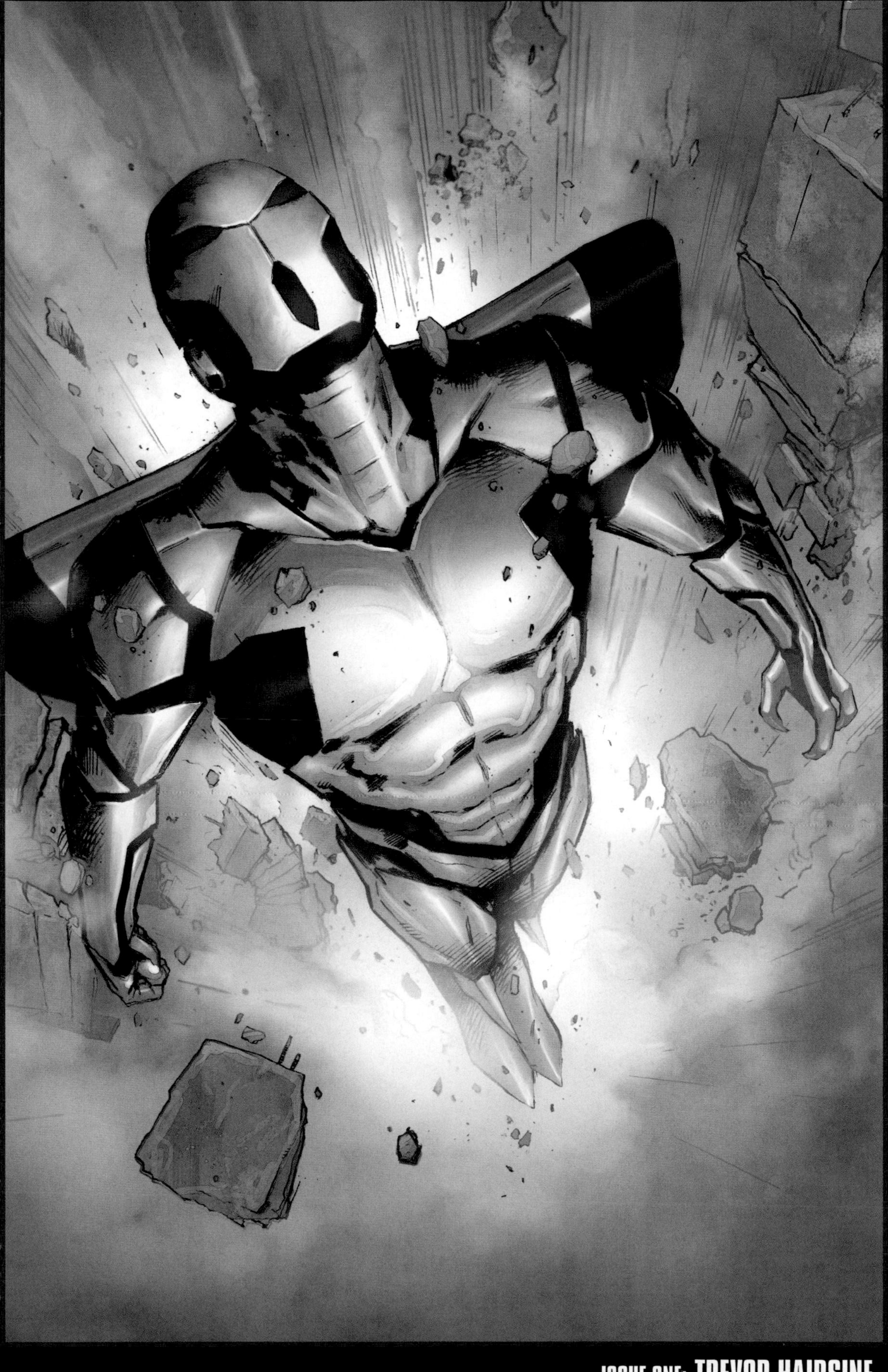

ISSUE ONE: TREVOR HAIRSINE
WITH ALFRED ROCKEFELLER

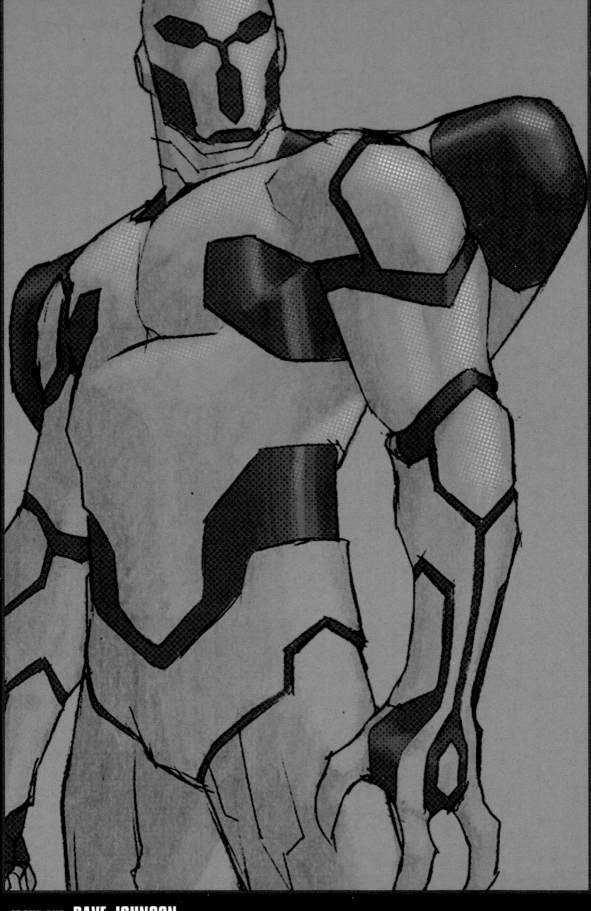

ISSUE ONE: **DAVE JOHNSON**

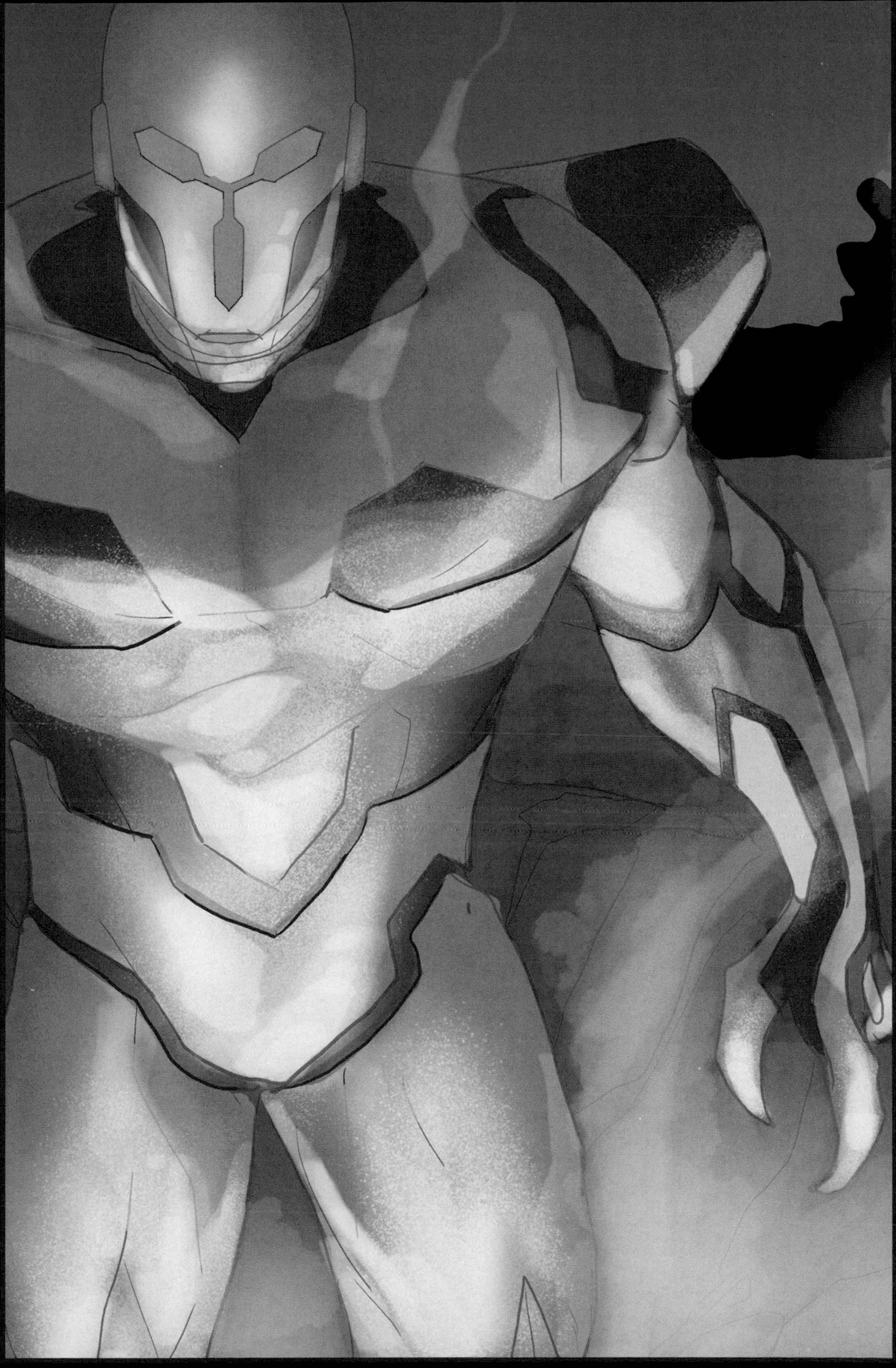

ISSUE ONE: PHIL NOTO

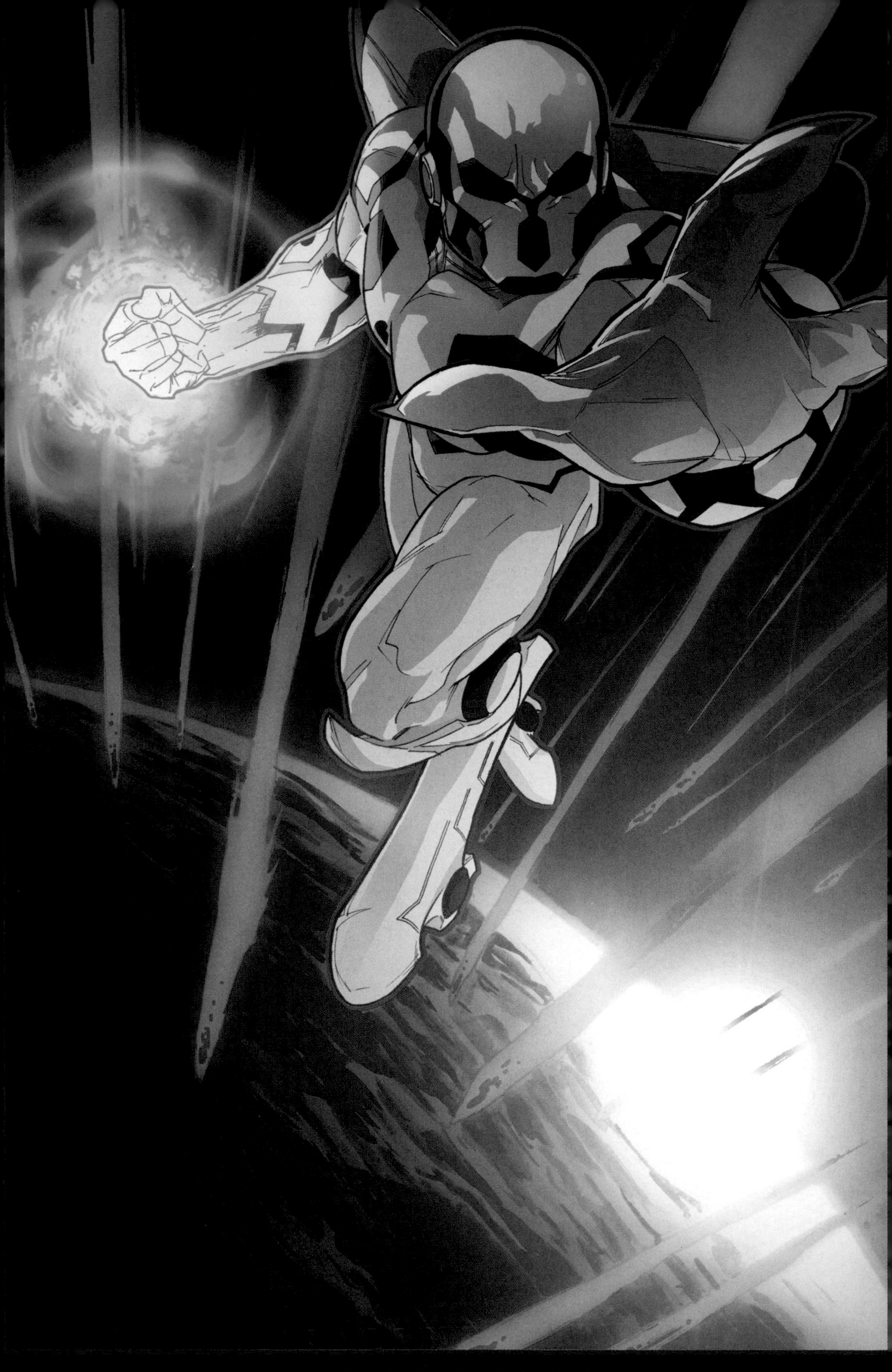

ISSUE ONE RETAILER INCENTIVE VARIANT: KALMAN ANDRASOFSZKY

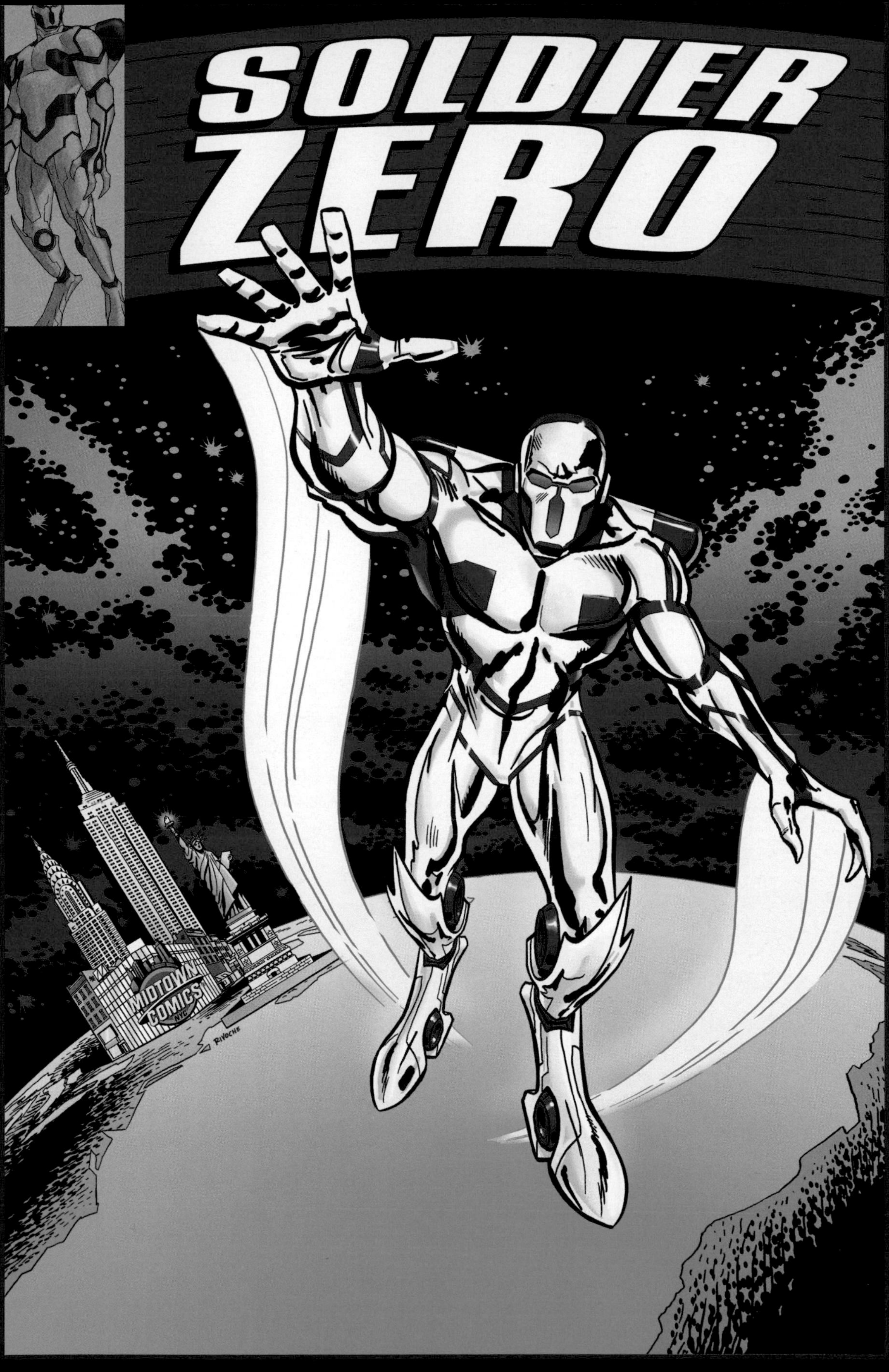
SOLDIER ZERO
MIDTOWN COMICS NYC
RIVOCHE

ISSUE ONE MIDTOWN COMICS EXCLUSIVE VARIANT: PAUL RIVOCHE

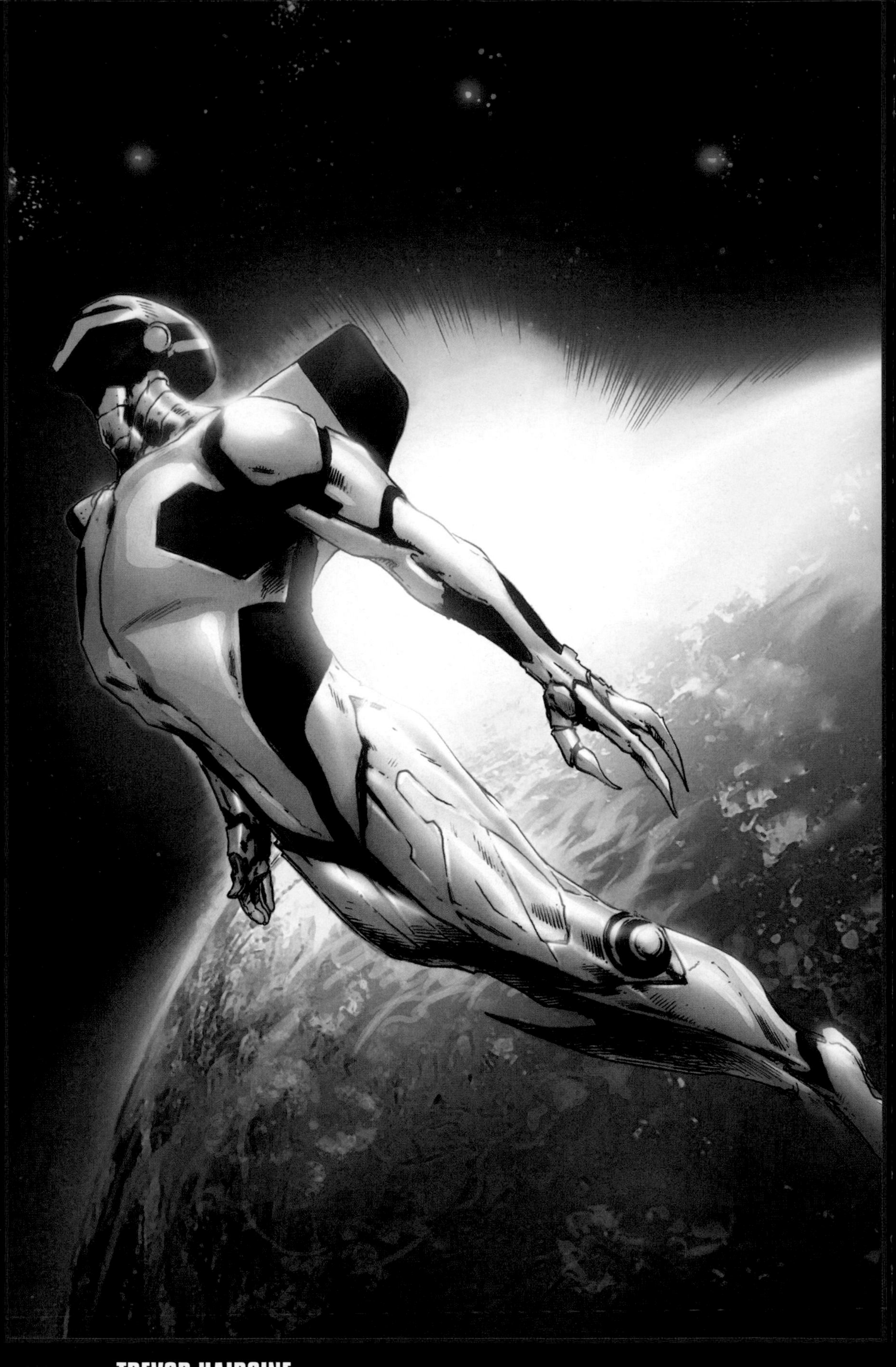

ISSUE TWO: TREVOR HAIRSINE

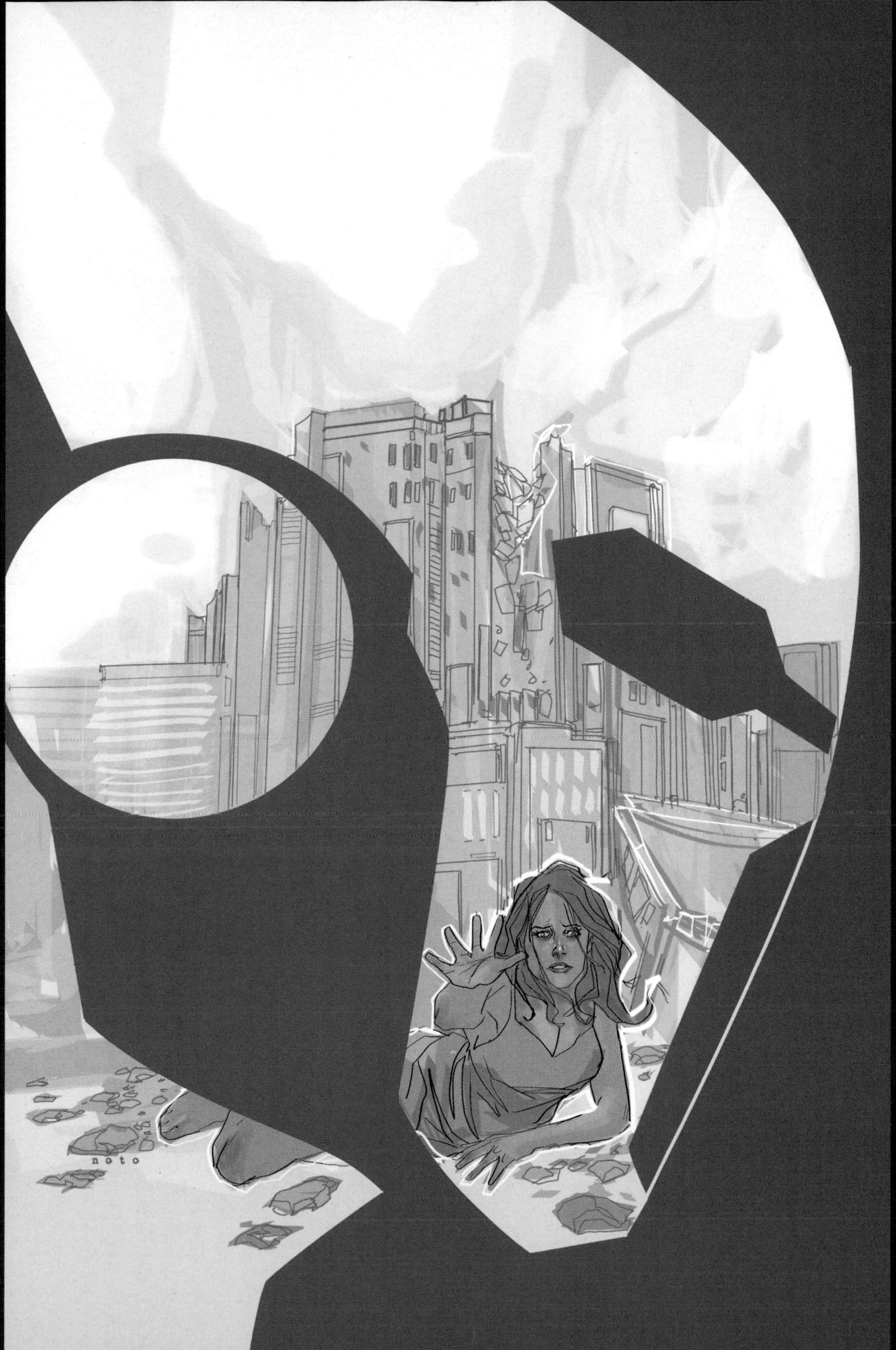
noto

ISSUE TWO: **PHIL NOTO**

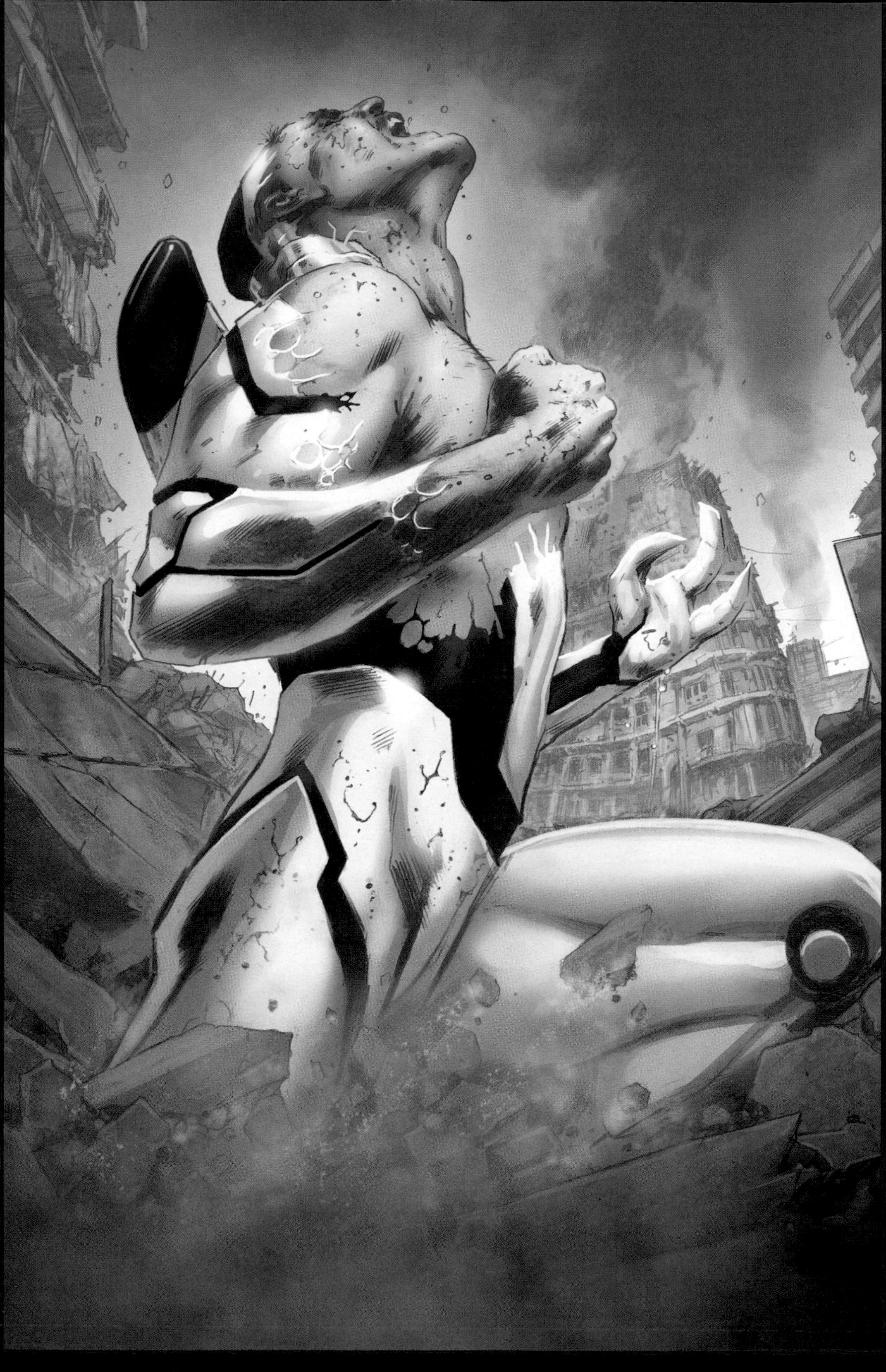

ISSUE THREE: **TREVOR HAIRSINE**

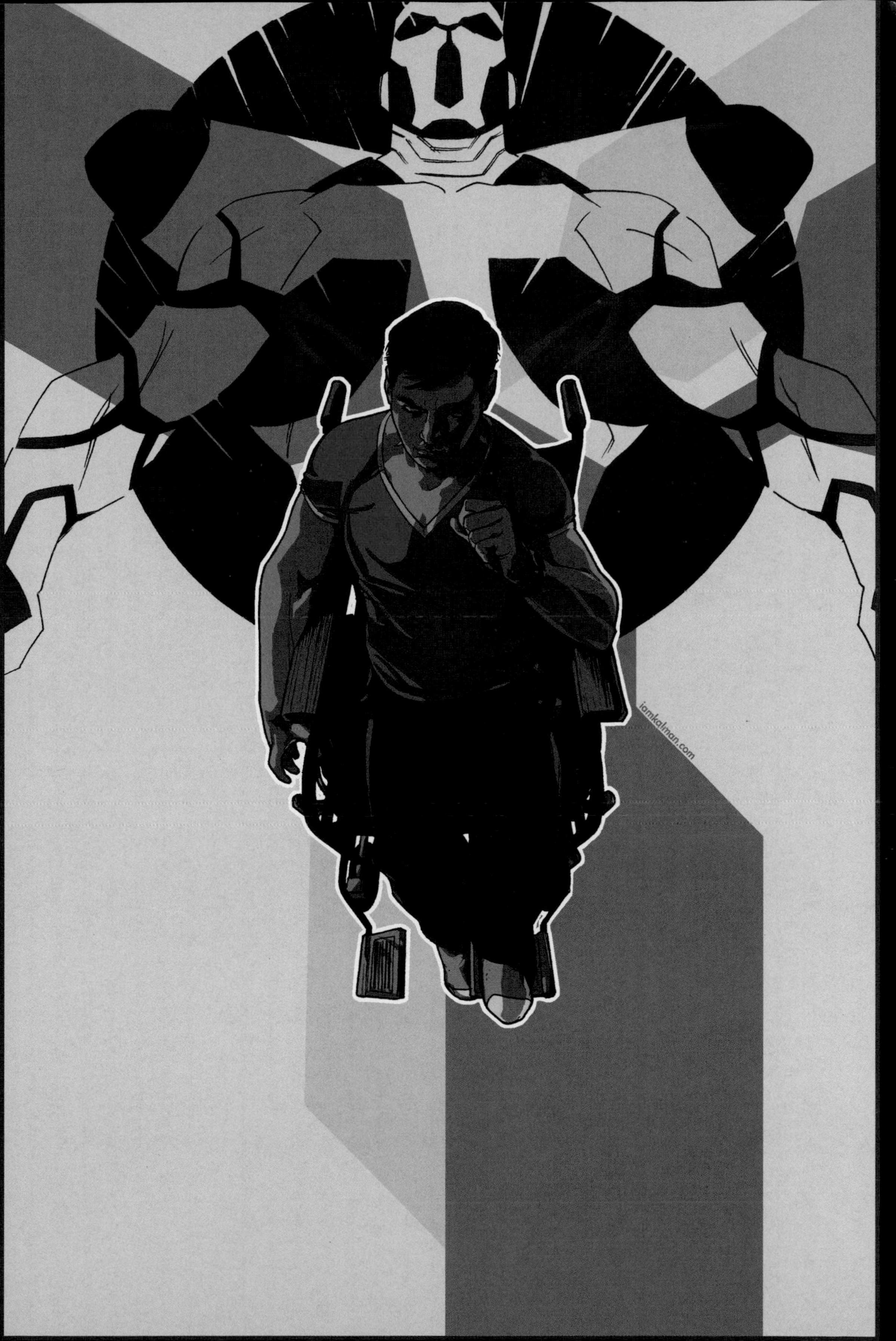
iamkalman.com

ISSUE THREE: **KALMAN ANDRASOFSZKY**

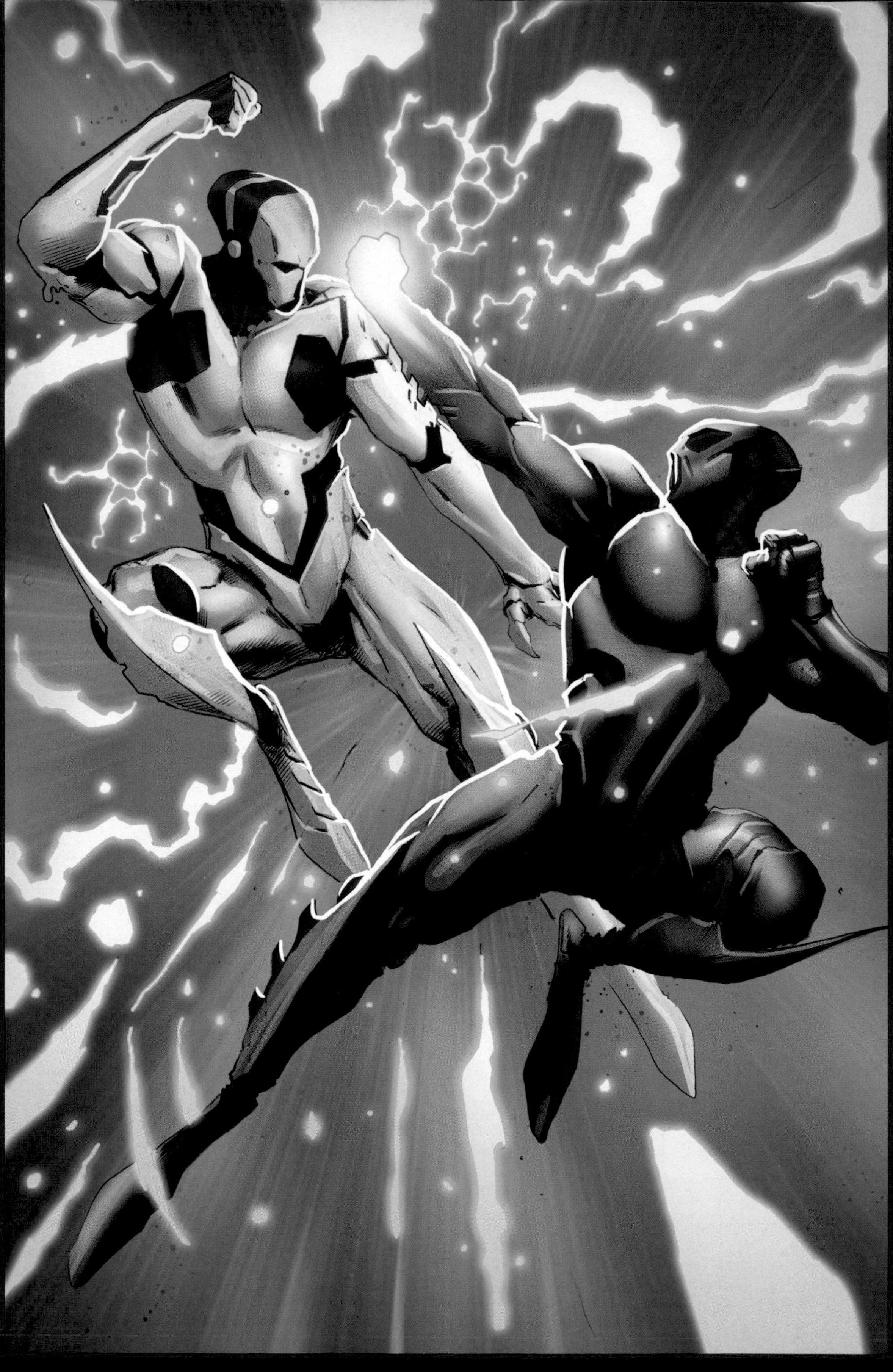

ISSUE FOUR: **TREVOR HAIRSINE**

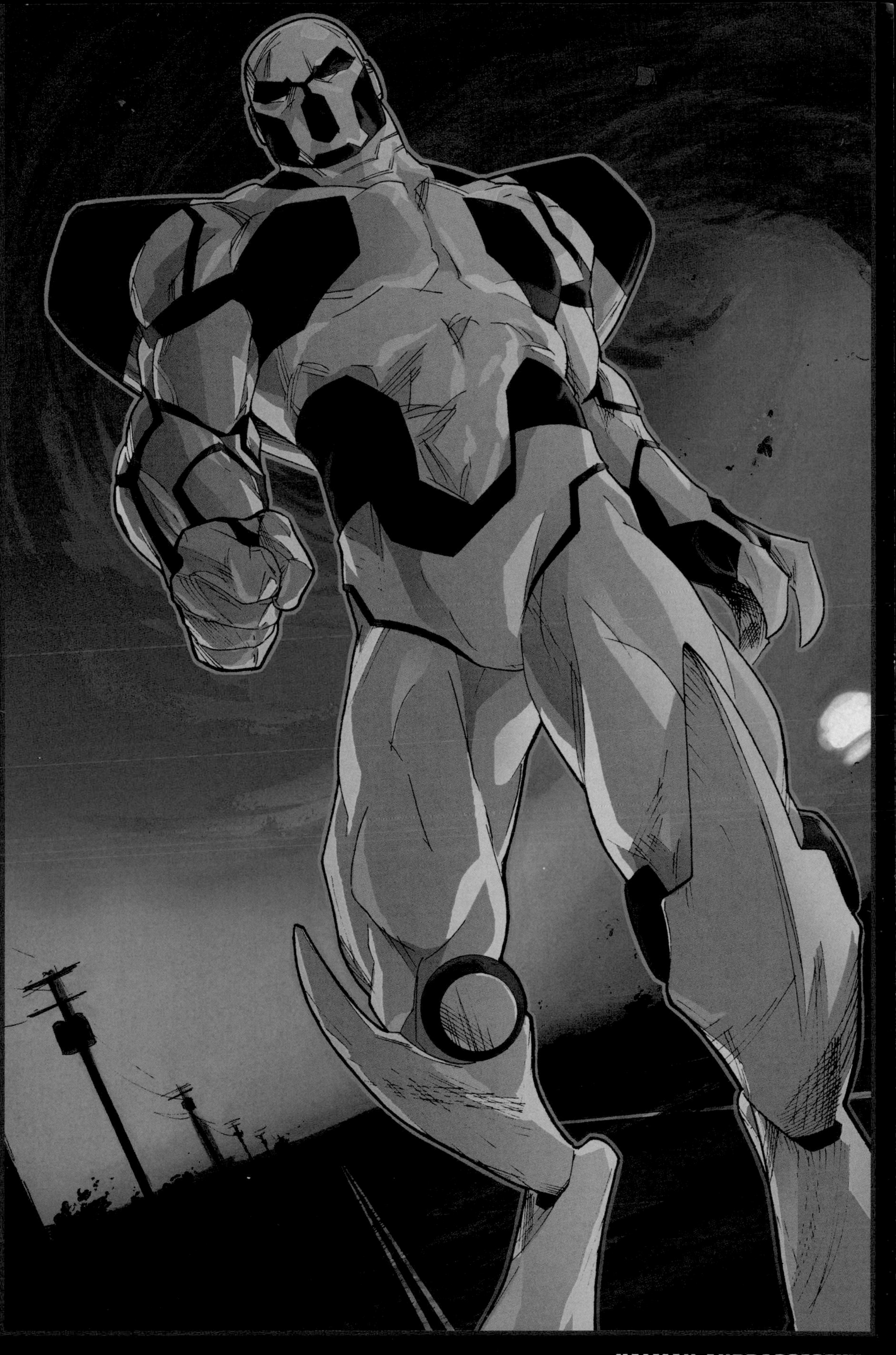

ISSUE FOUR: KALMAN ANDRASOFSZKY

ARTIST GALLERY

DESIGNS AND SKETCHES FROM
DAVE JOHNSON, JAVIER PINA & SERGIO ARIÑO

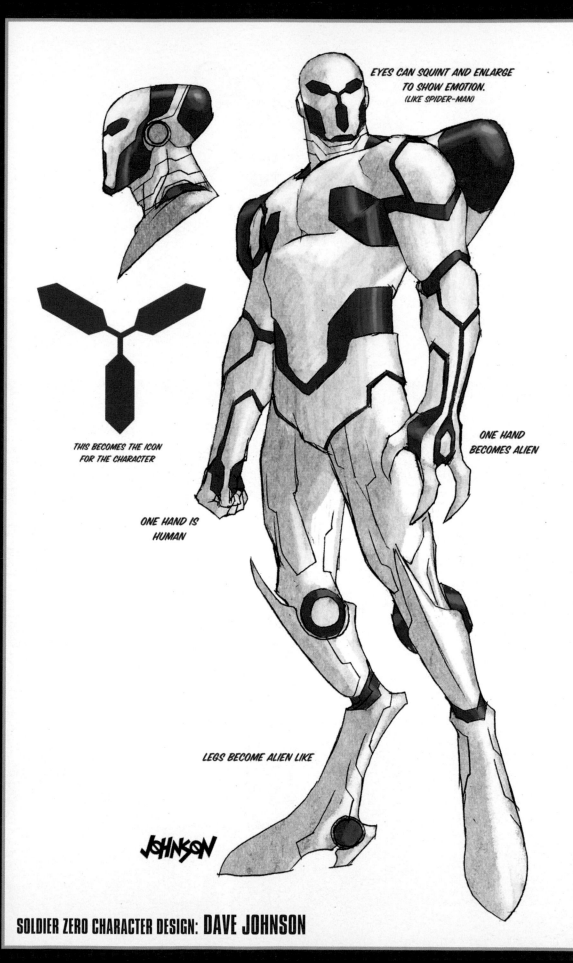

EYES CAN SQUINT AND ENLARGE
TO SHOW EMOTION.
(LIKE SPIDER-MAN)

THIS BECOMES THE ICON
FOR THE CHARACTER

ONE HAND
BECOMES ALIEN

ONE HAND IS
HUMAN

LEGS BECOME ALIEN LIKE

JOHNSON

SOLDIER ZERO CHARACTER DESIGN: DAVE JOHNSON

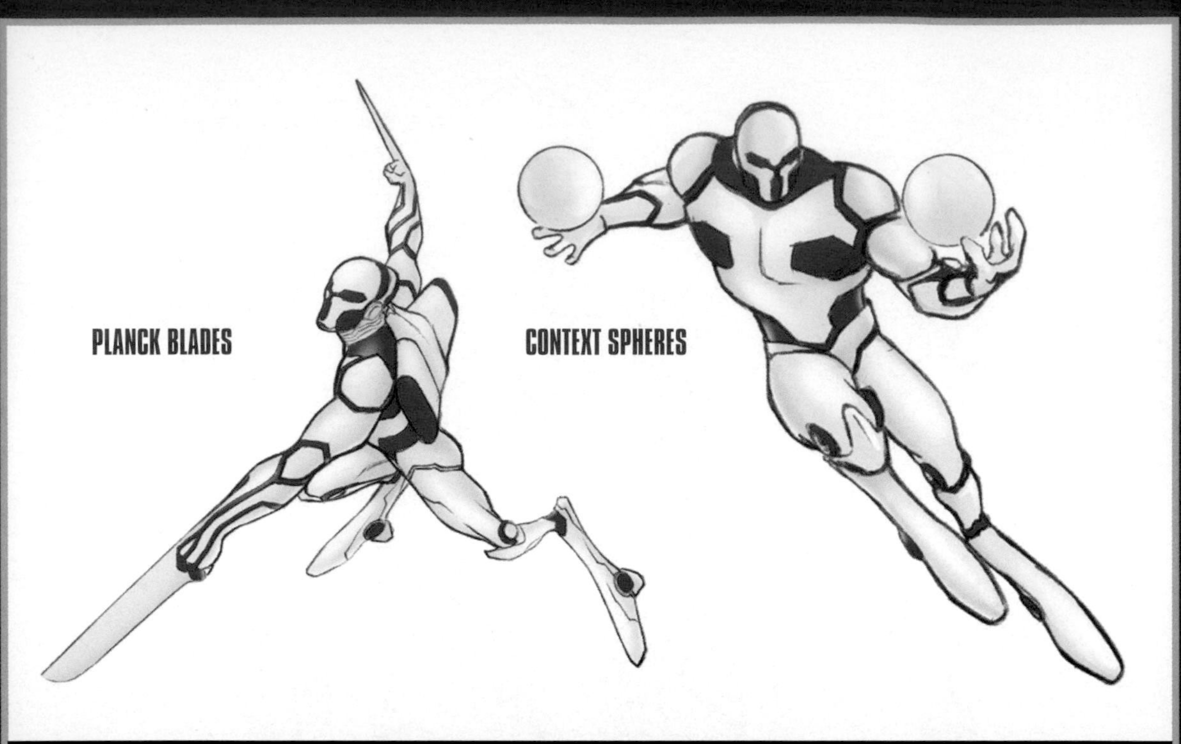
PLANCK BLADES
CONTEXT SPHERES

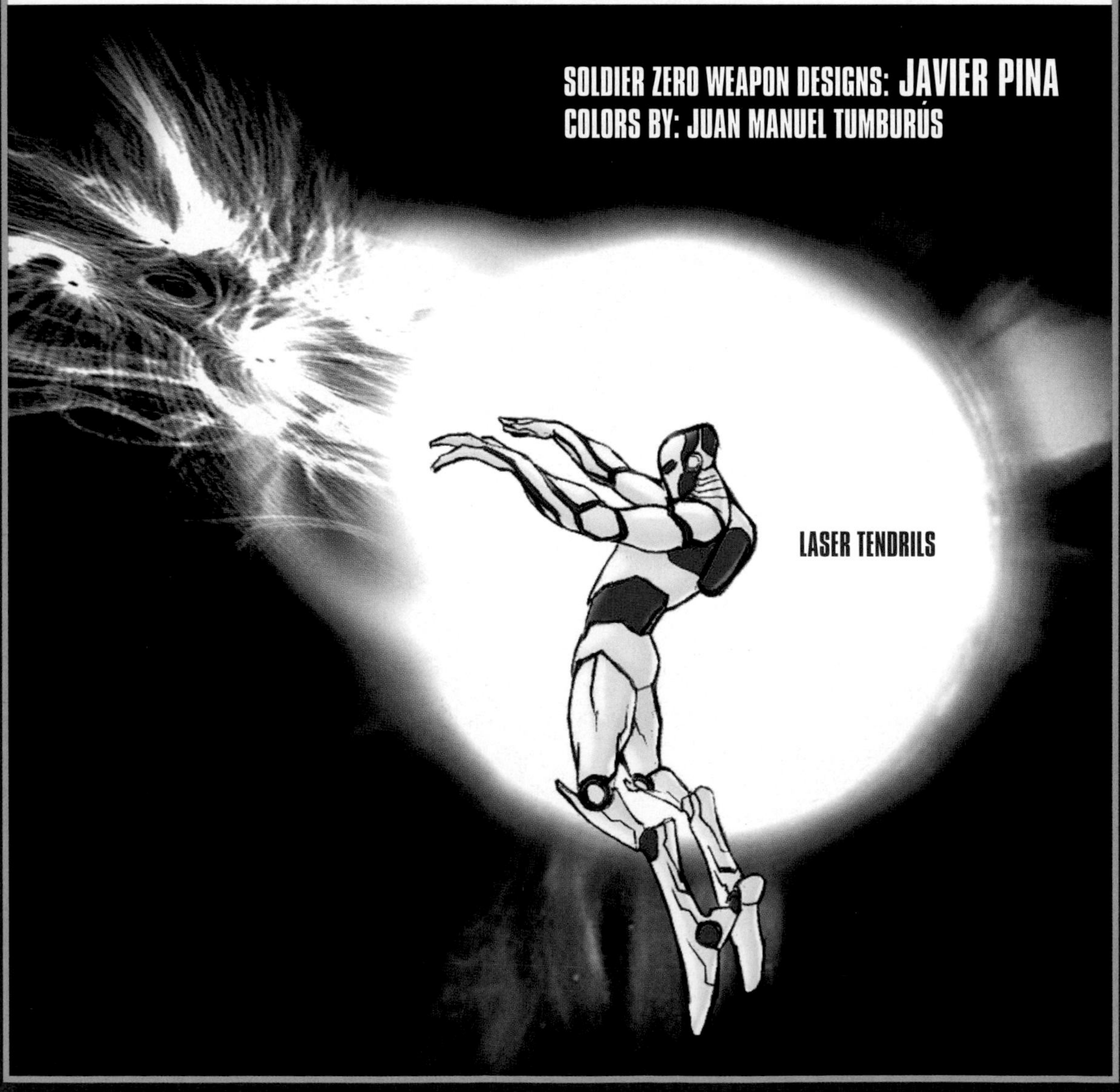
SOLDIER ZERO WEAPON DESIGNS: JAVIER PINA
COLORS BY: JUAN MANUEL TUMBURÚS
LASER TENDRILS

STEWART TRAUTMANN CHARACTER DESIGNS:
JAVIER PINA

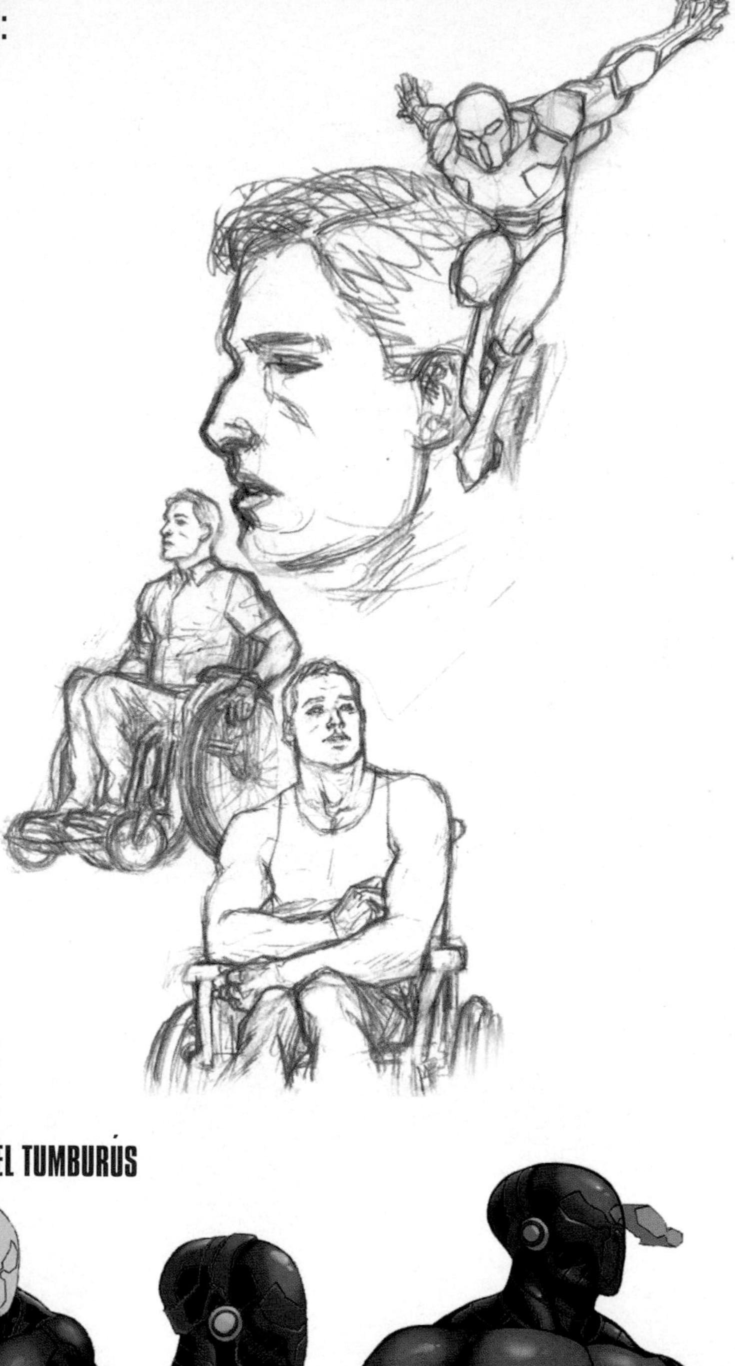

SOLDIER ONE CHARACTER DESIGNS:
SERGIO ARIÑO
COLORS: JUAN MANUEL TUMBURÚS

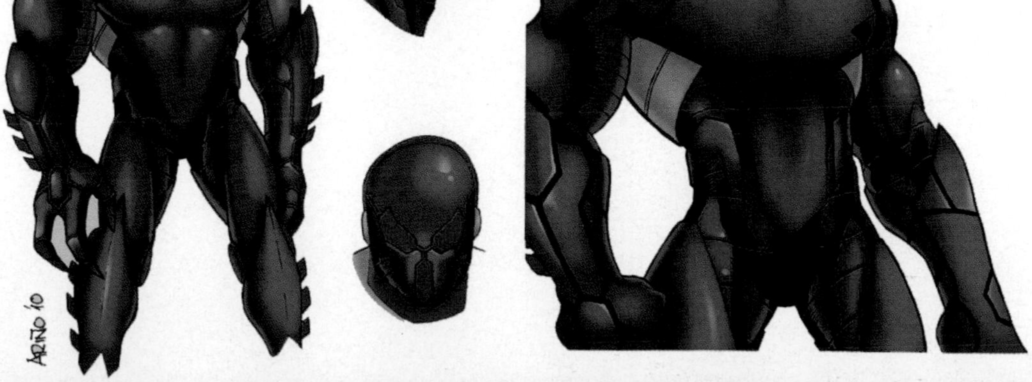

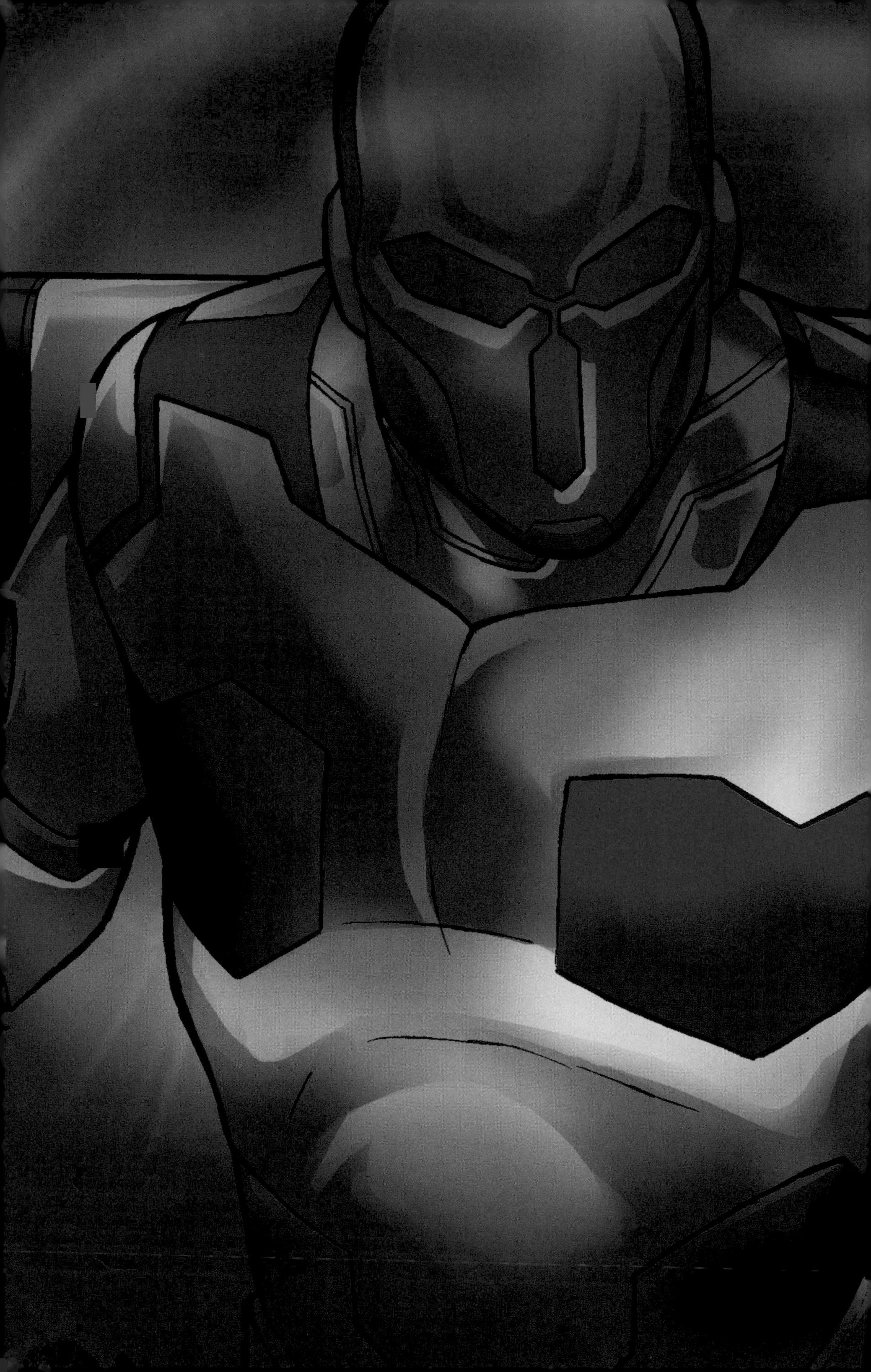

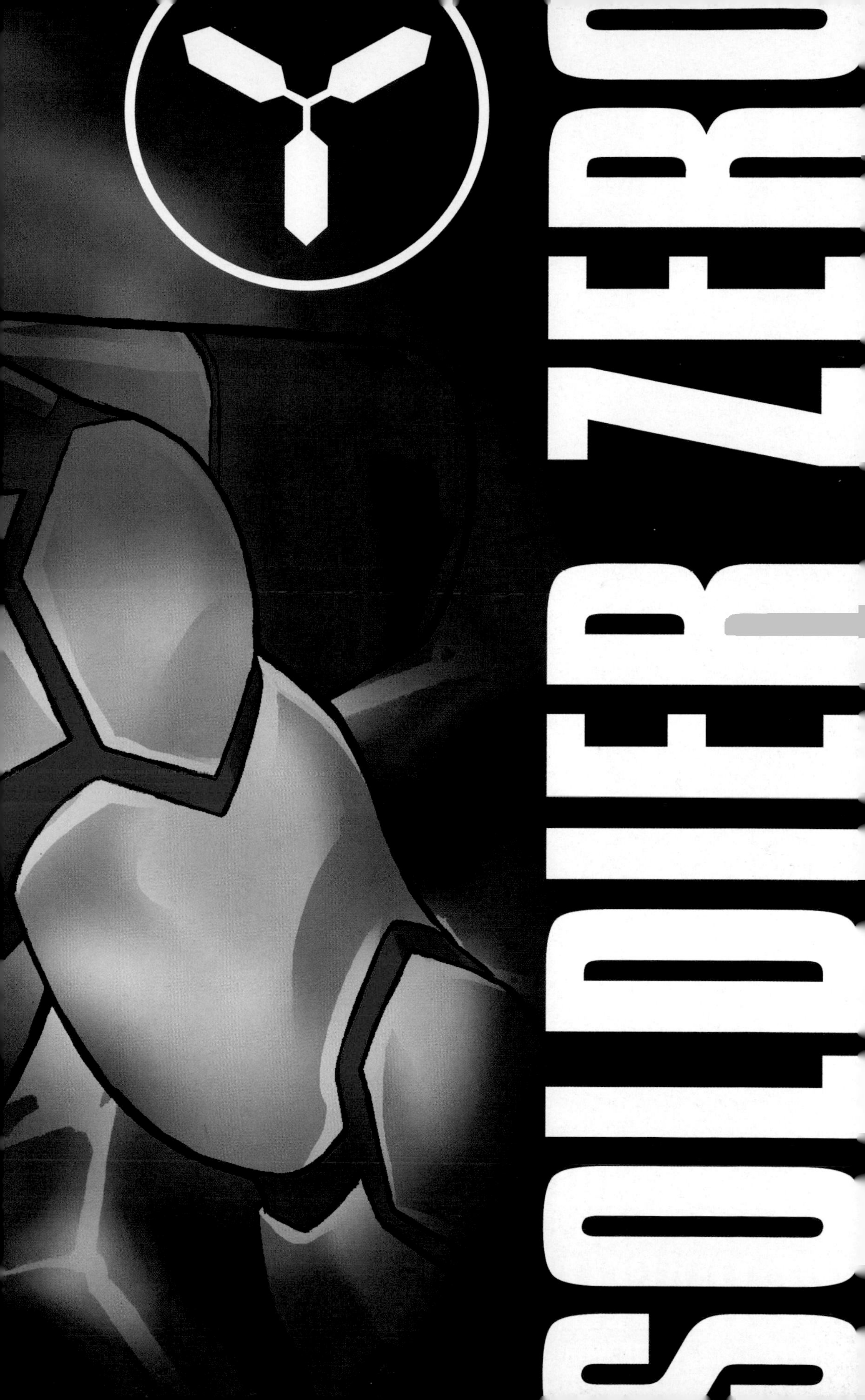
SOLDIER ZERO

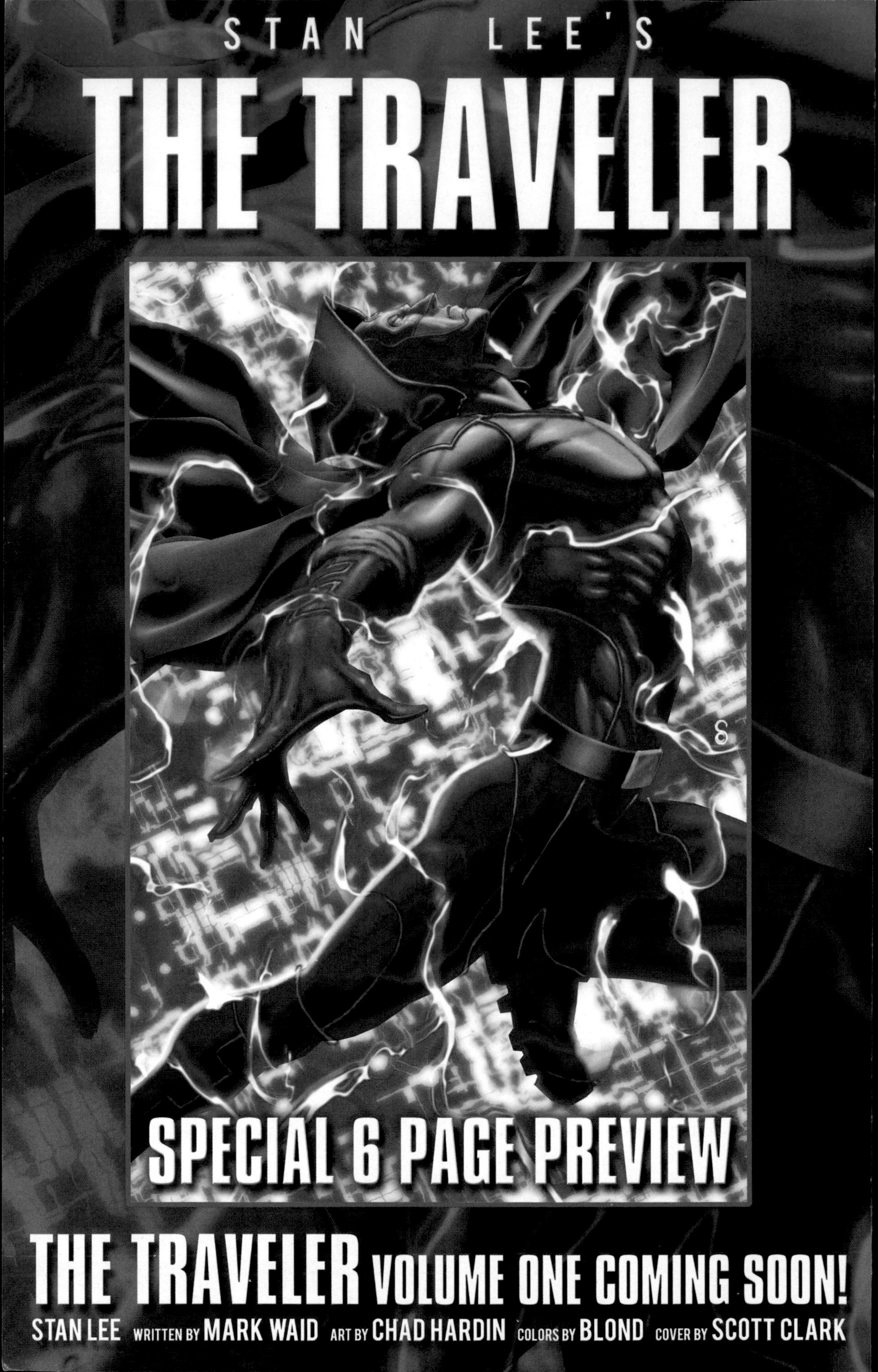
STAN LEE'S
THE TRAVELER
SPECIAL 6 PAGE PREVIEW
THE TRAVELER VOLUME ONE COMING SOON!
STAN LEE WRITTEN BY MARK WAID ART BY CHAD HARDIN COLORS BY BLOND COVER BY SCOTT CLARK

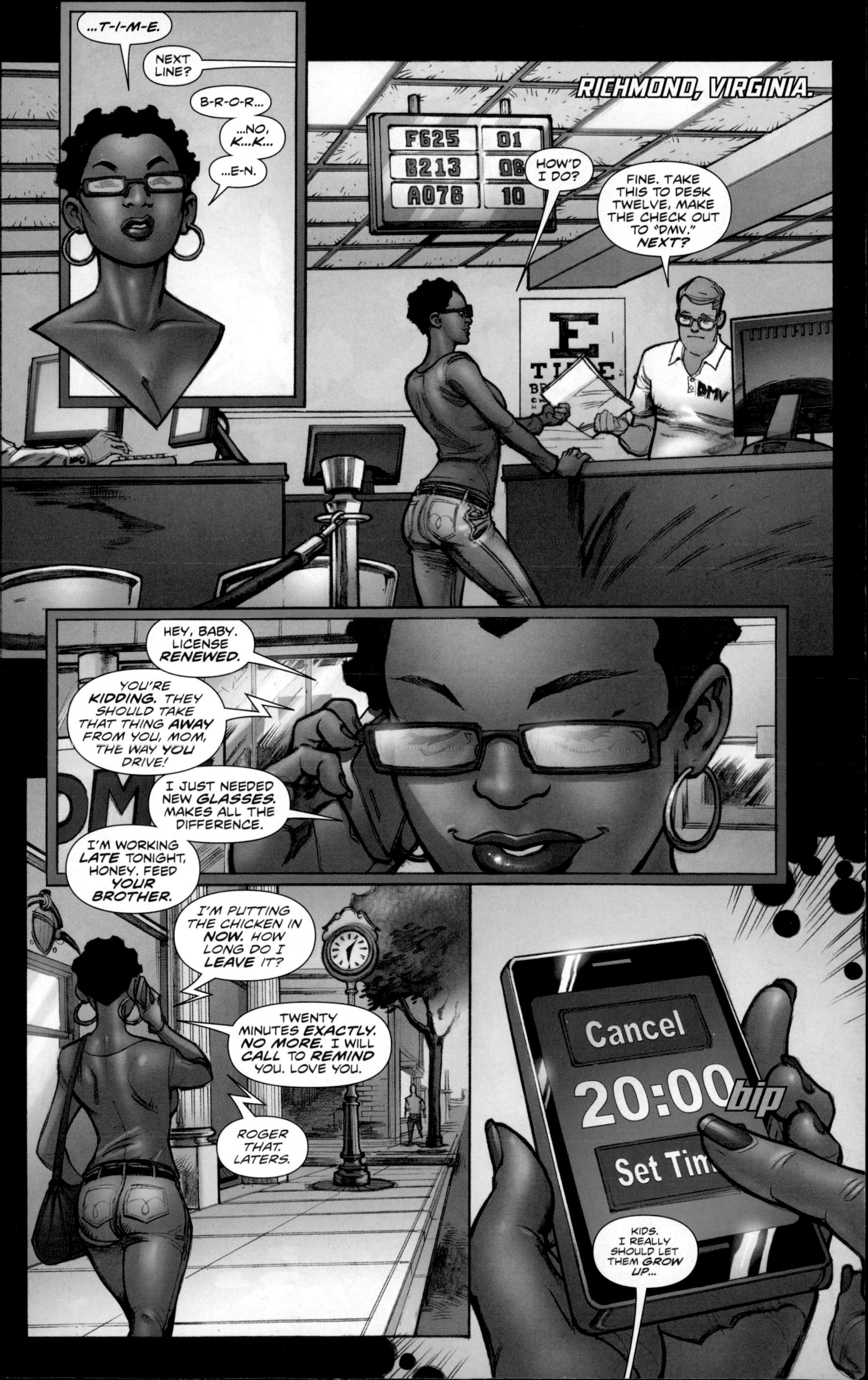
...T-I-M-E.
NEXT LINE?
B-R-O-R...
...NO, K...K...
...E-N.
RICHMOND, VIRGINIA.
F625 01
B213 06
A076 10
HOW'D I DO?
FINE. TAKE THIS TO DESK TWELVE, MAKE THE CHECK OUT TO "DMV." NEXT?
DMV
HEY, BABY. LICENSE RENEWED.
YOU'RE KIDDING. THEY SHOULD TAKE THAT THING AWAY FROM YOU, MOM, THE WAY YOU DRIVE!
I JUST NEEDED NEW GLASSES. MAKES ALL THE DIFFERENCE.
I'M WORKING LATE TONIGHT, HONEY. FEED YOUR BROTHER.
I'M PUTTING THE CHICKEN IN NOW. HOW LONG DO I LEAVE IT?
TWENTY MINUTES EXACTLY. NO MORE. I WILL CALL TO REMIND YOU. LOVE YOU.
ROGER THAT. LATERS.
Cancel
20:00
bip
KIDS. I REALLY SHOULD LET THEM GROW UP...

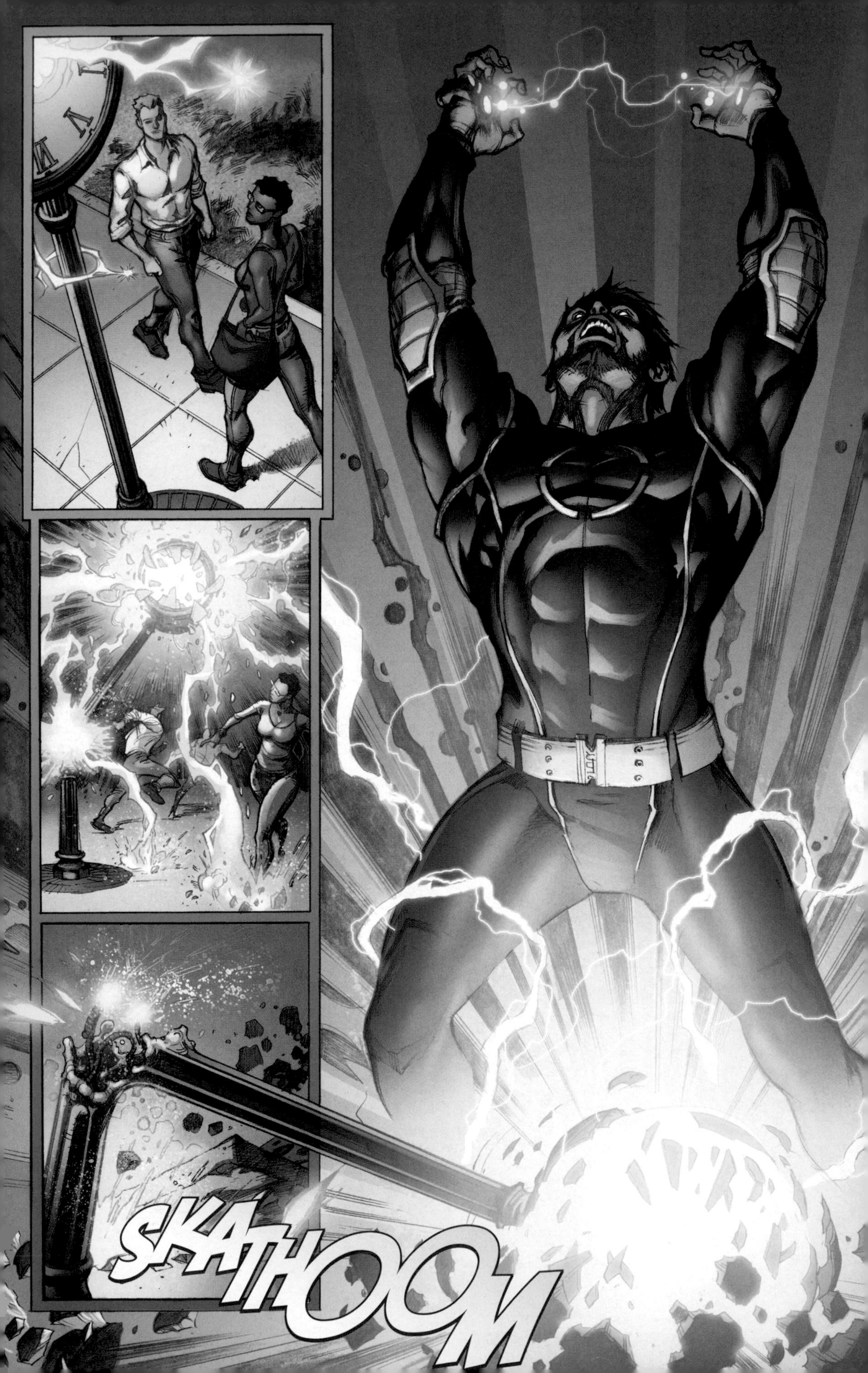
SKATHOOM

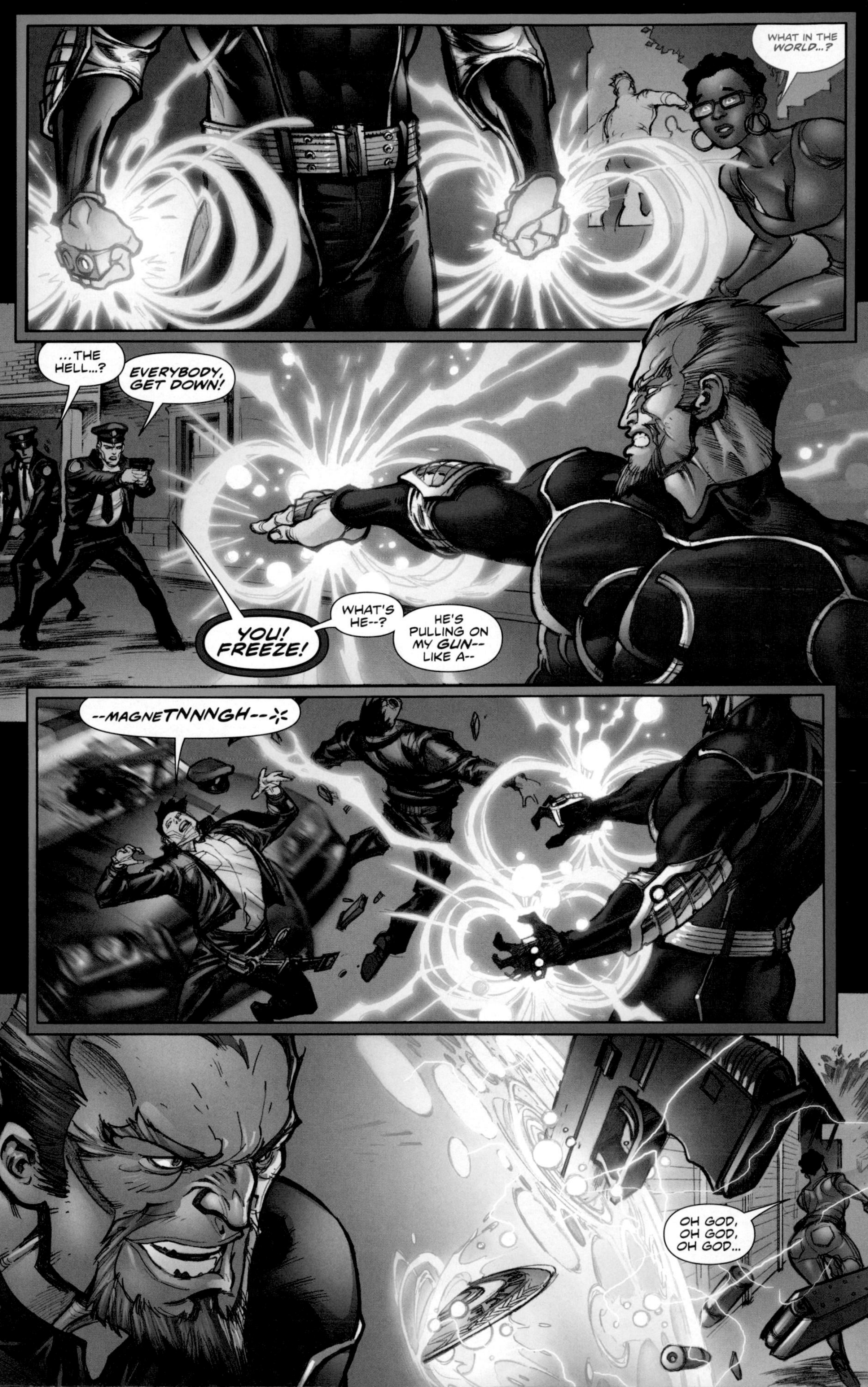
WHAT IN THE WORLD...?
...THE HELL...?
EVERYBODY, GET DOWN!
YOU! FREEZE!
WHAT'S HE--?
HE'S PULLING ON MY GUN-- LIKE A--
--MAGNETNNNGH--
OH GOD, OH GOD, OH GOD...

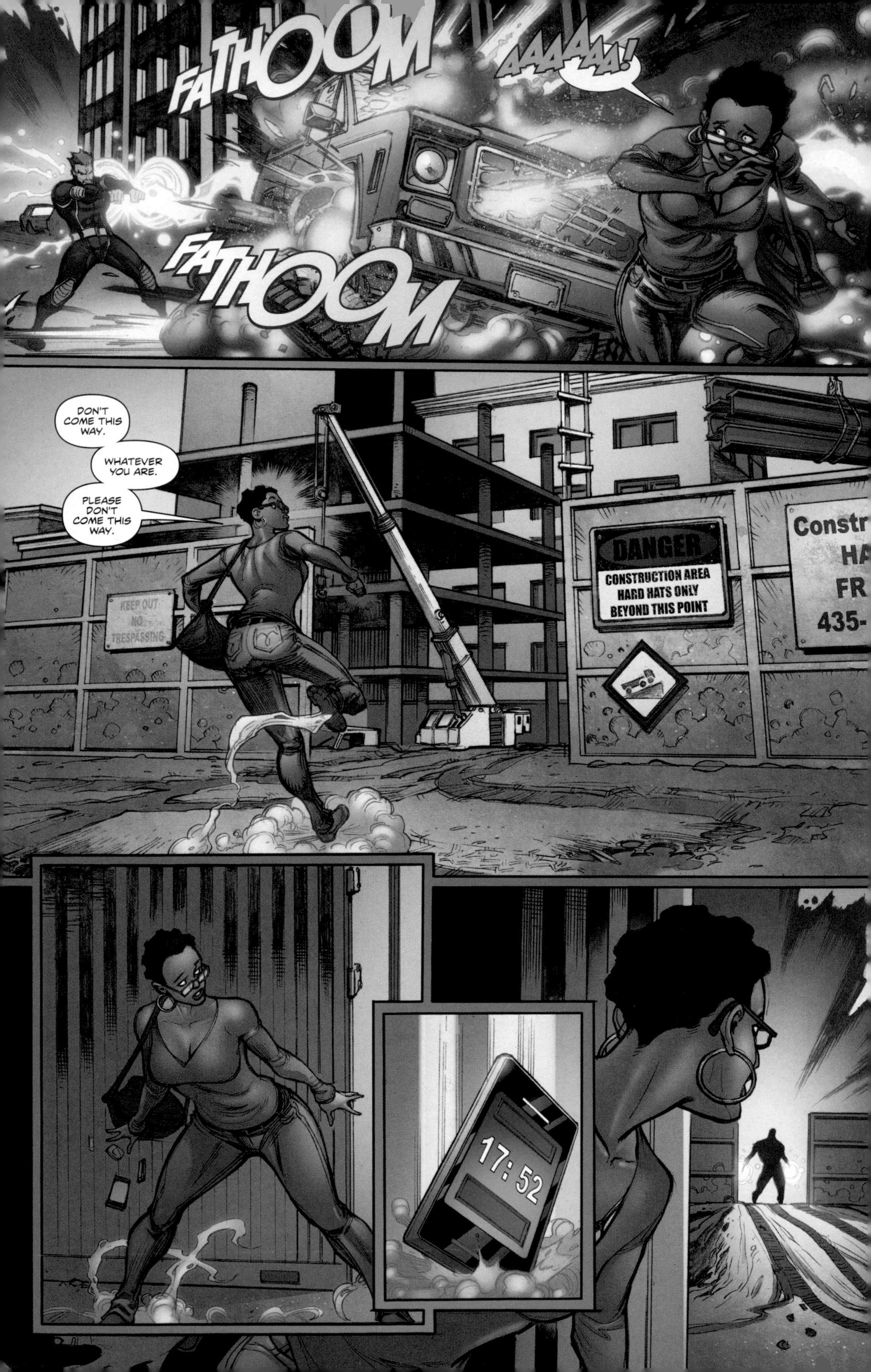
FATHOOM
AAAAAA!
FATHOOM
DON'T COME THIS WAY.
WHATEVER YOU ARE.
PLEASE DON'T COME THIS WAY.
KEEP OUT NO TRESPASSING
DANGER
CONSTRUCTION AREA HARD HATS ONLY BEYOND THIS POINT
17:52

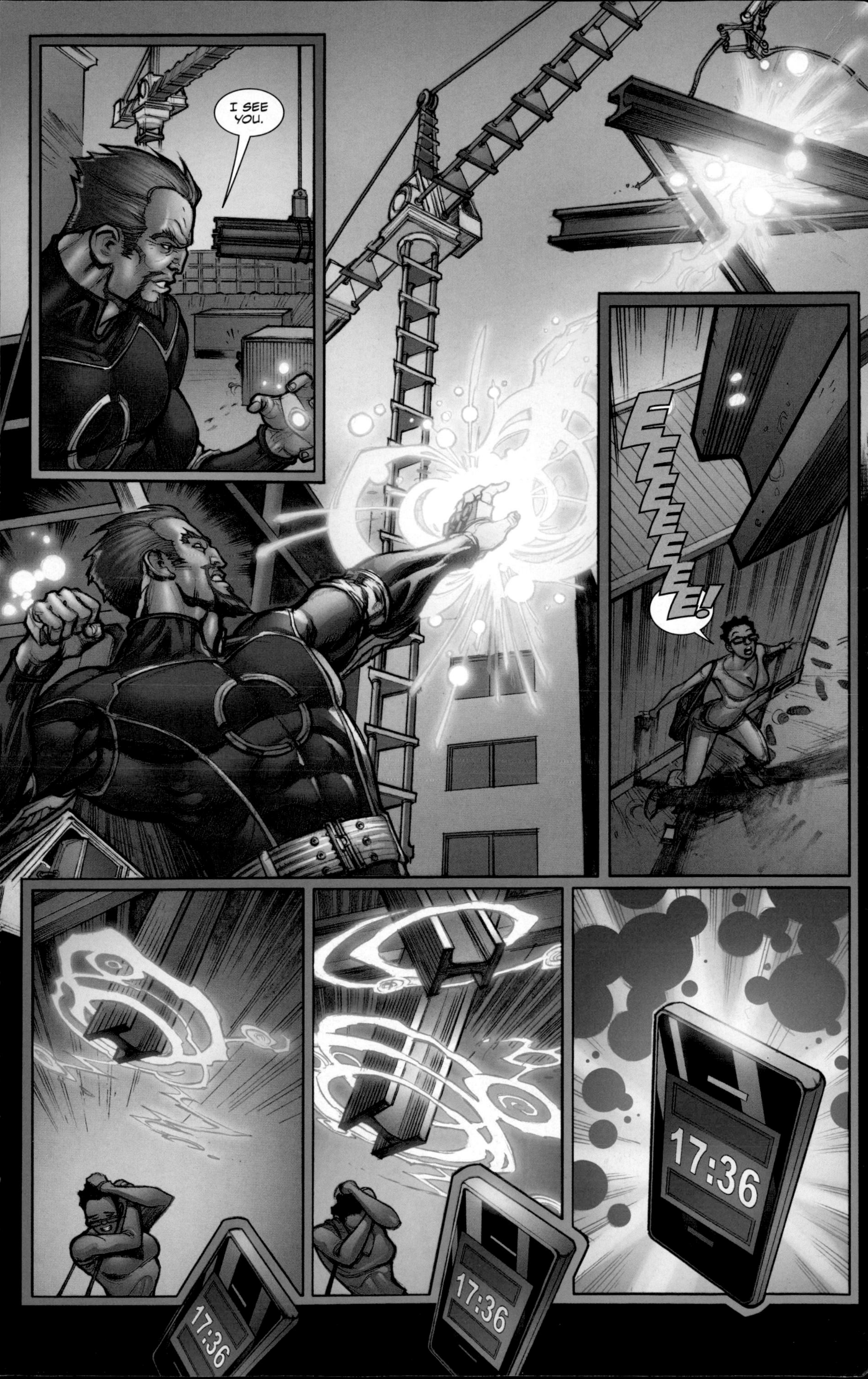
I SEE YOU.
EEEEEEE!
17:36
17:36
17:36

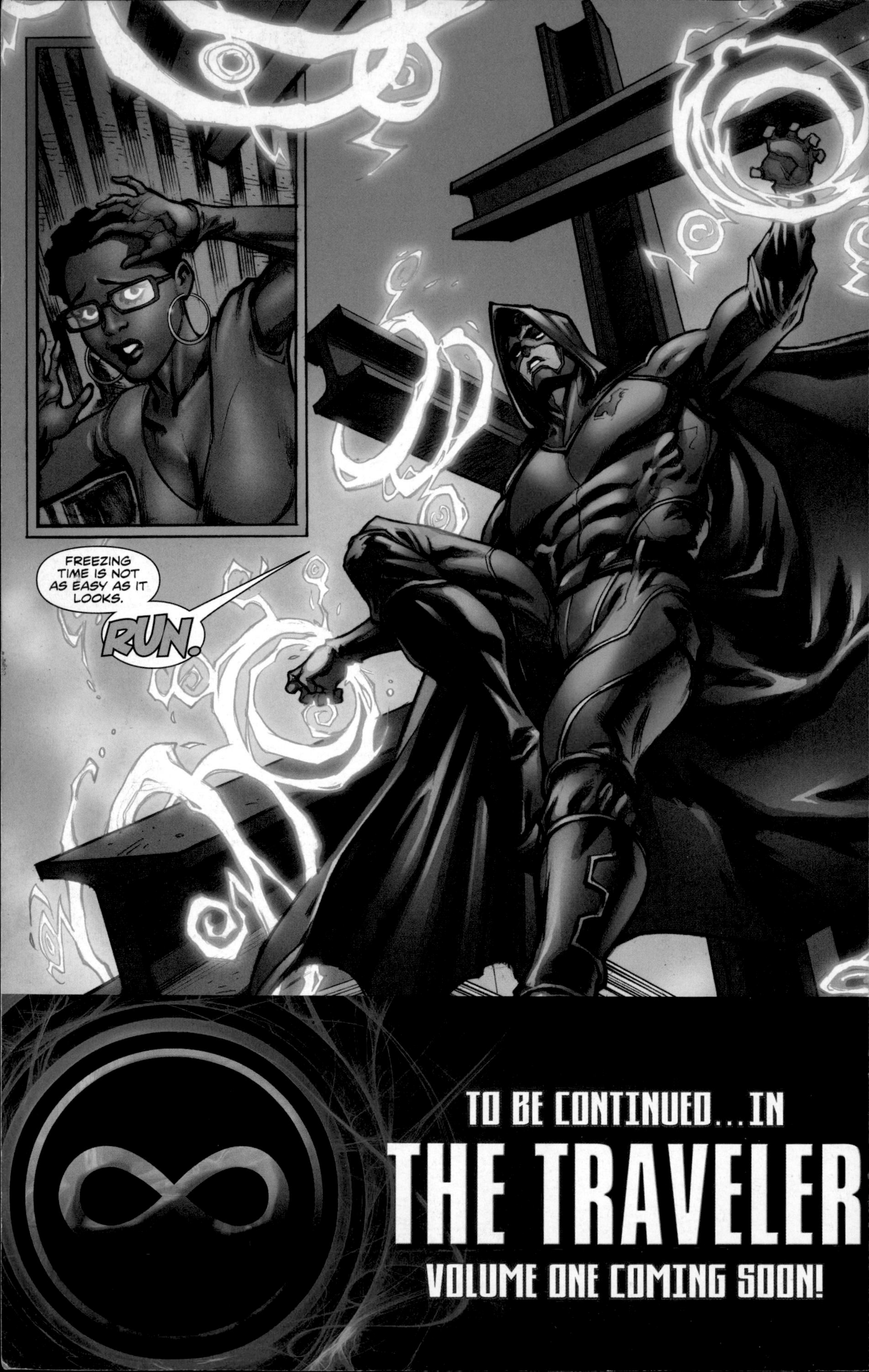
FREEZING TIME IS NOT AS EASY AS IT LOOKS.
RUN.

TO BE CONTINUED... IN

THE TRAVELER

VOLUME ONE COMING SOON!

Stan Lee